If You Meet George Herbert on the Road . . .
Kill Him!

If You Meet George Herbert on the Road ... Kill Him!

Radically rethinking priestly ministry

JUSTIN LEWIS-ANTHONY

Published by Mowbray, a Continuum imprint
The Tower Building, 11 York Road, London SE1 7NX
80 Maiden Lane, Suite 704, New York NY 10038

www.continuumbooks.com

First published 2009

British Library Cataloguing-in-Publication Data
A catalogue record for this book is available from the British Library.

ISBN 978-1-9062-8617-0

Typeset by Kenneth Burnley, Wirral, Cheshire
Printed and bound by MPG Books Group

Contents

For Alistair

with whom, over rough red wine and posh crisps,
many of these ideas were first expressed.

Acknowledgements

I was heartened to see in the acknowledgements to Dom Christopher Jamison's *Finding Happiness* that writing a second book was quantifiably (ten times) harder than writing a first: so not just me then? Even so, I have been immeasurably assisted by numerous people in the thinking, reading and writing which has gone into this book. First, I thank those clergy who have lived with the legacy of Herbert, and shared their experiences and insights with me, especially: Nick Stacey, who was so generous of his time and support; Bob Jeffrey, who read, commented and added unique insight to the workings of the twentieth-century Church of England; members of my cohort from theological college: Alistair Fuller, Steve Mason, David Munchin, Brian Cunningham, Jeremy and Ellen Clark-King, who argued with and honed my assumptions; Sam Norton, priest and sage of Mersea, who was a catalyst upon some of my early ideas; the clergy of deanery chapters, in this country and abroad, who nodded wryly during presentations of my ideas and so encouraged me to believe that it wasn't just me.

Ideas have to be underpinned with fact, and, if not fact, then footnotes. Scholars who have assisted me include Michael G. Cartwright, Mark Chapman, Elizabeth Clarke, Leslie Francis, Chris Hodgkins, and Douglas Turton. Professor Hodgkins invited this Daniel to participate in the presumed lions' den of the George Herbert's Living Legacies conference at the University of North Carolina in Greensboro in October 2008, where I learned from, among others, Chauncey Wood, Erik Ankerberg and Kenneth Graham. However, while corrections may be credited to the scholars, the mistakes remain my own.

The Dean and Chapter of Christ Church, Oxford, unknowingly allowed me two periods of residential research in House accommodation (through the good offices of Philip Tootill, House Manager).

I couldn't have found a more supportive publishing house than the team at Continuum.

Finally, in my last book, I thanked my family: this was too vague to satisfy my children, so I wish to pay tribute to the patience, and inability to leave me completely alone, of Arwen, Rosa, Jonas, and Hannele Lewis-Anthony.

Part 1

DEATH TO HERBERTISM

For 350 years the Church of England has been haunted by a pattern of parochial ministry which is based upon a fantasy and has been untenable for more than 100 of those years. The pattern, derived from a romantic and wrong-headed false memory of the life and ministry of George Herbert, finally died on the South Bank of the Thames in the mid-1960s – and nobody noticed.

I was walking across Hyde Park with a friend. He was having a hard time in his parish ministry, feeling that the standards he had set himself, and the standards which were being set for him, were impossible to fulfil. In favour of a quiet life, I was trying to persuade him to go easier on himself. He objected. 'But when you think about what George Herbert was able to achieve . . .' I cut across him: 'If you meet George Herbert on the road, you have to kill him!'

Afterwards I wondered to myself from where such a violent, angry image had come. I soon realized the image was abroad in our culture. Sam Norton, who writes the blog *Elizaphanian*, had, very shortly before my meeting with my friend, written a post about the burial of George Herbert.[1] Sam's post set off a flurry of responses. I realized that there was something happening here, something being experienced by priests in parish ministry, which could be best described as the desire and the necessity to 'kill George Herbert'. Why? What had led to such a depth of feeling among a certain number of parish clergy? Was this anything more than mid-career pique?

I began to think about, discuss and study the patterns of clerical ministry that were being followed in the Church of England today. I talked to friends, my contemporaries and those of a much older, senior ministry. I asked them what they thought was the role of priests today; how had it changed over the course of their ministry, what was good about it, what was bad, what was to be celebrated and what ought to be put down? I asked everyone I spoke to about their reaction to the original imprecation: 'If you meet George Herbert on the road, kill him!' It was their reactions that caused this book; anecdotal evidence, the stories of friends and colleagues, showed me that George Herbert had to die. All I needed to do now was to show why!

Because my training is in history and theology this book is not the result of an empirical survey of the attitudes and experiences of parish clergy in the Church of England today (although it uses the conclusions of other such surveys). It is a work of history and theology, setting out to show one possible route by which we arrived where we are, what might be the theological implications of the position in which we now find ourselves, and one possible way ahead. As someone once said, you must always step forward from where you stand.

The first section of the book will examine the history and structure of the false pattern (which I have christened 'Herbertism'); it will recount the *real* life and ministry of the saint of Bemerton; look at the changes in the status and functioning of English parish clergy in the last 150 years; and will mark the true death, the moment of passing, of 'Herbertism'.

None of this story happens without a cost, and the survey of 'Herbertism' will conclude with an accounting of the personal cost of 'Herbertism' in the lives and emotions of the clergy of the Church of England today.

The second section of the book will explore the beginnings of a new conceptual framework for ministry, based upon a lecture given by the Archbishop of Canterbury in 2004: a sustainable pattern for ministry will be grounded upon the three Ws of *Witness*, *Watchman* and *Weaver*. These images will be unpacked, using a catholic range of writers, thinkers and pastors as guides, measuring the images against the realities we have described in the first section.

The final section of the book will become practical: the sustainable pattern of ministry, which I have christened KGH, will be laid out, with strategies for managing the constant temptation to fall back into Herbertism.

But before describing the cure, the diagnosis needs to be confirmed: if Herbertism is a real and damaging condition, then we should indeed seek to kill George Herbert – and we should start by finding out why.

1

Lin-Chi, the curate and the Anglican divine

The young curate was very excited. He had spent the day at a post-ordination training day, normally a deadly dull occasion (workshops on 'new ways of being church for Generation FLK',* 'Fresh Expressions for the Cappuccino Church', or 'Pixellating Networks for Time-Poor Professionals') brightened only by opportunities for the diocese's curates to complain about their training vicars. This day was different; it had actually been engrossing – a study day on the life, work and example of the Anglican Divine, George Herbert.

'George Herbert is so great', the curate burbled to his vicar. 'He turned down a life at court, he worked in a poor rural parish, he wrote loads of great hymns, his congregation loved him and even stopped work in the fields to say their prayers when he rang the evensong bell, and he wrote this brilliant book on how to be a country vicar which is full of really good advice.'

His training incumbent, relieved not to be on the receiving end of projected disappointment and misplaced stress, coughed, turned over a page in his copy of the *Church Times*, and said, 'If you meet George Herbert on the road – kill him!' The curate was shocked. Was there no limit to his vicar's cynicism and philistinism? He added a new grievance to his store, and resolved that day to make George Herbert the model, and his incumbent the anti-model, for his own ministry.

The years passed and rough edges were rubbed off the curate. He worked in positions of increasing responsibility, sometimes sought and sometime thrust upon him. He watched as synods of the Church discarded all the new initiatives which had seemed so bright and productive in the first years of his ministry. He watched as bishops rediscovered all those initiatives and introduced them as the next best hope

* Doctors' shorthand for 'Funny Looking Kid'.

for the salvation of the Church. He was even allowed, occasionally, a curate of his own, to train and to encourage and to form (although the Church hierarchs never used such a hierarchical verb as 'form' any more).

One day this latter-day curate returned from a post-ordination training day, which had been spent on the spirituality of the Anglican Divines, and as his curate spoke of his enthusiasm for the poetry, prose and example of George Herbert, he found himself saying

'If you meet George Herbert on the road – kill him!'

And so it goes, Herberticidal thoughts all the way down.

Is this just mere clerical cynicism, or passive-aggressive vicars? Pause for a moment, and wonder whether something else might be going on here. Perhaps in this flippant, throw-away remark, a spiritual truth can be glimpsed. Perhaps the two priests, the first incumbent and the curate in his later life, half remembered a story about a Zen Master, and applied it to their own situation and religious tradition: inculturating the Zen story, as the jargon goes.

This is the story: Lin-Chi was born in Shandong province of China during the Tang Dynasty (AD 618–907). He trained as a Buddhist monk, in the Zen school. Partly because of the particular Zen tradition in which he was trained, and partly because of his character, his own teaching was marked by abrupt, almost absurd, sayings, and deliberately provocative behaviour. He wanted to surprise his disciples into enlightenment, make them realize that the Buddhist doctrine of non-attachment meant not being attached to *anything* in this world of illusion and self-deception. He even went so far as to seemingly deny fundamental Buddhist doctrines. For example, his students recorded this *koan*, or saying:

> Followers of the Way,* if you want to get the kind of understanding that accords with the Dharma,† never be misled by others. Whether you're facing inward or facing outward, whatever you meet up with,

* That is, disciples of the Zen path to enlightenment.

† Either, the repository of the Buddha's teaching and traditions surrounding it, or the ultimate principle behind the created order of the universe.

> just kill it! If you meet a buddha, kill the buddha . . . If you meet your parents, kill your parents. If you meet your kinfolk, kill your kinfolk. Then for the first time you will gain emancipation, will not be entangled with things, will pass freely anywhere you wish to go.[1]

Lin Chi was not advocating patricidal, matricidal, genocidal behaviour here. Rather he was saying, if you think that you have reached enlightenment, and if you have a vision of the Buddha, be very careful; that vision is more likely to be a projection of your own fantasy buddha onto the matter of the world. It is more likely to be an expression of your own prejudices than a genuine manifestation of the Enlightened One. Purge yourself of even these illusions!

Lin-Chi's teaching is not so very different from another description of discipleship, which can cause so much difficulty for conscientious preachers:

> To another Jesus said, 'Follow me.' But he said, 'Lord, first let me go and bury my father.' But Jesus said to him, 'Let the dead bury their own dead; but as for you, go and proclaim the kingdom of God.' Another said, 'I will follow you, Lord; but let me first say farewell to those at my home.' Jesus said to him, 'No one who puts a hand to the plough and looks back is fit for the kingdom of God.' (Luke 9.59–62)

To be fit for the kingdom of God, the spiritual equivalent of the Buddhist goal of enlightenment, seems to involve renouncing all those ties which make us human; our involvement within a wider society, our responsibilities to our family, our duties in work, culture and religion. It seems that Jesus here is advocating a posture of non-attachment, rather like the Buddhist doctrine of *dukkhanirodha*, the third of the Four Noble Truths which lead to freedom from the inevitable suffering and impermanence of this life. Perhaps it is good to examine our attachments, every so often, if not frequently, to see what things we have elevated to the positions of importance or pre-eminence in our lives.

But why kill George Herbert? What possible danger can the saint of Bemerton, courtier, poet and parson, pose to Christian ministers today? Is there really something more than sneering clerical cussedness going on here?

The answer lies in the way in which Herbert has been, and continues to be, used as an exemplar, *the* exemplar for the English parson. Whether you are High Church, Low Church, Evangelical, Charismatic, whatever, Herbert is portrayed as the prototype of the pastor, teacher, preacher, almoner, negotiator, gentleman, scholar. He is *Ur*-Vicar, the *Echt*-Rector.

I think that there are at least three reasons for this. First, Herbert's *The Country Parson* itself inevitably drew attention to the nature of Herbert's own parochial ministry. We infer the validity of his teaching and the authenticity of his suggestions from what we believe of the manner in which he lived his life. We know that Herbert, in that horrible phrase, 'walked the talk'. But, as his time in parochial ministry was so short, the walk not very long, we inevitably read *from* the text back *into* the life. *The Country Parson* tells us about the country parson, as it were. This is certainly what Isaak Walton did in his life of Herbert. For example, Walton tells a touching story of how, one evening walking to a musical soirée in Salisbury, Herbert stopped to help a 'poor man with a poorer horse'. The parson took off his 'canonical coat', reloaded the burdened animal and became 'soiled and discomposed' in the process. He told his friends that such an act of charity 'would prove music to him at midnight', and thanked God for the opportunity to comfort a sad soul.[2] This has all the hallmarks of an exemplary tale. If it *didn't* happen, Herbert was the sort of man to whom it *ought* to have happened.

Second, Herbert died young and in post. This has always been the fast-track to canonization in the folk religion of the Church of England. The story goes that in the Roman Catholic Church the source of all authority is the pope; in nonconformist churches the source of all authority is the Bible; and in the Church of England the source of all authority is the previous incumbent. If the previous incumbent has died in harness, then all the guilt and wonder at his vicarious sacrifice becomes transformed into hagiography. Herbert died before his parochial ministry could be compromised; not just by the ructions and turmoil of the English Civil Wars, but also by the regular, mundane bruises and cavils and accommodations that make up everyday life in a community of sinners trying to be saints.

Third, and on a wider plane, Herbert fits in, like the keystone or a linch-pin, to what Diarmaid MacCulloch calls 'the myth of the English

Reformation'. The myth appears in one of three, related forms; that 'the English Reformation did not happen, or that it happened by accident rather than design, or that it was half-hearted and sought a middle way between Catholicism and Protestantism'. The myth is a question of the identity of the Church of England, its understanding of where it came from, and who it is. According to MacCulloch, the myth formed in two distinct periods; the first in the middle years of the seventeenth century under Archbishop William Laud and after the Restoration, the second in the first third of the nineteenth century under the influence of the Oxford Movement. In both these periods Herbert's work was extremely popular and influential.

The myth emphasized the continuity of the Church by sharply defining who was part of the Church's story and who was not: Christians who remained loyal to the authority of the Bishop of Rome were traitors, and Christians who wished a more thorough reform on Genevan lines were condemned as somehow not fully members of the Church of England. Later historians built on this threefold division, so that the Elizabethan and Jacobean Church was viewed through 'a Laudian prism' in which the mainstream Calvinist characteristics of the Church of Herbert's day became somehow marginal.[3] MacCulloch points out the widespread nature of Puritan iconoclasm, the sheer amount of hard work, by lawful authority, which went into refitting medieval church buildings for reformed worship, and the Calvinistic tenor of the Elizabethan Prayer Book. He concludes that the true nature of the Elizabethan and Jacobean Church, in which Herbert worshipped and worked, was 'a church which found the Swiss Reformations more congenial than the German, which reflected this alignment in its theology and practice, and in which discontinuity with the pre-Reformation past was more characteristic than continuity'.[4]

If the reality was discontinuity, and a later establishment of the Church wished to emphasize or discover continuity, then an example of continuity had to be found: people were posthumously co-opted in support of positions which they would have been very surprised by in their lifetimes.

Enter Herbert. One of the most interesting aspects of Herbert's posthumous reputation has been his adoption by the Laudian 'High Church' strand of the Church of England. Elizabeth Clarke has uncovered the extent to which Herbert's social circle, his writing and his

2

'. . . how many live so unlike him now . . .'

> I have now brought him to the parsonage of Bemerton, and to the thirty-sixth year of his age, and must stop here, and bespeak the reader to prepare for an almost incredible story, of the great sanctity of the short remainder of his holy life; a life so full of charity, humility, and all Christian virtues, that it deserves the eloquence of St Chrysostom to commend and declare it . . . [I] profess myself amazed when I consider how few of the clergy lived like him then, and how many live so unlike him now.
>
> (Isaak Walton, *The Life Of Mr George Herbert*, 1670)

If you think the Angel Gabriel in Jacobean clothing is an over-the-top description of our subject, look at this passage from an early-twentieth-century edition of Herbert's poems:

> Here, as the cattle wind homeward in the evening light, the benign, white-haired parson stands at his gate to greet the cowherd, and the village chimes call the labourers to evensong. For these contented spirits, happily removed from the stress and din of contending creeds and clashing dogmas, the message of the gospel tells of divine approval for work well done . . . And among these typical spirits, beacons of a quiet hope, no figure stands out more brightly or more memorably than that of George Herbert.[1]

The reality of Herbert, his life and ministry, is, of course, a lot less bucolic, and because of that, a lot more interesting.

George Herbert was born on 3 April 1653 at Montgomery to Richard and Magdalene Herbert. His family were a collateral branch of the Earls of Pembroke; his paternal grandfather, Edward, was constable of Montgomery Castle, and his maternal grandfather, Richard

Newport, was a descendant of Welsh royalty. He was part of a large family, the seventh of ten children. When he was less than four years old his father died, having been injured in a robber ambush some years before. His mother was two months pregnant with his youngest brother Thomas. The family moved to live with his maternal grandmother in Eyton-upon-Severn in Shropshire, but following his grandmother's death in early 1599 the family were obliged to move again.

This time Magdalene took her family to Oxford, where George's eldest brother, Edward (later first Baron of Cherbury) had already matriculated at University College. According to Herbert's later, and not always reliable biographer, Isaak Walton, it was while living in Oxford that Magdalene Herbert became friends with the young courtier and diplomat, John Donne. Many years later Donne was to deliver the eulogy at Magdalene's memorial service.

By 1601 the family had moved again, this time to a house in Charing Cross, then a rapidly developing suburb between the two cities of London and Westminster. We have an illuminating picture of life in the Herbert household. Magdalene began a 'Kitchen Book' in April 1601 which records household expenditure, living arrangements and even guests for dinner. The household was large and hospitable, perhaps too much so. Edward Herbert acerbically recorded many years later that,

> My mother together with myself and wife removed up to London where we took house, and kept a greater family than became either my mother's widow's estate or such young beginners as we were, especially since six brothers and three sisters were to be provided for.[2]

It seems clear that Magdalene was in her element. Her son grudgingly admitted that she brought her children up carefully, and dedicated them to learning. She led a life that would have been denied to her as the child-bearing wife of a provincial gentleman. The 'Kitchen Book' records that in their first year in Charing Cross John Bull and William Byrd of the Chapel Royal were guests at dinner. George was put to the study of Latin and rhetoric: the 'Kitchen Book' records payments to tutors and booksellers. William Camden, the historian, was also a guest at dinner.

By 1604 George entered Westminster School as a day pupil. The headmaster at the time was Lancelot Andrewes, Dean of Westminster and afterwards Bishop of Chichester and Winchester. George excelled at his studies and was elected a scholar (residential pupil) in 1605. In May 1609 he matriculated at Trinity College, Cambridge, where there was a tradition of Westminster boys. When he graduated in 1613 it was as second of 193 graduates. He remained at Trinity as what we would call now a teaching assistant, until in 1618 he was appointed deputy to the University Orator. The Orator was responsible for all the University's communications with Crown, government and benefactors; the equivalent of modern-day public relations, although with a firmer grasp of classical oratory. One of Herbert's earliest letters as Orator in his own right was to the King, James I, thanking him for the King's gift of his *Opera Latina*; Herbert shows a fine gift for the rhetorical pyrotechnics and obsequiousness that such a task required:

> Scotland was too narrow for thee to be able to fully unfold thy wings from the nest . . . What didst thou do thereupon? Thou didst take possession of all the British Isles.[3]

It would seem at this time that Herbert's career was following a conventional enough path: Oxbridge, preferment, court and diplomacy. It was the career of his older brother, Edward: by 1620 Edward was English ambassador to the French court. Certainly, in surviving letters to his stepfather, Sir John Danvers (Magdalene married again in 1609, to a man who was two years younger than Edward and only nine years older than George), Herbert seems to be pleased with the status and gaiety of the position of Orator.

However, the pleasure and the ambition did not survive. In the late 1610s and early 1620s Herbert lost a number of relatives, including four of his siblings. His health, never strong, suffered in the murk and mists of Cambridge. After 1621 we have precious little record of his official work as Orator. The Herberts' star was on the wane. Edward was blamed, unfairly, for the initial failure of the marriage negotiations between the Prince of Wales and Princess Henrietta Maria, and was recalled to England in disgrace and financial hardship. Henry Herbert, as Master of the Revels (court-appointed censor for the theatre) had permitted a play satirizing the increasingly ill King James. George, meanwhile, had offended Charles, Prince of Wales and the influential Duke of Buckingham with an oration extolling peace when the two were looking for war against Spain. He was elected to the House of Commons as MP for Montgomery in the inconclusive Parliament of 1624, which was then prorogued. Herbert's career was going nowhere. No wonder he then explored the only avenue of advancement left open to him: the Church.

When he had become a major fellow of Trinity in 1616 the college statutes required him to be ordained within seven years. Herbert missed the deadline. We don't know why: perhaps it was his poor health. In any case, in November 1624 he petitioned the Archbishop of Canterbury for permission to be excused the statutory notice period for ordination as a deacon (a year) and for him to be allowed to be ordained at any time by John Williams, Bishop of Lincoln. We have no record of when the ordination took place, although Williams presented Herbert with the living of Llandinam in Montgomeryshire in December 1624 (curiously to our way of doing things, Herbert need not necessarily have been ordained to receive the income of the parish!), and by July 1626 he had been made canon of Lincoln Cathedral and held the benefice of Leighton Ecclesia (Leighton Bromswold) in Huntingdonshire. (His installation in the cathedral had to be by proxy, as that day he was delivering the University oration to the Duke of Buckingham.)

At first, Herbert seems to have taken on his parochial responsibilities as no more than a means of accessing some money: with the canonry and the parish came stipends. Even so, the stipends were not large, and with them came the responsibility to rebuild the decayed chancel of Leighton, estimated at more than £2,000. Some friends organized the appeal for him, the seventeenth-century equivalent of the thermometer outside the church building. Leighton had become more of a drain than a resource. Again, Herbert had reached a dead end.

Then three things happened which changed the course of his life. First, he visited his great friend from university, Nicholas Ferrar, at Ferrar's new home in Little Gidding. Nick Ferrar had been a student at Clare College, and, following a number of years travelling on the continent (learning Dutch, almost dying of a fever in Marseilles, and walking the 500 miles from Madrid to San Sebastian when his money ran out), he had settled back in London working for the family merchant-adventurer business. Unhappily, with the failure of the Virginia Company in 1623, Ferrar's family lost an enormous amount of money. In an attempt to limit their losses, and to prosecute those responsible for the failure, Nick became an

MP, and with Sir John Danvers, Herbert's stepfather, he was a prime mover of the impeachment of the Earl of Middlesex, whom he blamed for his family's financial loss. By 1625 Ferrar had withdrawn from public life, moving to Little Gidding in Huntingdonshire with his mother and family. Once there, wishing to be chaplain to the large household, he had himself ordained deacon by William Laud, then Bishop of St David's, in Westminster Abbey. The small community, later mocked as an 'Arminian nunnery', lived a life of daily prayer (scrupulously following the rubrics of the Book of Common Prayer) and study, for which purpose Ferrar wrote a harmonization of the Gospels. Ferrar and Herbert shared a deep and abiding friendship. Herbert's second biographer (the first was Ferrar himself) wrote:

> . . . they loved each other most entirely, and their very souls cleaved together most intimately, and drove a large stock of Christian intelligence together long before their deaths . . .[4]

The example of his friend, withdrawing from public life, must have influenced Herbert greatly. Then in 1627 his mother died.

Magdalene had been ill for more than five years. The sorrow that her illness and death brought her son can be seen in the personal tributes he paid her: in 1622, the poem-letter 'To his Mother, in her sickness', and, following her death, a poem in Latin and Greek, published as '*Memoriae matris sacrum*'. This was Herbert's first 'personal' poem to be published. John Donne, by now Dean of St Paul's, preached at Magdalene's memorial service in July 1627. In his sermon, Magdalene is shown to be a well-rounded person, faithful, forbearing and lovable:

> . . . in the doctrine and discipline of that Church, in which, God sealed her, to himself, in Baptism, she brought up her children, she assisted her family, she dedicated her soul to God in her life, and surrendered it to him in her death. And, in that form of Common Prayer, which is ordained by that Church, and to which she had accustomed herself with her family, twice every day, she joined with that company which was about her death-bed, in answering to every part thereof, which the Congregation is directed to answer to, with a clear understanding, with a constant memory, with a distinct voice, not two hours before she died.[5]

By the end of the summer of 1627 Herbert had resigned from his university post. He turned from the possibility of both academic and courtly preferment. With the influence of Nicholas Ferrar, and sorrow of his mother's death and the impression made upon him by Donne's memorial, Herbert now committed his future to the Church: not for personal advancement, but, for the moment at least, in service.

Herbert moved to Wiltshire, to stay with his stepfather's elder brother. While at Dauntsey he met and married Jane Danvers in March 1629. The newly-weds lived with Herbert's mother-in-law until April 1630 when he was presented as Rector of the parish of Fugglestone-with-Bemerton near Salisbury. This was Herbert's first true 'living', as we would understand it today. He remained as Rector of Bemerton until his death.

From Herbert's reputation and role as the exemplar of Anglican parochial clergy, one might be forgiven for thinking that Herbert served the people of Fugglestone-with-Bemerton for many, many years. In fact, he remained in post for less than three years. When Herbert took the living he was still a deacon; he was not priested until September 1630, four months after his curate! And it should not be thought that Herbert lost himself in rural life, like a pastoral version of the slum-priests of the nineteenth century. Bemerton, now a suburb of Salisbury, was even in the seventeenth century only a short stroll from the Cathedral Close. Walton tells us that twice a week Herbert walked to the cathedral for Evensong, and then spent the evening playing the lute and singing with his friends, often in the South Canonry (now the house of the Bishop of Salisbury). Within his parish lay the village of Wilton and Wilton Hall, the seat of his relations, the earls of Pembroke. It was his well-placed family who requested Herbert's presentation to the living. He became confidant and spiritual director to Lady Anne Clifford, wife of the fourth earl.

Herbert's poor life worsened towards the end of 1632, when he was obliged to employ a second curate for the discharge of his duties. By late winter 1633 he was dying of consumption. He died on 1 March 1633, a month before his fortieth birthday – a priest for two and a half years.

So why should we remember this man? An academic who never fulfilled his schoolboy promise; a courtier who found the politics of court too difficult to break into; a clergyman who held benefices in plurality and *in absentia*; a parish priest for less time than a modern-day curacy; a parochial theorist rather than a practitioner?

'The poems!' is the easiest answer. The man was a genius poet, and his verse is one of the glories of the English language and of the English Church. As Kenneth Mason says, in a little pamphlet published by the Sisters of the Love of God, 'It is, indeed, through his poetry that Herbert continues to minister to us . . . his priesthood is in his poetry.'[6] Perhaps so, although it was not always thought to be the case. His major collection of poems, *The Temple*, was published posthumously in 1633, and went through thirteen editions by 1709 (Charles I even having a copy during his imprisonment at Carisbrook Castle during the English Civil War). But in the eighteenth century he fell out of fashion. There was no new edition of *The Temple* until 1799. He was thought to be no more than a clever, but ultimately sterile, technician: Dryden mocked the poets who lived in 'Acrostick land'. However, his star began to rise in the early years of the twentieth century. T. S. Eliot, who in later life came to champion Herbert, described Herbert's standing in 1930s England thus:

> . . . his figure is preserved . . . as one of genuine though rather conventional piety . . . we go to Donne for poetry and to Crashaw for religious poetry: but that Herbert deserves to be remembered as the representative lyricist of a mild and tepid church.[7]

Curiously, Eliot goes on to say that Herbert's poetry works precisely *because* of his faith. He doubts that Herbert would have been more than a versifier without the structure and focus of his faith: 'You will not get much satisfaction from George Herbert unless you can take seriously the things which he took seriously himself and which made him what he was.'[8] By 1962, Eliot had expanded the bounds of Herbert's explicability and applicability. It is no longer necessary to read Herbert solely as an 'aid to devotion', although his work functions very well for that purpose. Rather, now Herbert may be read as a guide, *the* guide, to spiritual struggle:

> When I claim a place for Herbert among those poets whose work every lover of English poetry should read and every student of English poetry should study, irrespective of religious belief or unbelief, I am not thinking primarily of the exquisite craftsmanship, the extraordinary metrical virtuosity, or the verbal felicities, but of the

> *content* of the poems . . . [They] . . . form a record of spiritual struggle which should touch the feeling, and enlarge the understanding of those readers also who hold no religious belief and find themselves unmoved by religious emotion.[9]

Part of this openness and approachability in Herbert comes from his use of the English language. Sometimes, reading him, it is difficult to remember that Herbert died before the English Civil War, that great convulsion of politics, society, establishment, and, not least, language. Often the 1640s acts as a watershed for the modern reader, after which English poetry and prose can be simply 'read off' the page and before which effort and concentration on the *process* of reading have to be paid in order to comprehend the writer's meaning. And yet Herbert, once he left the florid Jacobean requirements of the Orator's office behind him, seems to be immune to the syntactical complications and allusive vocabulary of his contemporaries. Look at this poem, 'Praise I':

To write a verse or two is all the praise,
That I can raise:
Mend my estate in any ways,
Thou shalt have more.

I go to Church; help me to wings, and I
Will thither fly;
Or, if I mount unto the sky,
I will do more.

Man is all weakness; there is no such thing
As Prince or King:
His arm is short; yet with a sling
He may do more.

An herb distill'd, and drunk, may dwell next door,
On the same floor,
To a brave soul: Exalt the poor,
They can do more.

Oh raise me then! Poor bees, that work all day,
Sting my delay,
Who have a work, as well as they
And much, much more.

Within the whole poem there is no word of more than two syllables. Simple phrases work as hard as the bees of the poem, with a plainness in what they signify, and yet, by their placing and their subjects, leading to layers of deeper meaning: 'help me to wings', 'may dwell next door', 'and much, much more'. Herbert writes in a vernacular voice, there is no special 'religious tone' and yet, as Peter Porter says, in this poem the 'metaphysical pressure is high'.[10]

Herbert's poetry is now part of the canon of English literature, familiar enough to be quoted in book titles and the names of radio programmes. He does not have quite the status of Shakespeare, but that has not stopped two American academics from producing a concordance of Herbert's vocabulary[11] – and none of Shakespeare's poetry appears in hymn books of the Church! Even so, it is not for his poems that Herbert is the target of any Anglican Lin-Chi. It is for a book published, like his poems, posthumously, *The Priest to the Temple*, or, probably more accurately, *The Country Parson.*[12]

Although the book was written during Herbert's time in Bemerton (the preface, from the author to the reader, is dated 1632), it was not published until 1652, as part of the compilation by Barnabas Oley, *Herbert's Remains*, which also included Oley's brief biography and Herbert's collection of proverbs, *Jacula Prudentum*. The year 1652 was at the height of the English Republic, and the Church of England had been suppressed; priests, bishops and liturgy, replaced by a Presbyterian establishment. It is probable that Herbert's work was published only because of his family connections to the winning side in the Civil War; his stepfather, Sir John Danvers, was a signatory to the death warrant of Charles I. Even so, *The Priest to the Temple* was presented as 'an act of homage to the pre-Civil War Church of England'.[13] The editor's supplied title, as well as being a canny piece of marketing, reminding readers of those lovely poems from *The Temple*, is also provocative: 'priestly' ministry was one of the hated tenets of the Laudian church, and had been abolished along with prelates and other popish practices. To call the book by that title was as goading as publishing a work entitled A *Jihadist's Handbook* in contemporary America.

And yet we should not think that Herbert is an unambiguous champion for the 'High Church' party. Although in the thirteenth chapter, 'The Parson's Church', he quotes the great Laudian slogan of 'Let all things be done decently and in order', he qualifies it with the addition, 'let all things be done to edification': the rituals of the Church were to some degree for the teaching of the congregation, unlike the Laudian ideal where they were for the glorification of God. Although the church should be well looked after, kept clean and in good repair, Herbert deliberately refers to a Communion table and not a (Laudian) altar; he denies the holiness of objects, instead preferring to 'keep the middle way between superstition and slovenliness'. Although he recommends kneeling to receive the sacrament, he refuses to demand it, saying that 'Contentiousness in a feast of Charity is more scandal than any posture' (ch. 22). He regards his stewardship of the church building, for the glory of God and the benefit of the parishioners, to be in keeping with scripture, unlike those who 'deny Scripture to be perfect'; that is, who prefer church tradition to be the guide in such matters. And the ultimate irony is that *The Country Parson* was refused a licence to be printed in 1640/1 by the Laudian authorities who appropriated him as their champion only a dozen years later![14]

The Country Parson is a comprehensive and concise work; 37 chapters, the longest no more than 1,600 words, with an assumption of the natural breadth of a parson's responsibilities. The work begins with a brief discussion of the nature of pastors and their diversity, chaplains (to universities and great houses) and parish priests. Herbert makes it clear in the first sentence of the work what he believes is the purpose of all these different types of parson: 'A Pastor is the Deputy of Christ for the reducing of Man to the Obedience of God' (ch. 1, 'Of a Pastor'). Then he passes through the nature of the parson's life ('holy, just, prudent, temperate, bold, grave in all his ways'), the range of his education, to the two major responsibilities of praying and preaching. The way in which the parson manages his time, leisure and work, and his household, demonstrates to his parishioners that 'his family is a School of Religion'.

Much time is spent on describing the responsibilities of what we would call pastoral visiting, but what Herbert refers to as being on 'circuit' or 'sentinel'. The priest is to visit his parishioners so that he may see them in their natural environment, away from their 'Sunday best' behaviour. His task is to exhort and teach in all his visits, even assisting in lessons for reading and writing. As for the parish poor, 'neither disdaineth he to enter into the poorest Cottage, though he even creep into it, and though it smell never so loathsomely. For both God is there also, and those for whom God died.' Visiting the poor is greater comfort to them than visiting the rich, and it aids in the parson's own self-humiliation.

This concentration on the (beneficial) effects of ministry upon the minister gives us a clue to a proper understanding of what *The Country Parson* (the book) and who the country parson (the person) both are. As Herbert himself says in the preface, 'I have resolved to set down the Form and Character of a true Pastor, that I may have a Mark to aim at: which also I will set as high as I can, since he shoots higher that threatens the Moon, than he that aims at a Tree.' The book and the person are ideals, marks at which to aim. This is not a simple practical handbook; it is, rather, a different genre, a 'character' book.

The 'character' genre was one of the most popular in the early seventeenth century. It was based upon the template set by the classical author Theophrastus (c. 370–c. 285 BC) in his book *The Characters*. There Theophrastus vigorously and bitingly describes the personification of various moral characteristics for the edification of his readers: although the pen-portraits might be entertaining, through wit, satire and abuse, character writing had an ethical purpose. Elizabeth Clarke makes this connection between *The Country Parson* and its parent genre clear. Herbert's original title for the work was *The Country Parson, His Character*; it is written in short, pithy chapters, each beginning with the subject under consideration, 'The Country Parson is sincere and upright in all his relations'; it was originally published in the most common format for character writing, duodecimo (handy, pocket size); each chapter is written in the present tense and concludes with a pithy, didactic ending (Clarke calls them 'sententious'): 'Do well, and right, and let the world sink.'

Much of the model that Herbert sets out shows his training and employment in rhetoric. In order for the pastor to be able, as the opening chapter says, to reduce man to the obedience of God, then the pastor needs to understand himself in didactic and rhetorical terms.

First, the parson lives an exemplary life, in which the Christian life 'is most seen' by his parishioners (ch. 3, 'The Parson's Life').

Second, the parson should study the reactions of his parishioners to all his teaching, spoken and modelled, and amend the mode of his teaching accordingly: 'He observes who marks, and who not; and with particularizing of his speech now to the younger sort, then to the elder, now to the poor, and now to the rich' (ch. 7, 'The Parson Preaching'). Although the parson's normal mood should be sadness, fixed as he is upon the cross of Christ and the sin and misery of the world, occasionally he 'condescends to human frailties both in himself and others; and intermingles some mirth in his discourses occasionally, according to the pulse of the hearer' (ch. 27, 'The Parson in Mirth').

Third, the parson should not be afraid of using correction and reproof in his dealings with his parishioners: 'the Country Parson, where ever he is, keeps God's watch; that is, there is nothing spoken or done in the Company where he is, but comes under his Test and censure' (ch. 18, 'The Parson in Sentinel'). He does allow the parson a modicum of leeway in when to censure: 'those that the Parson finds idle, or ill-employed, he chides not at first, for that were neither civil, nor profitable; but always in the close, before he departs from them' (ch. 14, 'The Parson in Circuit').

There is much in *The Country Parson* which remains of interest to the historian of the Caroline Church. It shows us examples of *via media* between Laudianism and the Calvinistic pressures of the Puritans in a typical parish. It gives us an idea of social relationships in the English countryside. It shows what skills and education were valued and available to the Church's clergy. There are also elements within it that remain useful for today's clergy: its understanding of human psychology still rings true. For example, the parson should, over the course of a year, invite the entire parish to dine with him, and he should make it clear that the entire parish will be invited, 'because country people are very observant of such things, and will not be persuaded, but being not invited, they are hated' (ch. 11, 'The Parson's Courtesy'). Furthermore, Herbert assumes that the parson will be and ought to be available to the whole of society. This is still part of the Church of England's self-understanding (formed in no small measure by the Church's devotion to Herbert's work).

But there are some passages in the work which only go to show exactly how separated we are from the time and values of Herbert. Which priest today would regard it as his duty to admonish his parishioners, when found in their work, to 'dive not too deep into worldly affairs', and reminding them not 'to labour for wealth and maintenance, as that they make not that the end of their labour, but that they may have [the] wherewithal to serve God the better, and to do good deeds'? (ch. 14, 'The Parson in Circuit'). Which priest today would tick off the gentry who arrive late for the service, and not expect to get his name in the local newspaper? Which priest today would regard it as even *possible* to make his children first Christians, then patriots: 'the one he owes to his heavenly Country, the other to his earthly, having no title to either, except that he do good to both'? (ch. 10, 'The Parson in his House').

But Herbert was a parish incumbent for less than three years, and a priest for even less time than that. He lived and worked in a community of no more than 500 people,* and he undertook his work with at first one and then a second curate. He had a private income, and, away from the intrigues of London, Westminster and the university towns, he ministered in a society that was stable after the chaos of the previous hundred years. Like all good popular icons, he died young, and left a beautiful body of work. It is instructive, although ultimately unfair, to imagine how Herbert would have managed parish life in the turbulence of the Civil Wars. Would he have remained loyal to the Crown (as his biographer Barnabas Oley did) and been evicted from his living, or would he have taken the side of the Parliament (as his stepfather John Danvers did), and been evicted from his convictions? Would the example of *The Country Parson* have been fatally compromised by the trimming, or otherwise, of its author?

There is no great fruitfulness in pressing this particular thought experiment. The fact is that Herbert died within three years of arriving in Bemerton, having had no time to seek preferment or employment away from his little Wiltshire suburb. We have the biography and the text we have, and 'George Herbert, Priest, Poet, 1633' is there in the *Common Worship* calendar for 27 February.

---

* And probably many fewer than that. Fugglestone with Bemerton had only 500 people living there at the time of the 1801 census, in 111 houses. John Chandler estimates that there were no more than 200 parishioners in the three villages of Herbert's benefice: see John Chandler, 'The Country Parson's Flock: Bemerton in 1632' (2007).

3

The only thing I don't run

> . . . the average country parson is now a comparatively poor man . . . he spends much of his time clerking, teaching, examining, or taking services in neighbouring parishes during sequestrations . . . simply for his own personal profit. His wife probably goes out to work; and if he inhabits a large rectory or vicarage, he can make a considerable income letting rooms. This is all wrong.
>
> (A. Tindal Hart, *The Country Priest in English History*, 1959)

In the autumn of 1988 I went to see the Diocesan Director of Ordinands to begin the process leading to ordination. During the meeting he fixed me with a steely glare and sternly admonished me: 'I hope you don't want to be ordained for the status that being a clergyman affords you, because the social status of the clergy is lower today than at any time since the Reformation.' I took him for his word, because I trusted his judgement and because I liked the man – though as it happens he went on to become, in short order, Bishop of Stepney, Bishop of London, Prelate of the Order of the British Empire, Dean of the Chapels Royal, Privy Counsellor, and executor of the will of Diana, Princess of Wales.

Even so, there is but one Bishop of London, and for the rest of us Dr Chartres's warning holds true; there is precious little status to be found in the life of a cleric today. This chapter explores how and why we have reached the status we do possess, and what that status might be.

I was ordained to a title parish (as a curate's first job is technically called) in Cirencester. Just outside Cirencester is a small village called Barnsley. It isn't one of the heart-stoppingly lovely Cotswold villages, and other than a well-known garden, it didn't attract coach parties of day trippers like Bibury just up the road. There was one road through Barnsley, and, except for the church, the only public amenity was the village pub, called, imaginatively, 'The Village Pub'. The name was painted on the sign which hung above well-tended baskets of flowers. It depicted the road through Barnsley. A car was parked on the road, complete with running boards and huge headlamps, a 1940s kind of car. In the foreground was a village bobby, again in a 1940s kind of uniform. He had his arm out to shake the hand of the village parson; tweed jacket, bald head, round smile, glasses. A 1940s kind of parson. The village pub, with its village policeman and its village padre. The glory of England, combined in one pub sign.

The glory of England is celebrated in a thousand different cultural artefacts. In literature, music, film, television, radio, plays, and memories, the village parson is present, in body if not in mind, for we all know that parsons, like all sky pilots, are likely to be a little eccentric. Thomas Hinde, in *A Field Guide to the English Country Parson* (a significantly zoological title, don't you think?) thought that the whole idea of village parsons was a social experiment: 'Give a reasonably educated middle-class Englishman a modest income, a house in the country, and job security for life, and see what he will do . . . the most important thing the Anglican Church gave England was a gentleman in every parish.'[1] Hinde's book then catalogues a fair selection of the mad, the bad, the learned and the depraved. Some clergy of this ilk remained in post even as late as the beginning of my ministry. A rector in a gaggle of parishes to the north of Cirencester had been in the living for 40 years or more; let's call him Edwards. A retired priest once told me he received a telephone call from Edwards: 'Could you take some services while I'm away on holiday?' 'Certainly,' my friend replied, 'just let me get my diary.' 'You'd better hurry up. The taxi's outside waiting to take me to the airport!'

For all that disorganization, Edwards was a rural parson of the old school; I am sure he would have done well in the competition organized by the genteel magazine *Country Life* in September 2005. The editors put out an appeal for 'Britain's Best-loved Parson'. They were overwhelmed with nominations for one man, Richard Morgan, Rector of Therfield and Kelshall in Hertfordshire. When the writer went to meet Mr Morgan's parishioners, they enthusiastically endorsed their man:

> 'He had his beard shaved off for charity in the village pub . . .' '[He] writes many of his own prayers and hymns . . .' '[He] gets involved in everything, in all the social gatherings – the village fête, the book

> club, he comes to watch the sports club, plays with the Therfield Thespians, leads the sponsored walks – you name it he does it . . .' 'He's everyone's friend, Anglican or not . . .' and that comment has all the parishioners nodding.

This enthusiasm was confirmed for the writers when they attended a service in Therfield for the beginning of a new school term: '. . . you understand immediately why his parishioners have warmed to him so much . . . From the moment the first hymn begins, and the rector starts waving his hands to mime the words "He's got the whole world in His hands . . .", his infectious energy and steady smile have everyone glued to their hard seats.'[2]

We can celebrate this eccentricity, just so long as we don't have to work with it; we can be cheered by this diversity, just so long as we don't have to worship under it; we can be comforted by this ubiquity, just so long as we don't have to believe in it.

For there is just one small problem. The vision of 'The Village Pub' and *The Field Guide* and *Country Life* is of an England which no longer exists; in fact, may never have existed. A parson in every parish was an invention of the nineteenth century, a time when there were many more clergy in England than there had been at any time since the Reformation (and many of those earlier clergy were monks or friars, whose vocation was emphatically *not* to parochial life). Some numbers: in 1841 there were 14,613 clergymen in England and Wales. By 1901 this had risen, not quite in line with the growth of population, to 25,235. That was the high-water mark. Thereafter the numbers are 23,918 (1911), 19,147 (1931), 13,429 (1961), 12,056 (1976). In the latest year for which there are figures, 2004/2005, the situation seems to have improved: 13,654 priests. However, the breakdown of that number is significant: 9,138 licensed stipendiary clergy, 2,888 licensed non-stipendiary clergy, 1,628 in chaplaincy and 'other ministries'. The remaining 4,468 are the 'active retired', clergy who have ceased full-time ministry (whether paid or not) but have permission to officiate from their bishop (there are another 4,215 inactive retired clergy).[3] There are, therefore, only about 400 more licensed stipendiary clergy than all the other types (non-stipendiary, chaplaincy, retired) combined. If 'The Village Pub' were to have an accurate sign, then the village parson would need to be shown as retired, or working in another profession.

The word 'parson' itself betrays the cultural context in which clergy ministered at first. 'Parson' is an Anglo-Norman word dating to the thirteenth century, which in turn comes from the Old French '*persone*' which meant, in this case, 'ecclesiastical dignitary'. Parson was, originally and simply, the person in the parish, the person who was there as the representative of the Church.

Anthony Russell's magisterial book *The Clerical Profession* explores the eight different ways in which the function and status of this parson/person was expressed in the late eighteenth and early nineteenth centuries. The parson was, primarily, a *leader of public worship*. Sometimes, most times, it has to be admitted that this was the sum and total of the parson's responsibilities. J. J. Blunt, writing in 1856, admitted as much:

> There was a period and almost within my own memory when a notion prevailed that the duties of the clergy were the duties of Sunday and little more; that their sphere lay pretty exclusively in the due performance of the public services of the Church. That was, I need not say, a very imperfect view of clerical obligations.[4]

Along with the public services of the Church was the obligation to take the *Occasional Offices*, what was known as 'surplice duties' in the eighteenth century. The clergyman received his stipend, variable from benefice to benefice, no matter how many services of public worship were taken in his church: surplice duty (for marriages, baptisms, burials and the churching of women) was an important source of additional income, if managed properly. Unfortunately, the management was often abused in order to maximize income: the rich were attended to, the poor were treated perfunctorily. We see this distinction made in John Clubbe's advice to a young clergyman (1770): 'Carry not a rich man into the church and read over him the whole burial service and huddle a poor man into his grace with a small portion of it.'[5]

The parson was expected to be a *preacher*: it was almost the 'charter role'[6] of the cleric, and in the eighteenth century churches were built or remodelled to aid the delivery of the sermon. In fact, the existence of pew rents (by which people paid for the rights to a particular seat in church, like a debenture seat in Wembley stadium) meant that many urban clergy were dependent upon their ability to attract people to hear them preach. Unhappily, and inevitably, not all clergy were up to the task, and other, entrepreneurial clergy made a tidy living by printing ready-made sermons in copperplate lettering, so that if the parson's text was overlooked, it would not be thought he was reading another's work.[7]

Preaching was superior to the other liturgical function of the parson, the *Celebrant of the Sacraments*. Holy Communion in the eighteenth century was not just a dominical sacrament; it was also an expression of national and social conformity. The Test and Corporation Acts of Charles II's reign meant that anybody holding public office in England must be a communicant member of the Church of England. By this requirement, the parson became the gatekeeper to social inclusion and exclusion: the Eucharist was a shibboleth. This also meant that if there was no pressing *social* need for a Communion service, there was no pressing *religious* need. In the 25-year ministry of the Revd R. W. Finch in Barrington, Cambridgeshire, there was no celebration of Holy Communion at all, and Thomas Secker, Bishop of Oxford (and later Archbishop of Canterbury), in his Visitation of 1741, pleaded with his clergy: 'One more thing might be done in all your parishes; a sacrament might be interposed in that long interval between Whitsunday and Christmas.'[8]

The parson was expected to be a *pastor*, but despite Herbert's advice and the advice of some of the other clergy manuals in the eighteenth century, it is apparent that this was not a duty much observed either. William Jesse, an Evangelical reformer, wrote in 1785:

> Very few of the clergy seem to have any idea of the necessity and importance of parochial visitations, that is of going from house to house to inquire particularly into the state of the people's souls, to teach and press upon their conscience truths which have been delivered from the pulpit in a more general way.[9]

The Canons of 1604 required every 'parson, vicar or curate' to examine the children of the parish in the articles of the faith; so the parson was a *Catechist*. It was an integral part of the parson's Sunday duties, supposedly to be held during Evening Prayer after the second lesson. The parson was enjoined to instruct in the Ten Commandments, the Thirty Nine Articles, the Lord's Prayer, as well as the Catechism in the Book of Common Prayer. With the decline of evening services through the eighteenth century there was a corresponding decline in catechizing. However, the parson was very often the only teacher of any kind in the parish, and so in the eighteenth century most parochial schools were run by clergy, and the private tutors of the wealthy were also clergy. Robert Walker of the Lake District held school in his church for five and a half days a week, using the altar as a desk, supplementing his income by spinning wool at the same time.[10] We can see in teaching the expansion of the parson's role into areas which we would now regard as wholly secular in nature: the parson had responsibilities beyond the church porch.

As, often, the only literate person in the parish, the parson acted as *Clerk* – registrar for births, marriages and deaths. The records he kept were the only legal record, and legacies and inheritances were often dependent upon his diligence. Often the parish registers were used to record parliamentary legislation, and the parson was the contact point for all people needing something from the state: the 'clergyman's signature was in constant demand on the papers of emigrants, sailors, soldiers, clergymen's widows, pensioners, lunatics, and persons wanting to keep a public house'.[11] Along with this implicit role as an officer of the state, often the parson fulfilled an explicit role, as an *Officer of the Law*, usually as a Justice of the Peace. Diana McClatchey has examined the records of the Quarter Sessions held in Oxfordshire in the eighteenth century. Whereas in 1775 only 31 per cent of the JPs were clergy, 83 per cent of convictions were overseen by them. In 1797–1800 the parallel figures are 28 per cent clergy JPs and 75 per cent convictions.[12] In other words, the clergy acted as magistrates in disproportionate occasions to their numbers. It is clear the clergy relished the opportunity to serve their society by this means; whether such a high conviction rate helped their Sunday duties is another question. Charles Kingsley certainly didn't think so. In an address to a clergy meeting in 1848 he said:

> It is our fault, our great fault, that you should sneer, sneer at the only news that ought to be your glory and your strength. It is our fault. We have used the Bible as if it were the special constable's handbook – an opium dose for keeping beasts of burden patient while they are being overloaded – a mere book to keep the poor in order.[13]

In the centuries before an integrated welfare state, the clergyman fulfilled three roles as *Almoner*. First, the Elizabethan poor laws required a local tax to be imposed by each parish's Vestry in order to pay for a workhouse or a poorhouse. The parson was the chairman of the Vestry. Second, a network of charities was in existence, founded by benefactors for the alleviation of suffering. The parson and churchwardens were frequently, if not always, the administrators of these monies. Third, it was expected that the parson, himself a member of the gentry, would have sufficient income to provide relief for the poor, the unemployed and the homeless directly. Gerard's handbook said: 'It is incumbent on a minister to search out the poor and indigent in his parish and to contrive means of supplying them.'[14]

Although it was not part of the clergyman's ordination charge, many of the handbooks of pastoral practice, from Herbert onwards, recommended that the parson have at least nodding acquaintance with the basic skills of medicine: the parson was an *Officer of Health*. Herbert advises his readers: 'If there be any of his flock sick, he is their Physician, or at least his Wife, of whom instead of the qualities of the world, he asks no other, but to have the skill of healing a wound, of helping the sick.'[15] Parson Woodforde had a great reputation in Castle Cary as a veterinarian, and Sidney Smith, when he moved to Combe Florey, set up an apothecary shop in the rectory, from which he spent much of his time dosing his parishioners. In 1820 there was published a guidebook for those clergy without Woodforde's or Smith's confidence: *Instructions for the Relief of the Sick Poor in some Diseases of Frequent Occurrence, Addressed to the Parochial Clergyman residing at a Distance from Professional Aid.* It was written by a doctor, so there seemed to be a tacit understanding that there need not be a demarcation dispute between parson and doctor.

The final role delineated by Russell is the parson as *Politician*. Before parliamentary reform in the nineteenth century the vote was restricted to those owning property worth more than 40 shillings a year. In many rural areas the clergy were the only men who qualified, and so the clergy vote was an important one for the political parties to woo. Very few clergy participated directly in the political process; only one was ever elected as an MP, the Revd John Horne Tooke of Old Sarum in 1801. This caused such disquiet that Parliament passed an act which fined him £500 a day unless he resigned his seat: Horne Tooke swiftly complied! Most clergy restricted themselves to canvassing support for candidates, especially those great men who could act as patrons for advancement in livings, and to agitating for the social *status quo*, especially after the horrors of the French Revolution: there was 'no body of men more active in supporting the established order and repulsing infidelity and revolutionary actions than the clergy'.[16]

At the beginning of the nineteenth century there was little to distinguish a clergyman in his day-to-day life from any other member of the gentry. His 'charter roles' were not the most important part of his function in society, and certainly were not the most visible. By the end of the century that had all changed. Industrialization, enormous population growth, the expansion of an urban environment and new discoveries in science, medicine and technology all led to the increasing complexity of Victorian society and the inadequacy of its governance by men whose chief qualification to govern was their status as gentlemen. Victorian society became 'professionalized'.

This doesn't just mean that society became more diligently managed, although that is the most common understanding of the word: to be professional means to be competent and efficient. The professionalization of society, in a technical sense, meant that different functions within civil society (like officer of the law, social worker, charity administrator, doctor) became much more tightly defined and entry into the new profession was closely controlled by either the executive or a professional governing body.

Richard H. Hall, an American sociologist, produced a model of what constitutes a profession in 1968.[17] The strength of Hall's model is that it includes not just what he calls the 'structural' characteristics of a profession (its governance, its formal educational and entrance qualifications), but also its 'attitudinal' characteristics, which 'reflect the manner in which the practitioners view their work'.[18] Hall describes five marks in these attitudinal characteristics. First, there is *professional reference*: the profession is itself the major source of self-definition and understanding for each individual, who seeks his ideas and judgements about his work from his colleagues. Second, a profession has a *service orientation*: there is a benefit to the public from the performance of the profession, and the performance is indispensable for a complete functioning of society. Third, a profession is subject to *colleague control*: fellow practitioners are the best people to judge a professional's performance. Fourth, a profession is an expression of a *vocation*: a professional is dedicated to his profession, and 'would probably want to do the work even if fewer extrinsic rewards were available'.[19] Fifth, a professional exercises *autonomy*, able to make decisions about his work free from pressure from clients, non-professionals, employers.

The *structural* professionalization of Victorian society meant that clergy divested themselves (or were divested) of what Russell calls their 'non-charter' roles over the course of the nineteenth century. It became less common, less expected, for clergy to function as the politicians, officers of the law, schoolteachers and social workers of a locality. (Although clergy still functioned in those roles, they did so as members of the professions which had taken on that function in society. When a clergyman taught in a school he did so because he was a schoolmaster, not because he was a clergyman.) Entrance to the profession was no longer guaranteed by the general education of the gentleman: taking a degree at one of the two old universities was no longer seen to be sufficient. The first theological college, Chichester, was founded in 1839 by Archdeacon Manning (who later crossed the Tiber). By the end of the nineteenth century there were 40 of them, catering to every flavour of churchmanship and academic ability.

The structural narrowing was matched by an attitudinal narrowing as well: clergy, to have any status in a professionalized society, needed to become a separate caste. Defining their place in society more narrowly, just as other professions had done, enabled them to *retain* a place in society. Both the Tractarian and the Evangelical movements found it necessary to emphasize, for very different reasons, this separateness. The most obvious sign was the growth in a special uniform for clergy in their everyday dress. Whereas in the eighteenth century clergy dressed like a sober country gentleman, in the nineteenth century they resisted changing secular fashions and affected the clerical collar. Clergy associations grew up, clergy newspapers were published, and even hotels which catered especially for clergy were opened.

By the end of the nineteenth century the social function of clergy was that permitted by their ordination, not by their previously existing status as gentlemen.

> No longer was the role legitimated principally by appeals to its social utility, but in terms of the spiritual and sacramental nature of the

> Church. If, in the eighteenth century, the clergyman had been a member of the leisured class free to indulge his interests in gentlemanly sports, the administration of the county, together with scholarly and social pursuits, the typical mid-nineteenth century clergyman was a man without leisure.[20]

The clergy of the nineteenth century became, in Martyn Percy's vivid phrase, 'technicians of the sanctuary'.[21]

The nineteenth century saw serious, wide- and deep-ranging reforms in the clerical profession, the hard work of the Tractarians and the Evangelicals, growth of the theological colleges and the missionary societies, at home and overseas, structural and attitudinal reforms. Even so, in 1900 *The Times* could authoritatively state that the average country parson was reckoned to work

> . . . perhaps three hours a day on weekdays and six on Sundays, the latter forming a demand on his powers for which the country parson generally feels the need of special rest and support.[22]

In 1925, J. W. Robertson Smith judged the place of the gentleman priest in a Cotswold living with these harsh words:

> The blunt fireside judgement of the mass of agricultural labouring families on many a parson is that he is witless and lazy, a self-satisfied drone, who, by the advantage of his social position, has secured a soft job.[23]

Adrian Hastings extrapolates from Robertson Smith's judgement:

> . . . clergy were 'good sorts', they visited the dying, they were kindly, a few were actually saintly, a few were scholarly, mostly in rather irrelevant matters. They were feeble preachers but – more important – many of them were far too obviously concerned with sport and with maintaining class. Some were quite definitely odd. They were a bunch of very ineffectual men.[24]

But at least they were a bunch of ineffectual men in a stable society, which, while not necessarily valuing their expertise, at least accorded them some service. They knew their place, and, once, their place was known: the village parson, immortalized on the sign for 'The Village Pub'. 'The Village Pub' sign depicts a profession with an expertise that is at least valued by society, if not regarded as indispensable to it.

But the high summer of 'The Village Pub' did not last: the changes of the Victorian Church did not stop there. Society became increasingly more complex, technology (and especially the technology of war) more advanced, education more widespread, and each one of these changes affected the status of clergy, both in their perception of themselves and as perceived by society.

It seemed at the time that the Church was managing this change. After the shock of the First World War, when expressions of hostile atheism became, if not commonplace, then certainly more common, the Church settled back into its comfortable groove of affirming the *status quo*. Clergy handbooks continued to be published, before and after the Second World War, in which the assumption was the Christendom model of ministry, the nation and the Church being almost exactly coterminous, and all that was needed was a little more and better organization. We can see this tendency very clearly in the most influential of the clergy handbooks of the post-war period, *The Parish Priest at Work*, by Charles Forder, Vicar of St Clement, Bradford, and later Archdeacon of York. The book is an exhaustive, and exhausting, encyclopaedia of actions, attitudes and achievements. The assumption throughout is that the mission of the Church in any given parish is the cure of souls, and that work is the responsibility of the priest. For example, in the section on church maintenance, Forder advises 'All churches need an annual spring clean, and *volunteers can be found to help*.'[25] It is the priest's job; laity will assist. Forder sets out this assumption explicitly when he turns from discussing administration (over which the parson has complete control), to ministry (in which he is dependent on the co-operation between parson and people):

> The parish is the world in miniature and contains wide varieties of people, and the difficulties of co-operation often lie not so much in the differences between clergy and laity, as in the vast differences among the laity themselves. It often seems in the parish that the parson's main task is the keeping together of all the people worshipping and working happily together.[26]

The influence of Forder's book on post-war ministry can be seen in the warm endorsement by Michael Ramsey, then Archbishop of York, to the second edition, in the days before such endorsements were ubiquitous. Even so, Forder's book appeared in a world which was still changing. Most sociologists, historians of religion and even some churchmen have characterized this changing as the process of secularization: inevitably and inexorably, as society became more technologically advanced and socially complex, public expression of religion decayed. Further changes will lead to further decay. The models and assumptions of Forder, Dearmer, Martineau, Hocking, and Southcott[27] and their ilk can no longer apply.*

This is not the place in which to rehearse the details and validity of the secularization theory; Callum Brown, Adrian Hastings and Martyn Percy all give excellent surveys of what we can and can't say about the changes of the last hundred years. What we should note, however, is the effect upon the status of clergy of these changes. The structure of the professions changed, but this time, clergy as a profession did not follow. Whereas in the nineteenth century the workplace of the professional was usually individual (the single-doctor practice, the accountant with his brass plate in the high street), over the course of the twentieth century professionals began to work in what Hall calls 'organizational bases': accountancy firms, solicitors' companies, multi-doctor clinics. The parson remained in solitary splendour.

Moreover, as our society was increasingly structured by and for the professions (look at the number of lawyers in Parliament who determine how our society is governed), the skill-sets of certain professions became indispensable for a competent functioning in society. Who would think of getting a building designed by someone who wasn't an architect, with structural stability and integrity assured by a chartered structural engineer, financially managed by a chartered quantity surveyor, built by a competent and accredited contractor? The skill-sets of these professions are valued and necessary: here we see Hall's 'service orientation' at work.

---

* There was such a spate of 'priest in the parish' books in the late 1950s and early 1960s that David Paton, editor of the SCM Press, and later Secretary of the Missionary and Ecumenical Council of the Church Assembly, observed, 'If a vicar writes a book about his parish, then it means he is leaving.' Paton was a shrewd observer of the Church of England. (Private correspondence with R. M. C. Jeffery.)

But what of the skill-sets of the 'technicians of the sanctuary'? What can we say is the 'service orientation' of the clergy, or, changing the metaphor to advertising, what is the 'Unique Selling Point' (USP) of the clerical profession?

My wife and I spent our honeymoon mountain walking in the Dolomites, where we met an American couple. 'Smoke' was in his late sixties, a mountain guide in his native Sierra Nevada in California. We accompanied them on two high-level walks, pushing through the snowfields, still thigh-deep even in mid-June. As I followed Smoke down the mountain I envied his mountain craft, his knowledge of what was safe to do and where was safe to go, and his ease in the mountains. I wondered what my equivalent skill-set was: Smoke could lead me through a mountain wilderness, but I could preach a really mean funeral sermon! Somehow there seemed to be no equivalence!

My encounter with Smoke, although a little self-regarding, has been replicated in parsonages up and down the country in the years since the Second World War. Even in, what we are now told, was the last golden age of public Christianity, the 1950s, clergy were finding themselves becoming increasingly marginal to the needs, desires and outlook of modern society. Paul Ferris, in his 1962 survey of the Church of England, reports a conversation with the Revd Morton Gervaise (a pseudonym), rector of a country parish:

> I was advised when I came to the country, never use a word that a child of thirteen can't understand. I never reproach and I never scold: they'll probably see it, in time. It's no good thundering in the pulpit. All you can do is strengthen the attitude of the faithful. It's a bit platitudinous, but you can't be concrete in a small community. People bring their children to be baptised, even though they never come to church. Ultimately one feels the outcome of these things is in the hands of Heaven. One's only an underling, a deputy and all that.[28]

Our shared values in society, insofar as we can say that we share any values, are based upon empirical knowledge that is falsifiable, the application of this knowledge through technology, governed by bureaucratic, democratic structures: that is, we all agree on the things we can measure, we use that agreement to produce commodities which have an inbuilt value, and the way we organize our society is based on principles that are, in theory, open to participation by all. In other words, it doesn't matter where you stand or where you come from, a pound's worth of bananas is a pound's worth of bananas, because the government has fixed our weights and measures.

Set against this materialist and empirical world, the values mediated by clergy are personal, based on precedence and transmitted authority, and point to an experience of transcendence which is, by definition, not open to all in the same, falsifiable manner. In other words, to use the banana metaphor, there may or may not be bananas in your shopping bag, but how you *feel* about bananas will depend upon the stories your community tells about bananas, and the role they play in your shared culture. None of this will, necessarily, be affected by their weight, length or cost.

No wonder the skill-set possessed by clergy is not valued by society. Precedence and tradition and transcendence are worthless currencies in our measured, democratic age.

It wasn't until the 1960s that this great change in values, this paradigm-shift, began to be recognized by large numbers of the clergy. The outward 'success' of post-war national religion (increasing numbers of ordinations, church building and attendance) camouflaged the underlying changes. Some clergy, heroically, recognized that what wasn't needed was 'more of the same': the world was transforming under the complacent eyes of the Church of England in the 1950s, with its 'renewed institutional confidence, its mildly anti-intellectual leadership, and its half-conscious complicity in the "end of ideology" mood in the wider intellectual climate'.[29] Attempts to deal with the shift, attempting to reformulate the Church's traditional teachings and practices in an attempt to become 'relevant' to the modern world, were tried throughout the Church of England, and nowhere with more energy and determination than in the Diocese of Southwark. The parishes and priests south of the Thames were so closely identified with the project, that 'South Bank Religion' became short-hand for anything that was perceived as innovative, shocking or slightly unhinged in teaching and practice. The great dynamo for South Bank Religion was Nick Stacey, Rector of Woolwich.

> He transformed his church into a centre of non-religious social activity, with coffee bars, advice bureaux and youth clubs. His innovations were met by much criticism, with one Southwark vicar threatening: 'If Stacey thinks he can build the Kingdom of God by frying eggs on the altar and percolating coffee in the organ pipe he should think again.'[30]

This was, unknown to its participants, the last feasible attempt to implement the Herbert model of parochial ministry. Stacey had subconsciously attempted to adapt Herbert's model for his day and time. He drew around him a multi-skilled and multi-disciplinary team, members of which were all exceptionally gifted university men (double firsts from the old universities were the rule), men who might have had profitable and prestigious careers as university orators. The pastoral care provided by the team was to be as much centred on physical well-being as spiritual: whereas Herbert advised his parsons to know something of law and medicine,* Stacey required his team to know how, for instance, to rehouse homeless people. This concentration of talent was not supported by the wider Church, morally or financially: the diocese would not pay their stipends, in an attempt to manage the resources of the diocese equitably, or just from plain irritation at Stacey's unilateral actions. The stipends were paid for with Stacey's own supplementary income from journalism: 'If the team was a taste of Heaven, then finding the money to pay for them was continual hell.'[31]

The only substantive difference from Herbert's model was that Stacey consciously set out to be ecumenical in outlook and practice: St Mary's, Woolwich, hosted a church-sharing scheme before such things became common (or even legal) in the Church of England. It was Stacey's invitation to the local Presbyterian church to worship in the parish church building which led to the passage of legislation through the Church Assembly and Parliament to permit the sharing of church buildings. I wonder how many local ecumenical projects around the country recognize their debt to Stacey and Woolwich?

---

* 'The Country Parson desires to be all to his Parish, and not only a Pastor, but a Lawyer also, and a Physician . . . Now as the Parson is in Law, so is he in sickness also: if there be any of his flock sick, he is their Physician, or at least his Wife, of whom in stead of the qualities of the world, he asks no other, but to have the skill of healing a wound, or helping the sick.' (Ch. 23, 'The Parson's Completeness')

As with the building, so with the staff. Stacey early on ensured that there was a Methodist minister on the team, and, in their later, secular-employment incarnation, he even managed to invite a Baptist minister and a Roman Catholic priest to share the work: 'With [the priest's] appointment we only lacked a Congregational minister to be able to include all the major English Churches. No other parish in England ever had such a team.'[32]

And yet, the fact remains that Woolwich was the last attempt in which the George Herbert model of parochial ministry might possibly have worked for the Church of England:

> The agony of so much of our pastoral work in Woolwich was that the things people did want from us – the name of a safe, cheap abortionist; the loan of £20; a roof over their heads, or a new husband – we were unwilling or unable to provide. But the things that we were able to give they did not appear to greatly want.[33]

After four years of backbreaking work, Stacey rethought the project. A bitter article in *The Observer* of December 1964, in which he lamented the failure of four years of social-praxis religion, was followed by another article for the newspaper in May 1965 entitled 'How the Church could Survive'. Now Stacey had three proposals, vitally important for the Church if it were to survive. First, he advocated that 90 per cent of clergy should seek secular employment, for secular jobs give better expression for 'challenging the mores of our society' by teaching, counselling and social activism: 'Few people – except perhaps in suburbia – any longer come to the clergy with spiritual problems.'* Second, the Church must divest itself of the burden of so many unnecessary buildings, expensive to maintain and irrelevant to the needs of 1960s Britain. This would allow the release of vast amounts of capital, to aid in the dispersal of the immigrant populations from the ghettoes of the

* There were and are dangers in this approach, neatly identified by Alec Graham in an article in *Theology* in June 1968: 'The clergy can still fill the gaps in the social services and act as a kind of ecclesiastical counterpart to the "God of the gaps", but this cannot compensate for the fact that clergy no longer figure prominently in the magistracy, no longer largely control primary education, no longer are responsible for poor-relief, nor do the Church's views on moral matters carry the weight that they once did' (p. 244). (We'll come across Graham's article again; see p. 77).

cities. Third, there needs to be a parallel theological 'stripping-down', of what is taught and what is believed in: 'Increasingly, thoughtful Christians find themselves believing more and more in less and less – more deeply committed to Christ, more ready to be reverently agnostic about much else. The maximum of faith and the minimum of dogma must be the keynote for the Church in the twentieth century.'[34]

Stacey's recommendations were not met with wholly willing acceptance. *The Observer* asked a number of commentators to respond the following week – some churchmen and some secular. Eric Mascall, doyen of the scholarly Anglo-Catholic wing of the Church of England, ridiculed Stacey's theological economies: 'Presumably then, the really modern Christian would be the man who had infinite faith in nothing at all.' Bryan Wilson, the sociologist Fellow of All Souls' College, Oxford, who had begun the serious examination of the decline of religious observance in England, wondered if Stacey's title was inapposite: not 'How the Church could survive', rather 'How the Church might surrender'.[35] Even the laity, the people for whom Stacey had expended his prodigious energy, questioned what he had achieved. A parishioner in Woolwich wrote, 'It was not surprising that, despite Mr Stacey's assurances *that their help was needed*, many hung back, feeling perhaps that better qualified people were now at hand to do the jobs they had previously done.'[36] (There is still a hint here of parish life being something done *for* and *to* the laity.) As James Bogle, a historian of the South Bank project, wrote, 'It may not have been a coincidence that the Bingo and the Samaritans, which both had substantial lay involvement, both flourished.'[37] Stacey himself admitted, in his autobiography published after he had resigned from stipendiary ministry and was working as Director of Social Services for the London Borough of Ealing, 'I plead guilty to underestimating massively the depth and significance of social pressures which keep the English working class away from the worshipping community of the Church.'[38] After the failure of the Woolwich project (and, despite the huge number of people who passed through the doors of the church every week, and the lasting impression on the people of south-east London made by the professionalism and pastoral care of the clergy, it was acknowledged then and now as a failure by Stacey himself), 'Herbertism' was bankrupt.

The clergy of the Church of the 1960s were assailed on all sides: the 1950s fashion for religious observance was in steep decline, the Church produced report after report that sought to change the basis of clergy pay, deployment and employment ('Paul' 1964; 'Morley' 1967; 'Tiller' 1983),* and for the first time since the English Civil War, anti-clericalism was a fashionable attitude to espouse: 'The irony was that it originated from people receiving their incomes from the Church.'[39] Transcendence and ritualism, the only possible skill-sets left to the clergy, were to be thrown over, and in their place came a rather etiolated form of social work. It was keenly satirized in *Prism*, normally the obedient house magazine for the South Bank Reforming tendency of the Church of England. A new liturgy called 'Neo-Matins' was presented, which concluded with this blessing:

> Go forth into the world, to proclaim that the only obstacles to Truth are Religion and the Church; and may the Depth of all Being grant you a modern outlook and a muddled mind, and keep you from coming here again to expose yourselves to this retarded and probably hypocritical congregation. Amen.[40]

Ironically, this attempt to redefine the USP of clergy in terms of social work, and counselling, and social activism, has been comprehensively

* The 'Paul Report' of 1964 was written by Leslie Paul and marked the first time that the Church had used the skills of a lay, trained sociologist and statistician. It was bitterly resented by most in the Church, partly for its conclusions (replacing freehold with a time-limited leasehold, increasing group and team ministries, and imposing regional patronage boards for the various confusions of lay, college and episcopal patronage), but mostly for its methods. The letters page of *Church Times* was filled for the four months after the report's publication. At first the writers, including a number of letters from the common rooms of theological colleges, were broadly in support of Paul's conclusions, but gradually opposition won out, and Paul's recommendations were watered down and set to one side and ignored until the decade was over. There is an irony in that, 45 years on and as most of Paul's recommendations are finally in place (especially with the introduction of the *Clergy Terms of Service* Pastoral measure in the 2004 General Synod), Paul was hopelessly and spectacularly wrong. His whole report was based on the assumption that the previous fifteen years' high numbers of ordinands would continue, in fact increase, in the coming ten years to 1971. Instead the publication of his report coincided with the precipitous collapse of ordination numbers. The 62 recommendations would have been impossible to implement without those increased ordinations. In fact, the difficulties of much of the last 40 years of 'clergy deployment' have come from attempting to square the circle of Paul's assumptions and the reality of numbers. As Adrian Hastings put it in his judgement on Paul: 'There is something rather pathetic, indeed a little ludicrous, about the Church turning for the first time, in this new age of efficiency, to lay sociology to obtain a thoroughly professional view of what it should be doing with its priests and how many of them it would have, and being quite so grotesquely misled' (Hastings, *History*, p. 535).

rejected by the laity for whom it was undertaken. What is more, the very attempt at redefinition by the clergy has lost them their status as moral exemplars or practitioners for society. Fay Weldon, after a lifetime of literary and feminist writing, came to faith despite, rather than because of, the clergy. In an interview with the *Guardian*, she described how the clergy were once central to our society's well-being. They were 'part of a very necessary socialization that brought civilization with it. We've abandoned the Church and I think abandoned a great deal with it.' But the problem is furthered by the failure of the clergy themselves. Clergy now refuse to engage with the great moral issues of our day, and she would never dream of seeking their direction:

> I wouldn't consult him [the parish priest]. Would you consult a priest on moral matters? They're all therapy and touchy-feely. They're not actually engaged in moral debate. It's my problem with the Church – I am a Christian, but I am afraid they have failed their flock in their inability to confront moral issues.[41]

Even so, clergy are still expected, vicariously, to be good, to be good on behalf of others. A number of years ago, when a newly appointed suffragan bishop was left by his wife for another clergyman, a local newspaper pompously and tendentiously wrote:

> In a world which seems to have forgotten basic Christian qualities, it is more important than ever for the Church to take a moral stand . . . Admittedly, it is a huge responsibility to place on its shoulders, but it is one it should accept gladly. After all, clergymen have preached hellfire and damnation from their pulpits for centuries. The Church has decreed a set of values to which we should all strive to live by. If its own vicars are incapable of toeing the line, what hope is there for the rest of us? That goes, too, for the wives of vicars.[42]

And yet, it is clear that the authority of the clerical profession has constricted away from the area of public morality. Like the narrowing focus of spotlight, the area illuminated by the special insight or *magisterium* of the parson has become smaller and smaller – even, finally and amazingly, so as to exclude the expertise of the sanctuary technician. A priest I know was told off, when asking his servers to sit with more attention and dignity during the Eucharist, for speaking to them like children. Another was thanked for his 'opinion' when teaching children and adults how to receive Communion, and the children received Communion according to their parents' practice. A third was told he was being unreasonable in encouraging people to come to church on Christmas Day as they had attended on the Sunday, only two days before. A fourth was asked why she wouldn't move the Eucharist of the Last Supper from Maundy Thursday to earlier in Holy Week so that the churchwarden might be able to attend a ballet performance for which he had already bought the tickets.

In case these stories are too anecdotal for you, Yvonne Warren published her PhD thesis in 2002 under the title *The Cracked Pot: The State of Today's Anglican Parish Clergy*. Her interviews with two sets of clergy, in a northern and a southern diocese, showed:

> Several clergy in the south expressed the feeling that the community they ministered to had no interest in whether the Church was there or not. They felt the institution they represented and the Gospel they preached were irrelevant to the way people live now.[43]

Clergy in both dioceses felt an insecurity about their ministry under the influence of five different contextual factors: the issue of relative poverty in an increasingly affluent society, in which disposable income was a measure of social status; the decline in a culture in which the Church, its ministers and its message, are understood and valued; the constant battle against declining numbers and the very real fear of the effect this will have upon the stipend; a sense of wasted effort, in that no number of new initiatives and strategies seem to have any effect upon the numbers of people attending, and the quality of people's understanding of the Church; and finally, the 'cognitive dissonance', the mismatch between what you believe and what you experience, that comes from the ideal of the Church as the gathered saints of heaven, and its reality as an incorrigible, quarrelling group of sinners.

The problem fundamentally comes down to two aspects of the clergyman's work: first, what the work represents; and second, how the work is expressed.

In a society where value is afforded to the empirically verifiable, the technologically innovative, and the socially novel, the Church and its clergy represent older, outmoded values of precedent, authority and hierarchy. Even the seeming interest in the 'spiritual', which was such a source of comfort to the leaders of the churches ten or so years ago, is now recognized to be more an expression of the self-focused and consumerist dynamic of our society: 'Look at me! I may have all the trinkets which our society values, but I am also a deep person!' So Paris Hilton, the apotheosis of consumption without responsibility and celebrity without cause, is photographed going to jail carrying a Bible, as a signifier of her personal quest to become a better person. Some clergy and ministers, particularly in the emerging church movement which set out to plough this particular 'Gen-X' furrow, are crashing straight into the barriers of consumerist Christianity: people 'church shop' with all the forethought and selflessness of window shopping. Skye Jethani, a pastor at an American 'destination church', describes in *Leadership Journal* how he was told by two members of his congregation that they had decided to shift their allegiance to another, larger, *better* church:

> Being fully formed in a consumer worldview, Greg and Margaret intuitively accepted that the personal enrichment and fulfilment of desire is the highest good. As a result, they chose the church that best satisfied their family's preferences without bothering to consult their community, the Bible, or the Holy Spirit to gauge the legitimacy of those desires. After all, in consumerism a desire is never illegitimate, it is only unmet.[44]

The second problem comes from the way in which the clergyman's work is expressed. There are many parishes in the country in which, during the day, during *working hours*, the parson may be the only person of working age present. His ministry happens among the retired, the unemployed, housewives or house-husbands at home looking after children. These are not working people, in the sense that our society means and values, people who are in paid employment outside the home, whose salary and job title gives them an immediately recognizable position in the pecking order of our society. This daytime work is very often invisible to parishioners who themselves are away from home working in those hours. The times when the parson encounters his employed parishioners is in the evenings, or at weekends, especially on a Sunday, which, despite the degradation of the differing character of the day from the rest of the week in the last twenty years, is still not recognized as a 'working day'. The parson 'works' at times when other people (most people?) aren't working. He encounters them when they are volunteering; their time and effort and money into PCC meetings, or charitable functions, or even Sunday worship. The parson holds the anomalous position of being seen to do his main work when everyone else is volunteering: and he gets paid for it!

So, in the years after the Second World War until today, we see this shift in the status of clergy. His social status is decayed:

> The old vicar had been, typically, a graduate, a gentleman living in a large if uncomfortable house, a sort of sub-squire excelling at cricket, where he could mix as an equal with his parishioners while still receiving a fair measure of deference. He was known . . . The new vicar was living in a comfortable but insignificant house – not necessarily near the church – with an assured but limited income. The image of the gentleman was gone. The vicar had almost ceased to be a figure of fun, but he had almost ceased to be a public figure at all.[45]

His educational attainment and standing have radically altered as well: 'He has rapidly passed from being the intellectual doyen of society to being a member of the profession with the lowest specialist educational demands.'[46] And, in a society which equates value solely with payment, clergy stipends say this:

> Salary may be an uncertain test of the social evaluation of the ministry, although in England it must be acknowledged that the salary of the clergy has fallen relative to that of the professions with which they like to be compared, and that society at large makes no effort and voices no concern about clerical stipends . . . the priest's work is not accorded much importance; society in general does not account its welfare to the efficacy of those who spend their lives praying for it, nor does it confer very high rewards on those who seek to bring men under the influence of God.[47]

The expertise that he might offer, the 'service orientation' of the profession, is no longer contained within the 'closed shop' of clergy:

> . . . the clergyman, more than anyone else on the contemporary scene, is a jack of all trades. He occupies a unique position, but the uniqueness of his position has nothing to do with unique skills, or even with unique competence. There is nothing which he does that could not be done equally well by a lawyer or bricklayer in the congregation whom the bishop has ordained to the Auxiliary Pastoral Ministry. He does not have a job at all in any sense which is readily understandable today, and today, more than ever before, a person must have a job in order to fit into society . . . The clergyman . . . is in a position which is marginal to society and at the same time highly visible. He is a public person who, alone in our society, wears a distinctive uniform at all times. When he discards the uniform, as many clergymen do today, he evades the problem posed by his marginality, but he does not solve it.[48]

The parson is no longer the gentleman of the parish; he is no longer the professional 'person' of the parish, for the skill and knowledge which he possesses are no longer valued by a wider society.

And yet the show must be kept on the road. There is no vocation in the Church of England for church-closing: congregations must be pastored, taught and grown. We are presented with new challenges and new techniques for meeting these challenges. We are encouraged to find new ways of 'being Church'. We are to engender voluntarism in a society in which voluntarism is either dying or undergoing profound and, as yet, unmapped-out changes. All the while we need to keep the money coming in, the old people comforted, the young people entertained, the new initiatives staffed and old initiatives fresh. The Church is, in the provocative words of Rowan Williams, 'essentially a lot of people who have something in common called Christian faith and get together to share it with each other and communicate it to other people "outside" . . . a mass of individuals vaguely looking for things to do'.[49] It is the priest's role to hand out the jobs. For the priestly ministry in the Church of England is no longer *presbyteral*, in the sense of acting as an elder of a church community. It is no longer *episcopal*, in the sense, as some once thought it would become, a bishop-in-little, exercising oversight over the Christian witness of others. It has become *phulaxal*, which is the nearest Greek word I can find to 'wicket-keeper'. The parish priest is there, in his marginal and non-understood* occupation, to pick up the balls that go flying past the wicket when the other players wander off. He is the 'paid volunteer', an oxymoronic, marginal position.

So we arrive at a definition of 'Herbertism'. This is the dominant model of parochial ministry in the Church of England, a development which grew out of our reverence for the life and ministry of George Herbert, which, in turn, is an expression of the Church of England's need for ecclesial legitimacy in the years after the Reformation and Commonwealth. In Herbertism parsons are not just representatives of the Church of England, they *are* 'the Church of England' in any given place or, more precisely, the particularity of organized religion in a locality: think what the common attitude of 'Say one for me, vicar!' betrays about the relationship of the parson to the institution. The parsons' workplace is the parish church, in which they are readily found at all hours of the day or night. They officiate at the rites of passage of a community, or a family or an individual: they will bless the opening of a cricket pavilion as readily as a marriage or a birth. The religion and deity which they represent are both benign, and they, remembering the gentlemanly roots of their profession, will never behave in an indecorous or discomforting manner. They are well educated, highly educated even, although their education should never come in between them and their parishioners, for much education about God is the product of 'ivory towers' and is 'academic' and therefore repugnant to the needs of the church community. One acceptable characteristic of their learning is a tendency to be unworldly, and if this is expressed through eccentricity, then that is all to the good. They are ubiquitous, present for every activity in a community, whether 'church' or 'civic'. Their function in this ubiquity is to affirm and encourage, marking especially worthy contributions to community life by individuals or sections. They are society's *animateurs*, that wonderful French concept by which an individual is responsible for *'l'animation socioculturelle'*. Like Mr Grace in *Are You Being Served?* they should expect to be wheeled on at the end of any function to proclaim 'You are all doing very well'. In short, under

* Not 'misunderstood', because that implies an attempt has been made to understand. 'Non-understood', because it has not been thought necessary to make the attempt, or even that there is anything there to understand.

Herbertism the clergy of the Church of England are to be omni-present, omni-competent and omni-affirming.

Look at the following definition of priestly praxis given by a prominent layman of the Church of the 1960s:

> My parish priest enters completely into whatever activity he is engaged on at the moment, and *is felt by others to be doing so*: and yet he remains in a sense withdrawn, uncommitted. He can go from a funeral to a football match, from a committee to a confirmation class, *giving to each all he has*, as though their concerns were the only thing that mattered to him. He can switch from one wavelength to another, as it were, at the turn of a knob.[50]

In Herbertism, the parish priest is no more than a particularly well-worked transistor radio.

A story is told of how every evening the parish priest takes a short walk to the railway line that runs through his parish. When he gets there he stops and waits for the London express to pass by. Night after night a friendly parishioner notices this routine, and, puzzled, one evening joins the priest at the level crossing. He asks the priest what is so fascinating about this particular train. The parish priest sighs. 'Today I have printed the parish magazine, visited three people in hospital, chaired a meeting of the school governors, attended a meeting of the deanery mission plan committee, written to the Sunday school volunteers with the new child protection arrangements, completed the diocesan census returns and interred some ashes. Sometime later this week I have to write a paper on the licensing regulations for the church hall, choose next month's hymns and write three sermons for Sunday. So it's pleasant to come down here and watch the only thing in the parish that I don't have to run.'

4

The Cult of Nice*

> . . . it is true, and not just cynicism, that an automated priest with a perpetual grin on his face, everlastingly wandering around the parish and automatically 'mouthing' what would be only quite a small repertoire of platitudes, would meet the vast majority of needs.
>
> (Nick Stacey, *Who Cares*, 1971)

By the beginning of the 1960s with the publication of the Paul Report,† it had become clear that the stresses and strains of ministry were beginning to have an unendurable effect on the clergy of the Church of England. Part of Paul's examination of the state of the Church was the first serious, statistically valid polling of the activities and morale of its clergy. Almost 1,000 questionnaires were processed in the summer of 1962 to become the statistical groundwork of Paul's recommendations. Thirty-two questions were asked, ranging from the simple, numerical (Easter communicants, full-time staff and so on), to the complex, attitudinal ('Are you able to secure a period of relaxation each day?', 'Do you have too little to do?').[1] Paul allowed space for the clergy to elaborate on these questions if they wished, and he reproduced some of their comments in the body of his report. They make heart-breaking reading, even after 45 years. Example 30: A town incumbent, who believes his to be a 'glorious parish':

> The parish will quite literally kill me one day and I am quite prepared for this . . . am in a chronic state of perspiration (so people will not approach me) and am so desperately tired . . . Oh how desperately I

---

* I am grateful to Dr Mark Chapman, Dr Robert Jeffrey and Mr Nick Stacey for their comments on earlier drafts of this chapter.

† See the footnote on page 40.

> need a holiday, or if not that, just a bit of interest on the part of anyone in the utterly impossible task with which I am confronted.[2]

Again, a town incumbent (Example 33):

> The time sheet shows an average week of 70 hours. When special events come round such as Lent, Christmas, Harvest, Confirmation, etc., this has to be stepped up to 80/90. It is not that one is unwilling to work these long hours, as the whole of one's life is dedicated, but the effect is disastrous. One feels a sense of being held fast in a machine that grinds endlessly on. Hobbies are impossible. Family life is neglected and worse still one becomes uninteresting and dull to other people. This feeling is made worse here by this unhappy parish. As my predecessor has said, he 'never knew what the crucifixion really meant until he came to Y . . .'[3]

And, to show that overwork is not the only cause of poor morale, Paul took into consideration those who felt themselves to be under-worked:

> It is questionable whether it is right to have a resident incumbent in many of these places. A man can easily lose heart when Sunday after Sunday he is ministering to fewer than six people at any one service . . .
>
> . . . after you are instituted they leave you alone . . . A small living is a pleasant enough life if you are content to simply plod on and minister to the needs of your flock, and spend the rest of your life in the garden or reading. However, if you are young and active – after a few years in such a parish you realise that there is really little else you can do and you begin to chafe at the bit. The problem then arrives, what are you to do? The only thing you can do is to see your bishop, and tell him that you would like to move so that you will not stagnate. He simply promises to bear your case in mind, and there the matter rests.[4]

When I was first ordained I had a burning desire to rectify the Church of England. When friends (materialist lawyers and accountants all) asked me why I wanted to be ordained, I said that it was too important a job to be left to the people who were already doing it (honestly!).

I saw the elderly and the retired priests in my title parish, and, being the Cotswolds there were a lot of them, and I thought to myself, 'You are the ones. It was on *your* watch that the ship sailed into the rocks. It was while *you* were sat on the committees and synods and councils that the Church of England drifted and failed. What have you to teach me?' Many years on from then, and looking at the books and journals and newspapers of the early 1960s, when the elderly and retired priests were as young and fired up as I was, I can see how they wrestled with the same problems I saw facing me and my time. I even recognized some of their names in the radical journals of the day. And I realized that it was not the men, it was the structures that stagnated and stifled all that talent and energy. Some even recognized the distinction between people and structures at the time. Michael Hare Duke, later to be Bishop of St Andrew's, wrote in *Prism* in November 1964:

> The present structure of the Church of England allows no way out of this intolerable situation. Hence the many pleas for administrative reforms; for groups of priests to work together, for a 'rediscovery' of the role of the laity. However, it is not simply the machinery which must be changed. The pattern is deeply embedded in our whole theology of the ministry, which takes for granted a hierarchical, almost paternalist, pattern.[5]

Since Paul's survey an immense amount of work has been done on the structure of the Church of England: most of his 62 recommendations have been put into place, with the greatest and most intractable, the replacement of the freehold with a leasehold (in Paul's words) or Common Tenure (in General Synod's words), grinding its way through General Synod as I write. One would think then, with the healing of the structural iniquities of the Church of England, the burdens of isolation and marginality so vividly described by Paul would have also healed. Not so, for as we saw throughout the previous chapter, the stresses and strains upon the clergy are not just the result of badly organized working conditions (although these persist). The clergy are in a bad way because of deeper, more existential problems. As it was put so vividly to me on a chapter retreat, 'Even if I clear all the paperwork from my desk, there are still 5,000 people out there who need visiting.'

The depth of the problem can be seen in two works of pastoral psychology of recent years: *The Cracked Pot* (2002)[6] by Yvonne Warren, and a chapter, 'On the Analyst's Couch' by Sara Savage in *The Future of the Parish System* (2006).[7] Both works are based upon practitioners' experience: in Warren's case, the result of a survey she undertook of a representative sample of clergy in two dioceses in the Church of England between 1996 and 2000; Savage is Senior Researcher in the Psychology and Religion Research Programme at Cambridge University. These women know what they are talking about.

Both acknowledge and celebrate the great benefits found in the parish system of the Church of England. Clergy consistently report high job satisfaction in comparison with other professions, occupations or trades, and Savage and Warren celebrate this in the lives of the clergy they meet. Savage in particular recognizes that the parish as a human institution has much to commend it by developing healthy social and psychological processes: the parish church as a building is a landmark 'owned' by all in a neighbourhood; occasional offices are an opportunity for outreach and service; the normative, low-key, Anglican church culture is in tune with the mood of a 'privacy-loving culture', allowing introverts the protection to be part of a larger body; the system of church governance in the Church of England minimizes instances of pastoral, sexual or religious abuse; even the Church's breadth of theological opinion and praxis is a strength, speaking of 'a diverse, organic and supple community'.[8]

However, she also recognizes that each one of her six social/psychological strengths also comes with an underside, and that 'the burdensome costs of the positive features are borne mainly by the clergy'. Thus, a sacred landmark for all the people in a locality can spill over into a vicarious religion: 'My parish church (or *my* vicar) will do my religion for me.' Not for nothing are clergy universally referred to as 'vicars'. The sense of connection to a building can be very focused, with an inability to see beyond the bricks and mortar of a particular place; and the sense of ownership can go back generations, without any apparent intermediary connection between parishioner and church.* Even the gathered churches, to which people may travel many miles to attend, are not

* When the Church of England eventually gives permission for the reuse of closed churchyards, we will see this ownership springing to life again, like the dragon's teeth sown by Cadmus: 'How dare you reuse the grave of my great-great-great-Uncle Bert!'

immune from a form of this ownership. In the gathered churches, noted for great children's work, or a particular worship style, or a particularly gifted preacher and so on, the sense of ownership attaches to the 'stream' represented by the church community: 'If another church nearby (perhaps of a different denomination) is seen as a better exemplar of the "stream", then church-hopping readily occurs . . . members demand much from their church involvement and, as consumers, will go elsewhere if their desire for a transformed personal life and a caring community go unmet.'[9] We have seen an example of this in Skye Jethani's experiences.

The 'fuzzy boundaries' of most church communities within the Church of England allow for the timid and the uncertain to 'taste and see' without feeling overwhelmed by doctrinal or practical commitments. But the same fuzzy boundaries also allow the previously committed to slip away, through physical removal to another home, or emotional removal following a life milestone, such as a serious illness or a death in the family.

Church communities also share, inevitably, in the behavioural and value norms of the society in which they are to be found. What appears to be the ethos of a community at worship (discipleship, service, spiritual pilgrimage), can very quickly, after the service is over and the coffee is served, fall into 'traditional British cultural norms'. For anyone who takes the ethos of worship at its plain value will find this 'culture switch' difficult to take: 'The more innovative or religiously intense parishioners often give up and go elsewhere. Within the soft embrace of an acquiescing majority, a great deal of social loafing can occur.'[10] It is the responsibility of the clergy, sometimes explicitly stated, more often implicitly realized, to prevent this sinking into an unthinking replication of the values of a wider society.

And so on. Savage very properly pays tribute to the positives of the parish community, and very realistically acknowledges that the heavy cost of maintaining this open generosity often falls upon the clergy. But the parish as a community also has its out-and-out negative aspects. Here we enter the inner sanctums of what I call the Cult of Nice.

Savage enumerates seven factors at work in the Cult of Nice. First, the Church remains, at its core, a *hierarchical* society, with layers of social accumulation and historical resonances. A hierarchy is a set of rules allocating people to fixed roles; but no set of rules is flexible enough to encompass the full range of people's abilities and needs, and so people learn to 'play' the hierarchy in order to accommodate these needs. This 'playing' is expressed by 'status seeking, fawning, bullying, passivity, blaming others, fearing criticism and gossiping'.[11] There is, then, a gap between a worldly culture in which identity and status are mutable, contingent upon choice and wealth, and a Church in which the 'Body of Christ' metaphor applies fixity to who we are and where we are allowed to be. Across the gap are straddled the clergy, themselves players in the game of subverting hierarchy (for they too are formed in the milieu of 'portfolio identities'), but also umpires of the old rules. Occasionally the Church attempts to wriggle itself out of the hierarchical model, but with very little success. Two examples: a senior priest was completely convinced by the need to develop collaborative forms of ministry, within the large clergy team of his parish, and between clergy and laity. He was so convinced of this, that when mischievously introduced as 'my boss' by a curate, he would object 'No! No! We're colleagues.' One day they were both to attend a meeting exploring the possibility of a new chaplaincy with a secular organization. The boss/colleague was late for the meeting, and when he arrived he was introduced to the others as 'a colleague'. 'Hallo,' he smoothly added, 'I'm the Vicar of Y; Fred is my colleague.' There was just the faintest emphasis on the possessive. Collegiality in a hierarchical organization is an irregularly declining verb: 'I am the Bishop of X; you are the Vicar of Y; he is our colleague.'

The second example: there is a fashion now, following the example set by the Archbishop of York, for the liturgical ceremony marking the arrival of a new bishop into a diocese to be called an 'inauguration',* rather than an 'enthronement'. But no amount of insisting on this use will remove the echo of 'enthronement' from people's memories. Just as Towler and Coxon said, in relation to a distinctive clergy dress (on page 45 above), to discard an enthronement evades the problem posed by a hierarchical Church, it doesn't address it.

This is not a new phenomenon. One of Paul's correspondents said:

* Curiously for a Christian ceremony, the word 'inauguration' comes from the Latin, *inaugurare*, to take omens from the flight of birds. It is slightly better than the legally valid word 'installation' which has echoes of the delivery of a fridge.

> . . . let the bishop be the bishop. Let the reorganization, or whatever it is that the present move is seeking, be a setting free of the bishops from all the numerous committees, financial bodies, and supervisory administrative duties that at present make it quite impossible for them to be Fathers-in-God to their clergy.[12]

Warren's survey of her clergy's relationship with their bishops shows this anxiety, even more deeply wrapped in psychological maladaption. Again and again for her interviewees the role of the bishop was seen as a father-figure, not just Father-in-God, but father-in-psyche. Bishops were absent fathers to men who had experienced absent fathers as children. Because of this transference of childhood needs into adult relationships, guilt was a major motivating factor in most of her respondents' lives:

> Guilt is often a major preoccupation for clergy. They feel that they have 'let God down', and others also, and that they can 'never get it right' or do enough.[13]

Sometimes, a priest's childhood was filled with an inadequate father, and Warren reports the adult priest being, as a result, 'a sad, hurting man'. One priest experienced his bishop as a judgemental father; the pastoral relationship was complicated by the fact that he was twice divorced, and anything other than unalloyed approval would have appeared to him as a rejecting judgement. Often there appeared to be a dynamic of rebelling against an authoritarian parent:

> Though some of the clergy described themselves as rebels, none of those interviewed appeared to act adversely against the authority of the bishop or the Church. Some were quite vocal in voicing dissent from their bishop's pronouncements but without engaging directly in anarchy. All appeared to value and need the parameters the Church sets, and also to advocate such a stance within their own parishes.[14]

I think this is a very trusting interpretation of the priests' attitudes and actions. Martyn Percy has a more realistic analysis of rebellion, following the work of James C. Scott. In the face of perceived authoritarian or distant structures, petty acts of resistance become a 'hidden transcript' or a message, showing the impossibility of the situation:

> Small acts of resistance may begin to accumulate and occur when clergy feel that they are no longer themselves; that they have become 'lost' in the expectations, demands, projections, desires and routines of others. There may never need to be a decisive moment when this point has been reached – the Rubicon crossed, as it were. It is more like the steady accumulation of snowflakes; eventually, something gives.[15]

Allowing 'something to give', taking pastoral risks in other words, is a whole extra factor in the Cult of Nice (see p. 63 below).

Percy adds a useful viewpoint on the functioning of bishops from the position of the exercise of power.[16] There are three *modes* in which a bishop may exercise the power that he has, or is *perceived* to have. First, power may be *monarchical*, in which the bishop operates either by divine diktat or aloofness. This is not an abrogation of power, although it might feel like it ('Why do we never get a direction from him?'), but rather it is the exercise of power through not exercising it. Like the Queen, whose constitutional authority is mostly expressed in its potential rather than its actual exercise, a monarchical bishop's power is not entangled in the divisive or the contentious. It is a form of *traditional* authority, in which the office, not the person, is the locus of power. Second, power may be *executive*, through which the bishop acts as a hands-on manager, making key strategic decisions, and operating within a model derived from business or education. This is a form of *rationalized* authority, and its characteristics are reviews, mission statements and strategic appraisals. It is worth noting that this mode, seemingly the norm today, did not exist before the 1970s. It requires a secretariat, and until the late 1960s 'a diocesan office was often not much more than an archdeacon with a typewriter, the Bishop's chaplain and a legal secretary'.[17] Third, power is *distributive*, in which the main expression is through facilitation, relating one part of organization to another. In this model, power becomes 'enabling capacities and its generative reticulation (i.e. the energy derived from and through networking, making connections, etc.)'.[18] It is a form of *charismatic* authority, in which the ability to make this reticulation depends upon the gifts and personality of the individual, and not just the position he may hold. We shall come across this idea again, in a slightly different form, in the chapter on the 'Weaver' on pages 123ff. below.

The social jostling that comes in managing a hierarchical society is managed in the Church of England by a liberal dose of *niceness*. Giles Fraser, with his usual penchant for rhetorical flourish, characterized its clerical manifestation in this way:

> There was a time when the country vicar was a staple of the English dramatis personae. This tea-drinking, gentle eccentric, with his polished shoes and kindly manners, represented a type of religion that didn't make nonreligious people uncomfortable. He wouldn't break into an existential sweat or press you against a wall to ask if you were saved, still less launch crusades from the pulpit or plant roadside bombs in the name of some higher power.[19]

So niceness is not a new thing: Nicolas Stacey had diagnosed the pernicious influence of the Cult of Nice, as we saw in the quotation at the head of this chapter. His image of the grinning, inane automaton of a parson is a haunting one, especially to any minister who has gone round the supermarket smiling at all the other shoppers so as not to offend an unfamiliar parishioner ('I saw that vicar who took Dad's funeral last year in Asda, and do you know, he cut me dead! That's the last time I'm going to his church!'– until the day they are brought into church in the box themselves). Clergy are expected to be nice; it 'softens the impact of hierarchy, while preserving it'.[20] Niceness is the way to manage volunteers, and especially volunteers mostly made up of the retired or those at home with children. For niceness attempts to take the sting out of disagreement, and remove the possibility of conflict. Niceness oils the cranking mechanisms of hierarchy in a non-hierarchical society. Niceness allows the validity of everybody's opinion and everybody's behaviour. There is no opinion too obtuse or behaviour too outrageous that cannot be comprehended with a good degree of niceness. If we could all sit down with a nice cup of tea, I am sure that we could sort this out.

It doesn't always work. The *Church Times* hit an unexpected raw nerve in 2005 when it asked for examples of rudeness in church life. The editor was swamped by the response: the curate told by a member of the congregation 'Don't you start talking about Jesus to me in here!'; the vicar told off for encouraging new families to attend; worshippers tipped out from pews because the place 'belonged' to someone else; children told to 'Shut up!'. The collected incivilities were published under the heading 'Going to church? Wear your thickest skin'.[21]

Every parish priest can testify to similar experiences, where the conventions of niceness and gentle irreligion don't actually manage the cracks in the social/psychological ecology of the parish. In my first parish I was told of a woman who hadn't been to church for 30 years because she fell out with the curate over the flower rota; I was once criticized for my grammar in the announcements at the beginning of the Eucharist ('I am *so* disappointed with you; I thought you were an educated man'). A woman once returned a parish mailing with a refusal to read it as she had been ill for a month and the priest hadn't been to visit her: she was a twice-yearly worshipper in church, and hadn't, as far as could be told, missed one of her visits.

Church life is, as we all know, on one level the life of a voluntary organization. Voluntary organizations are made up, not surprisingly, by volunteers who, by definition, don't need to be there. Volunteers only remain associated with an organization for two reasons: first, they perceive a need in themselves which can be fulfilled by what the organization offers; and second, if they feel themselves to be needed by the organization, and that need *is sufficiently clearly expressed*. Churches do things, and doing things involves procedures, and as most of the things churches do are to do with people rather than, say, mechanics, there will always be more than one way of doing the things that need to be done. More than one way will lead to more than one opinion of how to do things. In the past, differences of opinion were settled by the hierarchical power attributed to the clergy: 'Father knows best'. That cannot be used today, and even if you work in a parish where 'Father knows best' is traditional, it still cannot be used. For it is now, in our time and culture, the nuclear option, with a difference. It doesn't work. Even if Father says what will happen, people will still behave just as if Father said nothing at all: fuzzy boundaries, loss of deference and subversion of hierarchies apply to parishes High and Low alike.

Of course, differences of opinion need to be managed, and most parishes, according to Savage and Warren, manage them badly by *conflict*. There are relatively few parishes in which toe-to-toe stand-up rows are the norm. We know this to be so because every single instance of these conflicts is reported in local, national and church press (usually with a headline including 'unholy row'). However, just because open warfare is relatively rare in our churches doesn't mean that conflict by other means is not being waged. Here, though, it is indirect conflict, a general, low-grade, grumbling hostility. Gossip (and the intercessions!) tend to be the forums of choice for the laity, the parish newsletter (and the pulpit) for the clergy. We have all been in churches, have we not, where the sermon has argued for one particular policy for the church, national or local, and the intercessions have immediately contradicted it, with only the Creed in between acting as peace keeper.

Warren's interviews convince her that conflict is the dominating social and psychological mode of discourse for clergy today, and this discourse is both *external* and *internal.*[22] The expression of external conflicts is mainly descriptive of the sorts of areas we have already seen in the changing status of clergy and the Church. Warren's interviewees find themselves in conflict with a society which has very little interest in the gospel which they are charged to proclaim. Their working lives are not understood by people inside or outside the Church (explaining for the umpteenth time that 'working one day a week' is a joke and not a job description). In her interviews, any residual status of clergy as the 'professional' person was no longer borne out by the laity's behaviour: 'the anecdotal expectations of the laity have appeared to rise in proportion to the decline in church attendance'.[23] There was an experienced confusion of roles between those to whom the parish clergy are accountable and who also offer pastoral oversight: this dissonance will presumably have deepened since the passing of the Clergy Discipline Measure in 2003 (in force since 2006), when it is now explicitly stated that the bishop who is your 'Father-in-God' will also be the man who judges any complaint made against you. Balancing the demands of parish and family life were no longer tolerable, especially through living in tied accommodation, when the parsonage house is either much larger, or much less well appointed than others in the parish. Residual expectations still run high, and even if there isn't a tradition of 'open house' at the parsonage, there will be a tradition of 'neighbourhood watch' upon the comings and goings.

There is another factor in the parsonage house which Warren's study didn't touch upon. As a tied house it represents a benefit of the parson's employment (and is certainly counted as such in all the calculations of parish share, diocesan quota and Church Commissioners' reimbursements), and yet it is a benefit that only accrues in the living in of it. The parson and his family have no access to the capital that it represents. I don't mean that the parson should be able to sell the parsonage, although, in recent years of pension scandals and stock market under-performing, more and more people outside church employment use property as a means of saving for the future. Rather, most banks offer extremely cheap loans secured against property ownership: one can borrow money against the value of your house in order to improve the house, or pay for a holiday or a car loan, or even simply to pay off debts. As long as the mortgage is long enough, and property prices continue to appreciate, the cost of the loan is almost as small as it could possibly be. Try borrowing using an unsecured loan: interest rates are up in the dizzy heights of credit card APRs. In Canterbury a number of socially concerned and thoughtful people decided to set up a Credit Union. The instigator came to speak to a fellowship meeting of my church: he used as an example of need the fact that some people had to take unsecured loans at exorbitant interest rates. Everyone agreed that this was unacceptable; everyone in the meeting owned at least one property – everyone except the rector, who had just finished paying off an unsecured loan at an exorbitant interest rate. As a benefit in kind, in a society in which owning property is both a means to save and means to an income, the benefice house is no such thing.

But this all comes under Warren's 'external conflicts' heading. There are also *internal* conflicts: the plea at the Chapter retreat is a common one; parish ministry, by definition, is impossible to complete. (Is this why so many clergy throw themselves into building projects? Here is something concrete, measurable, that will leave a lasting effect, for good or ill, within the parish, and everyone can see when it has been completed.) There is the psychological dissonance that comes from preaching upon and modelling the life laid out in 1 Timothy (be 'above reproach, married only once, temperate, sensible, respectable, hospitable, an apt teacher': 1 Timothy 3.2) and yet dealing with inner frailties, and a set of disciplines (prayer, study, spiritual direction, confession) which potentially provide a piteously honest examination of those frailties. The priest is also a representative of a belief system that builds upon a transcendent, supernaturalist understanding of the world and human society: is it possible to maintain an intellectual and pastoral honesty for the sake of others if dealing with doubts of one's own?

The turmoil of the 1990s over the ordination of women to the priesthood raised questions of gender identity and authority. Some of Warren's respondents were bitterly disappointed by the ordination of women, and felt the decision of the Church was a keenly felt wound to their understanding of the priesthood (in abstract) and their own priesthood (in particular). Perhaps the strength of opinions expressed was a product of the time in which Warren undertook her research; and ten years on, matters have settled. Perhaps.

The management of conflict is of such importance to church life that we need to devote a whole chapter to it below. In the meantime, let us agree with Sara Savage when she says that too often people within church communities do not wish to admit to conflict, for in the building of a Christian community it is seen as a failure. During a free and frank exchange of views in a PCC meeting you can rely on at least one voice to say wistfully, 'Look how these Christians love each other', thinking that they are quoting Scripture.* It is as if conflict, or even disagreement, is never permitted in the Christian fellowship, by the very nature of that fellowship. Therefore, we tell ourselves, because we are not susceptible to conflict, we need do very little to learn from conflict. And yet 'conflict is a growth point; it is a rare arena in which religious people are forced to relate honestly to one another'.[24]

Of course, not all conflict is the result of well-thought-through opinions, honestly held. Some conflict in church (most?) is the result of DIFFICULT PEOPLE. Now, one man's difficult person might be another man's projection. Even so, Savage tells us that a small proportion of the general population falls within a range of psychological disorders, which 'while not psychotic (in other words, they are in touch with reality) have developed inflexible, maladaptive personalities with a striking inability to reflect on their own need for change'.[25] If this is true of the population as a whole, then how much more so must it be for the church community, a society which explicitly welcomes the marginalized and the misfit, and allows opportunities for all kinds of volunteering. Managing such

---

* It is actually Tertullian, who isn't famous for avoiding all disagreements (*Apologeticus*, ch. 39, sect. 7).

maladaptive personalities requires anything but niceness: 'Form a real relationship with them, and then sit on them'![26]

Even those who are not clinically maladaptive may display other, unappealing social pathologies: VANITY and a tendency to DISUNITY. Vanity finds its expression in 'taking a stand' on points of theological principle. This is a good camouflage: 'I am not behaving this way through self-aggrandizement. I am behaving this way because I am a principled and honest broker of a particular (the correct!) theological understanding of the problem.' As Savage says: 'Leaders, at all levels in the hierarchy, may seek to advance their own theological orientation in such a way as to disadvantage others. Clergy intuit this, and feel they have to fight their corner.'[27] Occasionally, cultural differences may intervene, to cause misunderstandings in the expression of vanity. On Christmas Day 2006 an interview with the Rt Revd Peter Akinola was published in the *The New York Times*, during the course of which Akinola denied that his actions in the Anglican Communion were the result of vanity: 'Self-seeking, self-glory, that is not me . . . No. Many people say I embarrass them with my humility.'[28] Let us assume that the genuine modesty in that statement was lost in translation.

Sometimes the translation is lost, not between people but *within* a person. In other words, we are all subject to UNCONSCIOUS PROCESSES as a result of our birth, upbringing, moral choices and development. These processes include our understanding of God and his community, a 'God image', which then acts as a lens through which our relationships with God's representatives, other Christians in general and clergy in particular, are refracted:

> It is normal that God's 'representatives', the clergy, evoke strong feelings, and that emotions from significant past relationships are transferred on to them. This process of transference may be signalled by inordinate love towards the minister, or, if failing to comply with a person's particular God image, inordinate hate.[29]

The same subconscious processes are also acting upon the clergy, but with an added burden of living up to serious expectations. The Ordinal makes this explicit in the introduction to the ordination of priests:

> Priests are ordained to lead God's people in the offering of praise and the proclamation of the gospel. They share with the Bishop in the oversight of the Church, delighting in its beauty and rejoicing in its well-being. They are to set the example of the Good Shepherd always before them as the pattern of their calling.[30]

We can see concrete examples of this pressure to conform in Warren's research. Between 1996 and 2000 she wrote to a representative sample of 347 clergy in two dioceses, one in the northern and one in the southern province, inviting them to participate in a study no more explicit than 'the way clergy live today and the problems confronting them'. She received a 76 per cent response, very high for this sort of exercise, of whom 170 were willing to participate. She eventually interviewed 60 priests. The interviews make disturbing reading. The occasional happy, integrated personality is so rare as to be remarked upon. Some clergy are obviously in the throes of a deep neurotic breakdown; their answers are monosyllabic, or stereotyped, their engagement with anybody outside their own heads limited. Of course, some of this is predicated, it seems to me, by the nature of the exercise. If you feel neglected, isolated and bowed down, and someone writes to you to elicit your opinions on the problems facing the Church today, then you are very likely to agree to co-operate. If you are busy, and happy in your business, then you are unlikely to see the need to participate. Petitioners to Parliament very rarely demand that things should stay the same! As Warren records of one of her respondents: 'One reason for his desire to take part in this research was a wish to communicate his feelings of hurt to the Church'.[31] Leslie Paul saw something of this self-selecting phenomenon, when he recorded one reply to his questionnaire concluding with: 'I'm thrilled to be one of those chosen to send in a reply'.[32]

Even so, the majority of Warren's respondents seemed to her to have been ordained so as to deal with brokenness in their lives: the Church was seen, subconsciously in most cases, consciously in some, as a refuge, an alternative family, or the means to social mobility. This is not a healthy body of people.

A combination of subconscious processes and an externally imposed, but never conclusively defined conformity, leads to the clergy always being on best behaviour, and ultimately to an 'erosion of the freedom to be an authentic self'.[33] The individual priest, who may already be dealing with the other negative social/psychological aspects of parish life, begins to substitute a 'religious performance' for an integrated performance of his personality. He begins to operate with such erroneous beliefs as 'I must be successful in everything I do. Everyone must accept me. Everyone must love me. If I make a mistake I am a total failure. If I disagree with someone, they won't like me. My value as a person depends on how other people view me.'[34]

This is the Litany of the Cult of Nice.

So, we can see in Savage and Warren a real dichotomy between external and internal conflict, public and private discourse, conventional niceness and subconscious processes. These splits are difficult for Warren's clergy to manage. She sums it up thus:

> Being a priest is internal. It is how the clergy feel about themselves, which is expressed in their priestly persona. However, being a vicar/rector is public. It is to do with how others see them, and more than that, it affects others as well – community, congregation, and the wider Church. It is often not possible to hide feelings of fragility or incompetence.[35]

Clergy cannot find affirmation in completing the task, because the task of the Good Shepherd can never be completed. Good relationships with the hierarchy are hard to make and keep when the roles of pastor, manager and judge are confused, and we live in a society which has broadly rejected hierarchy. Clergy spend a disproportionate amount of time with people who exhibit borderline sociopathic attitudes and behaviour. If all these things are true, then is it any wonder that some clergy find themselves taking foolish RISKS IN THEIR PASTORAL MINISTRY?

Losing objectivity, a sense of appropriate pastoral boundaries, or even the boundaries of personality between pastor and person cared for, has been called 'pastoral lust'.[36] The giving and receiving involved in a pastoral relationship becomes imbalanced, and the pastor's need for affirmation, to be needed, disguised as a virtuous sacrificial giving, becomes the drive behind the relationship. Savage reports a survey in which 37 per cent of clergy in the United States admitted to inappropriate sexual involvement in a ministerial role:[37] this is three to four times more than other caring professions. Why?

There must be some kind of answer in the extent of the psychological brokenness in her respondents' childhoods uncovered by Warren. The deprived child finds expression in the inherited emotional deprivation of the adult priest. The clergy described to her, wittingly or unwittingly, many different ways in which they sought affirmation through their pastoral relationships, although all affirmed that they would be aware of an absolute boundary that must not be crossed.

Deliberate risk-taking in ministry has been identified by Dean Hoge and Jacqueline Wenger as one of the main contributing causes to clergy leaving full-time ministry. One of the ministers they interviewed for their study of *Pastors in Transition* mused, 'I have often wondered if having an affair isn't a sick way of relieving the stress, that to shoot yourself in the foot is the only way to get out of a terribly stressful pastoral situation you're in. It's "I can't handle this, but I can't say, let me out".'[38]

Sick ways of relieving stress are matched by sick ways of experiencing stress. This is called 'burnout', and it is such an important factor in clergy life today that we need to look at it in detail in the next chapter.

5

A little soft round the edges

> At times I wonder whether we are all going a little soft round the edges. What our parents and grandparents put up with or had strategies to deal with, we find it really difficult to cope with . . . I have to say that I do hear a lot of grumbles about stress and pressure and burnout . . . and I do sometimes wonder where is the cutting edge, where is the resilience and stamina, where is that stickability which I learnt years ago from my training incumbent when I was a young curate.* God never promises us an easy journey in carpet slippers but the way of a cross. . . .
>
> (The Rt Revd David Bentley, *Gloucester Diocesan News*, February 2002)

The Bishop of Gloucester swiftly retracted his words. Sort of. In the following month's diocesan newsletter he wrote, 'The last thing I want to do is to cause offence, particularly to clergy or their families, and, if I did so, I am very sorry.' The Bishop's spokesman, John Horan, underlined his boss's apology. Sort of: 'Some people agreed wholeheartedly with what Bishop David said in his article, and applauded him for saying it; others felt offended. The Bishop's response was to apologize for causing any offence.'[1] This is a mealy-mouthed sort of apology: I am sorry that people were offended: the substance of my caricature remains.

It is all very curious, because the Bishop of Gloucester, as a member of the House of Bishops, had commissioned a report in 2000 on the Church's healing ministry, *A Time to Heal*. When it was published, all the publicity concentrated on the (small) section on the Church's

* This incumbent was Michael Hocking, the author of a whole series of parsons' handbooks (*A Handbook of Parish Work*, *A Handbook of Pastoral Work*, *The Parish Seeks the Way*), none of which mentions 'stress and pressure and burnout'.

ministry of deliverance (exorcism, as the papers described it). Overlooked was the section on the effect of providing long-term, unrelieved, pastoral and practical care. The context was not parochial ministry, but there are hints that this may have been a sub-text. The report described the process of burnout, following, although not crediting, the work of, either Herbert Freudenberger, who first coined the term 'burnout' in 1973, or Christina Maslach, whose work was the first qualitative analysis of the phenomenon.*

It is important to note that 'burnout', however we write it, is not an invention of the late twentieth century, a sign of our decadent modern times. A collection of poems published in 1599, and attributed to William Shakespeare, contains this couplet:

> She burnt with love, as straw with fire flameth,
> She burnt out love, as soon as straw out burneth.[2]

Eric Partridge's *Dictionary of Slang and Unconventional English* records 'burn oneself out' as late-nineteenth-century slang meaning 'to work too hard and die early'.[3] Graham Greene wrote a novel in 1960, *A Burnt-Out Case*, in which the architect Querry's attack of ennui and indifference is likened to the hopeless lepers by the doctor of the leper village in the Congo: 'You heard what the doctor called me just now – one of the burnt-out cases. They are the lepers who lose everything that can be eaten away before they are cured.'[4]

Herbert Freudenberger, an idealistic psychiatrist who worked in both private practice and the free clinics of Manhattan, first applied the expression to a psychological phenomenon in an article in *Psychotherapy*

---

* There is intriguing evidence of conceptual development in the changing orthography of the term 'burnout'. It began as two separate words, 'burn out', with quotation marks around them, showing that it was a metaphor, taken from the physical process of burning an object such as a match. It then morphed into a hyphenated word, 'burn-out', sometimes with and sometimes without the quotation marks. This showed that it was changing from a metaphor into an objective concept; there was only one possible direction of burn, and that was 'out'. The diagnosis does not yet appear in the handbook of the American Psychiatric Association, *Diagnostic and Statistical Manual of Mental Disorders* (version IV, published in 1994, contains 297 disorders), but when it does it will be as Burnout, with proper noun capitalization, to show it has become an objective reality. (Disappointingly, although burnout has achieved official status in the World Health Organization's *International Classification of Diseases* (ICD), as disease Z73.0, it is as 'Burn-out: State of vital exhaustion'. Which spoils the theory, somewhat.)

in 1973:[5] 'Some years ago, a few of us who had been working intensively in the free clinic movement began to talk of a concept which we referred to as "burn-out".' He began to spell out the implications of the syndrome in *The Journal of Social Issues* the following year.[6] From the first, Freudenberger's analysis was based upon the character traits his patients had in common. Those most likely to burn out were:

> . . . idealists, perfectionists, and compulsives. These individuals were said to suffer from narcissistic disturbance, low self-esteem, childhood difficulties in development, high idealism, and Type A personality.*[7]

Burnout was limited to those who exhibited 'dynamic, charismatic, goal-oriented men or women or to determined idealists'.[8]

For Freudenberger, driven and successful people lose sight of their 'real selves', the shadow side of their personalities, for whom the drivenness and compulsion to succeed is a subconscious attempt to placate basic psychological needs left unfulfilled by damage in childhood. The burnout candidate has a strongly idealized picture of him- or herself and uses coping strategies to bridge the gap between image and reality. Those coping strategies – disengagement, distancing, dullness, deadness – ironically lead to greater stress, until their emotional resources are utterly depleted. They are burnt out.

Freudenberger's idea struck a chord, and from the late 1970s and through the 1980s book after book began to describe the phenomenon. However, work based closely upon Freudenberger suffered from his initial lack of 'a coherent psychological explanation of burnout . . . [and] his rather loosely formulated principles'.[9] In the end, 'the blurred, all-encompassing meaning of burnout and the unempirical nature of [Freudenberger's] clinical approach led academic critics to disparage the concept of burnout or even dismiss it entirely'.[10]

The clinical discovery of burnout was given intellectual and empirical credibility by the social psychologist Christina Maslach, in the face of much resistance. When she and her collaborator, Susan Jackson,

* A personality type first described by two cardiologists, Friedman and Rosenham, in the 1950s. Type A personalities were susceptible to increased chances of coronary disease through a pattern of panicky behaviour, worry about status and time keeping, and highly developed sense of competition. Type As are sometimes, cruelly, called 'stress junkies'.

submitted their psychometric test for burnout to an academic journal, it was returned with the words, 'We don't do pop psychology'. Despite this initial reception, the Maslach Burnout Inventory has gone on to become the standard measurement of burnout.

Maslach defines burnout as 'a response to the chronic emotional strain of dealing extensively with other human beings, particularly when they are troubled or having problems'. It can be recognized in three separate areas of a person's normal emotional functioning: someone suffering from burnout experiences 'emotional exhaustion, depersonalization, and [a sense of] reduced personal accomplishment'.[11] Maslach believed that anybody who did 'people-work' was susceptible to burnout, and she included ministers of religion among her broad range of occupations.

But there may remain some who question, with the Bishop of Gloucester, the fact that burnout is a modern phenomenon. No number of allusions found in Shakespeare's poems, or Graham Greene's novels, will satisfy the suspicion that somehow we live in weaker, milquetoast, days.

Schaufeli and Enzmann in *The Burnout Companion* list seven possible causes for the increased presence of burnout in our culture.[12] First, a much greater proportion of the population earn their living through 'people-work'. In the European Union the proportions vary from a high of 69 per cent in the Netherlands; even in the mainly poorer and agricultural in Portugal 50 per cent of the population work in the service sector. More people working in people-work means that more people are exposed to the problems of people-work. Second, there has been a change in our culture which allows psychological problems to be labelled: think of the 'true-life' articles in newspapers and tabloid magazines which describe the difficulties an individual faces with a particular problem, and how grateful and relieved they are when the problem is given a name and a status in the eyes of physicians or psychologists. Third, at the same time our culture has eroded the communitarian structures of the past in favour of allowing (making?) individuals define their own roles and status. We live in 'a narcissistic culture that is characterized by the increasingly transient, unrewarding, and even combative nature of social relationships'.[13] This 'individualization' leads to greater emotional and psychological frustration, for which people are less equipped to deal, a 'perfect recipe for burnout'.

Fourth, changes in methods of working, with the increased presence of advanced technology, and at the same time combined with increased competition for the attention of consumers, means that modern people-workers are required to do two non-complementary tasks: highly advanced cognitive duties and unlimited 'emotional labour' in keeping customers or clients happy. In the past it was enough to do the job; now the job has to be done with sympathy. For example, in the past a proper attitude for a nurse would be to be 'responsible, orderly, tidy, neat, prudent, industrious, disciplined and sensible. Nowadays, nurses are [also] expected to be empathic, giving and in tune with the emotional lives of their patients.'[14]

People expect more from their people-worker than before, and sometimes the expectation is unreasonable:

> A young businessman said to a flight attendant, 'Why aren't you smiling?' She put her tray on the food cart . . . and said, 'I'll tell you what. You smile first, then I'll smile.' The businessman smiled at her. 'Good', she replied. 'Now freeze, and hold that for fifteen hours.'[15]

(Fifteen hours is a short shift for workers in the Cult of Nice.)

Fifth, at the same time, there has been a weakening of professional authority for *all* professions, and not just the clerical. Professional bodies, from the 1970s onwards, were thought to be more concerned with protecting their vested interests than in serving their clients. Unhappily, some actions by professional bodies have confirmed this suspicion: think of the public reaction to the Roman Catholic Church's decision in the 1980s and early 1990s to move priests accused of sexual abuse, rather than report them to the police.

The weakening of professional authority is connected to our sixth factor, the interaction of the people-worker, their clients and 'professional mystique'. This is the expectation, implicit, unspoken, in the minds of the clients about how the people-worker will behave or even think. If there is a shortfall between mystique and actuality, then stress will increase. The mystique can even operate upon the people-worker directly. There may be, for example, a very strong assumption that a priest's day-to-day work will largely consist of 'being alongside' those in need. What happens when administration, filing or form-filling become routine?

The seventh and final factor is what Schaufeli and Enzmann call the 'changed psychological contract'. This is the belief that a people-worker, an employee of a particular organization, might have about the reciprocal exchange of work and value: 'I will do this work in these hours for you, and in exchange you will provide me with a wage/status/stability.' This is something more than the written contract of employment; it operates, again, in the implicit and unspoken assumptions that people make. The psychological contract always lags behind the employment contract: people-workers will be labouring under the terms of the one, while simultaneously working under the assumptions of the other. What will happen when the new Terms of Service legislation is implemented in the Church of England?[16] How long will it be before the changed psychological contract ceases to be a factor in individual clergy's stressing?

Given these factors in the increased prevalence of burnout in our culture, what can we say about the manifestation of the syndrome? How does it appear in a burning- or burnt-out individual? *Time to Heal* gives us a process, and in doing so clearly follows the lead of Freudenberger and the clinical approach, with a concentration on the personal causes of burnout. The 'reason', if not the 'blame', for burnout comes from the individual's inability properly to integrate emotional needs and professional demands. Whereas Freudenberger's work gives twelve stages to the burnout cycle, *Time to Heal* succinctly reduces them to three. The first stage is a simple 'imbalance between the demands of work and personal resources'. The carer works longer hours, probably longer hours than strictly necessary for completing obligatory tasks, and personal time is squeezed. You eat meals in a hurry, and reduce time spent with family and friends. You may begin to experience physical symptoms such as altered sleep patterns, especially in getting to sleep, or niggling colds or cold sores. At this point it is important to prevent this pattern of destructive behaviour worsening; find time 'to take stock, seek God and the advice of those around us . . .'

It is rare that a carer, experiencing burnout for the first time, is actually able to do this. You need to have some explanation for what is happening to you, but human psychology means that the explanation usually doesn't take into account any complexity in the situation in which you find yourself. The simplest, most obvious explanation is a *personal* one. Maslach calls this the *mea culpa* response: 'I am incapable of handling what everyone else can.' It is a result of 'pluralistic ignorance': if you live with a reduced level of emotional functioning, then you will be unable accurately to judge the cloaked thoughts and emotions of other people. They become opaque, and you begin to think that you are the only person who feels this way. 'I am collapsing under the strain, but when my colleagues say they are coping that is because they really are coping. My failure to cope, to be like them, is a sign of my unique moral weakness.' Maslach gives an example of a nurse's reaction to the chronic stress of medical care:

> While we were in training, we were always being told to 'be professional'. No one ever said exactly what 'professional' meant, or how to be that way, but I guess we all figured out that it meant being cool, calm, objective – and not easily rattled by things. But I *did* get rattled and upset at times . . . and I would be panicky and angry and sad . . . Everyone else seemed to be handling things OK, which made me feel worse – like a real failure and a weakling who wasn't cut out for this kind of work.[17]

Unhappily, by the time you have reached this position, with emotions and judgement impaired, you will be rapidly entering stage two.

Here, increasing and intolerable stress is expressed in your behaviour to those around you: 'angry outbursts, irritability, feeling tired all the time and anxiety about physical health'. Although *Time to Heal* doesn't mention it, this is often a stage in which the stressed carer begins to self-medicate, with food (comfort eating), or alcohol (comfort drinking) or non-prescription drugs. You begin to use a different explanation to explain what is happening to you: you *blame*. Blaming forces you to become emotionally detached from those for whom you are caring; it provides a simple, tangible explanation for the emotional dysfunction of burnout, caused, in reality, by a chronic tangle of socio-economic, pastoral and theological factors. The tangle cannot be easily described in concrete terms, for, as Maslach puts it, 'It has no specific boundaries in time and space.'[18] Blaming the person with the difficult pastoral problem, the person for whom you care, allows you to comprehend what is happening to you: 'Why should I behave compassionately towards people like them? They have brought their problems on themselves.'

The third stage is grimly called 'terminal burnout'. Here you find it impossible to re-calibrate the balance between what is (perceived to be) demanded of you and the resources you have to offer. 'He or she goes into overdrive, works mechanically, by the book, lacking the fresh inspiration of the Holy Spirit. They tend to be late for appointments and to refer to those they are caring for in a derogatory manner, using superficial, stereotyped, authoritarian methods of communication.'[19] That's how it appears to those outside you; inside, it is much worse:

> On an emotional level, the carer becomes exhausted, incapable of empathy and overwhelmed by everyday problems . . . Persons in this situation put themselves down, feel discouraged and wonder how they ever achieved in the past. Problems pile up and paralyse the mind. Disorganization results in more precious energy being expended to make up for lost efficiency. Fatigue deepens and thought processes slow. Physically, an inner tension, an aching across the chest, weakness, headaches, indigestion and a lack of sleep are often experienced.[20]

This is a hateful and wasteful condition for anybody to find themselves in; hateful because it stirs up many emotions focused around (self-) loathing, and wasteful because of the sheer amount of physical and emotional energy which it eats up.

But is it sufficient to find the causes of burnout in the sufferers' personalities and psychological makeup? It certainly lets off the hook the organizations in which sufferers work; they can't be held responsible for an individual's failings. Furthermore, the clinical approach paradoxically applies another layer of stressing upon the sufferer: if burnout only happens to dynamic, charismatic and successful people, then my burnout and my suffering are somehow an achievement, a badge of status. It shows that I have reached the levels of omni-competence and drive denied to lesser mortals.

But Maslach, on the other hand, emphasizes the *structural* causes of burnout. In her analysis, burnout is neither something just 'happening in the mind', nor is it evidence of moral feebleness, theological vagueness or vocational weakness. For Maslach, burnout is less the result of the individual's incapacity for stress than it is the product of an organization's structural stressing:

Although personality does play some part in burnout, the bulk of

> evidence I have examined is consistent with the view that burnout is best understood (and modified) in terms of situational sources of job-related, interpersonal stress. The phenomenon is so widespread, the people affected by it are so numerous, and their personalities and backgrounds are so varied, that it does not make sense to identify 'bad people' as the cause for what is clearly an undesirable outcome. Rather, we should be trying to identify and analyze the critical components of 'bad' situations in which many good people function.[21]

To put it another, Wildean, way: to lose one cleric to stress may be regarded as a misfortune; to lose many looks like carelessness.

This is where burnout in clergy has another, externally imposed factor. Burnout in clergy can become spiritualized; that is, burnout may be treated as a problem that can be solved by the application of the correct spiritual, theological or biblical nostrum. BALM,* whose main work is to do with bullying in parochial ministry, says this about deficiencies of the spiritualizing approach:

> Nevertheless, it is not unusual for well-meaning Christians to focus only on the spiritual aspects of the problem. Often the approach is very judgmental – 'You are anxious, where is your confidence in Christ?', 'You are depressed, where is your joy in the Lord?', 'You are stressed, you need to pray for God's peace'. Judgement followed by prescription – and often backed up with Bible verses to strengthen the message. And all this with very little understanding of what psychiatric injuries really are!
>
> What happens? The wounded Christian feels guilty and begins to question if everything that has happened to them is in reality their own fault, and down to their own spiritual failure – a destructive process that is easily helped along by further 'spiritualizing' of the problems. Guilt feelings can very easily be induced in damaged, vulnerable people and doing so, even unintentionally, can (and probably should) be considered as a form of spiritual abuse. *Feeling* guilty is not the same as *being* guilty – but the damaged Christian may be unable to tell the difference.[22]

---

* 'Bullied and Abused Lives in Ministry': <www.balmnet.co.uk>.

This does not mean that burnout has *no* spiritual causes, and neither does it mean that it doesn't have spiritual *consequences*. Douglas Turton and Leslie Francis have mapped the relationship between a healthy prayer life and resistance to burnout: 'the empirical evidence suggests that people who pray enjoy a range of psychological benefits, including a greater sense of purpose in life, a higher level of satisfaction with life, and better psychological well-being'.[23] However, as we have seen in the stages of the burnout cycle above, taking time for something as non-concrete as prayer, in a world in which meaning is supplied by results, is a hard thing to do when maladaptive behaviours are being reinforced in the burning-out parson:

> Clergy work-related poor psychological health, stress, and burnout pose an increasingly serious problem for the leaders of denominations throughout the world, as the particular circumstances related to spiritual and religious leadership in the community have a special and unique dynamic. The Christian church, like most religions, has the unenviable task of looking back to its roots, living in the present with the constant changes associated with a modern community, and looking forward with eschatological confidence and hope, all at the same time. Combined with the sense of urgency attached to the church's mission, clergy and church leaders frequently become the victim of their own humanity and frailty. The challenge for researchers is to understand the nature of the problem in order to develop effective support and therapeutic strategies.[24]

This is the purpose of the remainder of this book.

Part 2

HERBERTISM HABILITATED

We have seen how the pattern of ministry in the Church of England has been dependent on an unrealistic memory of George Herbert's brief time in a rural parish in the early 1600s. We have seen how men (and latterly women) of integrity have attempted to apply this false pattern, 'Herbertism', in an industrialized urban society, with unimaginable (for Herbert) changes in economics, social structure and cultures. We have seen the cost of attempting to square the circle of Herbertism in the psychological studies of church life from the late 1990s and the description of burnout in the 1970s. You might feel, with me, that so far this has been an unremittingly negative process.

It is now time to sketch out the beginnings of an alternative way of being a parish priest. With 'a sense of urgency attached to the Church's mission' and a sense of urgency derived from the pain (at worst) and inconsequentiality (at middling) caused by exercising its priestly ministry, to answer this question: If we are to kill the George Herbert we meet on the road, then who or what do we put in the phantom's place?

6

+ABC and the three Ws

> . . . the ordained priest is called to reflect the priesthood of Christ and to serve the priesthood of the people of God, and to be one of the means of grace whereby God enables the Church to be the Church.
>
> (Michael Ramsey, *The Christian Priest Today*, 1972)

Over the course of 22 years as Bishop and Archbishop, before every ordination service he conducted in his various cathedral churches, Michael Ramsey gave a series of addresses to each cohort of ordination candidates. They listened to him reflect on what it meant to be a Christian priest for their days and times. The talks were so illuminating, and so worthy of a wider audience, that they were collected and published under the obvious title, *The Christian Priest Today.*[1] Ramsey made the purpose of his book clear in the rewritten introduction to the second edition, in which he adopted the words of a Congregationalist minister, P. T. Forsyth:

> As a priest, the ministry offers to God the Church's soul, as prophet it offers to it the salvation of God. In the minister's one person the human spirit speaks to God, and the Holy Spirit speaks to men. No wonder he is often rent assunder. No wonder he snaps in such tension. It broke the heart of Christ. But it let out in the act the heart of God.[2]

The heart of Ramsey's book is found in the second chapter, 'Why the Priest?': a compact and 'immensely rich' (according to Rowan Williams) exploration of what it means to be a priest. Ramsey's starting place was provided by the article in *Theology* we have already encountered by Alec Graham (then Chaplain at Worcester College, Oxford and later to be

Bishop of Newcastle).[3] Whereas Graham describes a possible model for priesthood in terms of experience and pragmatism (the priest fulfils a representative role by *displaying* a total response to Christ, by *enabling* the work of the Church to be done, and by *involving* the whole Church in his activity), Ramsey wishes to affirm the 'old doctrine that the ascended Christ gives the gift of ordained priesthood and calls men to it'.[4] Ramsey delineates this old doctrine in four parts and one whole.

First, the priest is to be a man of *theology*, a teacher and preacher, whose knowledge may not be wide but certainly will be deep. Ramsey makes it clear that this teaching role is emphatically not *ex cathedra*; the priest is not to hand down on tablets of stone esoteric knowledge to which the laity will have no other access. Rather, he tells us that Christian learning is a partnership in which the distinction between '*discens* and *docens*' (that is, student and master) is meaningless: 'the priest learns from the laity much about the contemporary world and about the meaning of divine truth in its human context'.[5] There is an assumption, however, in this definition of partnership which implies that the *laity* have a knowledge which is otherwise inaccessible to the clergy: there are hints of the unworldly clergy being tutored in the ways of worldly Mammon.

Second, the priest is to be the *minister of reconciliation*, and through the exercise of reconciliation the priest links the Church with 'the gospel of divine forgiveness upon which its common life depends'.[6] In this way the priest, while not denying the uses and insights of psychiatry, is able to provide the moral responsibility that a community, founded upon the reconciliation of Golgotha, is able to represent. Here the key text is 2 Corinthians 5.18f.:

> All this is from God, who reconciled us to himself through Christ, and has given us the ministry of [the] reconciliation; that is, in Christ God was reconciling the world to himself, not counting their trespasses against them, and entrusting the message of reconciliation to us.

Third, then, the priest is to be the *man of prayer*. This is not to deny the prayers of the laity; rather, it is to say that the priest as the man of theology should be connected directly to the proper subject of theology – that is, God himself, through his participation in the prayer of the

Church. In the priest 'the Church's prayer is expressed in strength, and it thereby becomes the stronger'.[7]

Fourth, and obviously, the priest should be the *man of the Eucharist*. In his role as celebrant the priest acts as 'the focusing of the Eucharist in the givenness of the historic gospel and in the continuing life of the Church as rooted in that gospel'.[8]

Some people might think that Ramsey has missed a vital part of the priest's vocation, that of a pastor. After all, shouldn't a pastoral heart be the main qualification for being a priest today? And yet Ramsey does not include the priest as pastor as one of his four divisions, for the simple and persuasive reason that 'pastor describes the whole'.[9] The priest is pastor when he is a man of teaching and learning, *and* when he proclaims the Church's task of reconciliation, *and* when he prays *and* when he presides at the Eucharist. To do all these things in a harmonious whole is to be a pastor.

Ramsey sums up the calling of the Christian priest thus:

> . . . today the ordained priest is called to reflect the priesthood of Christ and to serve the priesthood of the people of God, and to be one of the means of grace whereby God enables the Church to be the Church.[10]

Words which the present Archbishop warmly endorses: it would be 'hard to improve on [these] as a summary of what the Church asks of its priests'.[11]

Michael Ramsey's book has been immensely influential in the 35 years since it was originally published. Still in print, still bought, and yet (to be honest) more flicked through than read, marked, learned or inwardly digested. Even so, four generations of ordinands, of a particular churchmanship or of a particularly romantic cast of mind, have bought the book, hoping that it would provide some pathway through the thickets of discernment, interviews, selection conferences and training courses that line the path to ordination in the Church of England. *The Christian Priest Today* remains on the reading lists of diocesan vocations advisers and is still quoted in ordination charges. Ramsey's book is as close to an expression of ministerial theology as the Church of England has.

Which is why, as part of its 150th anniversary celebrations, my old theological college invited the present Archbishop of Canterbury to deliver a lecture on Ramsey's book, title and themes. In the first full year of his Archiepiscopate, Rowan Williams delivered many such lectures, talks and press releases. The secular media and the congregations of the Church of England were getting used to having an Archbishop who thinks (and clearly elucidates his thinking), and found the novelty disquieting. Even though the talk was later reproduced, as a chapter in a book reflecting on Ramsey's life and writing,[12] it is both disappointing and not surprising that the Archbishop's insights have not had a wider circulation among the clergy of the Church of England and those responsible for their selection, formation and continual training.*

Williams begins by noting the Church's perennial back-to-front approach on questions of ministry: reports are written on 'What ordained ministry does the Church of England require?' (sometimes we even get reports on how we should make the best fist of the ministry we already have). This should not be the preferred starting point for considerations of the Christian priest today; the Church should really be asking, 'What ordained ministry does *God* require?' or even, 'What *Church of England* does God require?' However, Williams sees a virtue from proceeding in this practical way. First, it is true to the incorrigible Anglican trait to be pragmatically minded: a church which finds its genius in the Elizabeth Settlement will always prefer 'what works' over 'what is systematic', especially if 'what works' allows a latitude of opinion and practice. Second, beginning with needs rather than doctrine allows the possibility that God will speak to the Church through the circumstances in which he places us. There is a willingness to deal with *givenness* in the pragmatic approach, and Williams detects this in his predecessor's method: 'Any reflection on the Christian priest today has to be a reflection not just on what we find helpful but on what has been provided for the Church.'

But there is also a balancing danger in the pragmatic approach, a way of thinking all the more dangerous because it is so pervasive; that is, treating the Church (and its ministry) as if it were a group of people

---

* Especially when compared with a book published after Dr Williams's talk was delivered, John Pritchard's *The Life and Work of a Priest* (London: SPCK, 2007). A senior priest of my acquaintance (a diocesan director of ordinands, no less) after reading this book, and looking at the busyness, and omnicompetent/omnipresent model of ministry it assumed, described it rather as *The Life and Nervous Breakdown of a Priest*.

who all believe the same thing, and would like to find a better way of sharing what they believe with those outside the group. The fact that this seems a reasonable (pragmatic?) description of the Church shows exactly how widespread it is and yet how it is, in Williams's words, 'very seductive and very damaging'.

An example. There is a website which, bizarrely and for inadequately explained reasons, has taken Edward Gibbon's monumental book *Decline and Fall of the Roman Empire* and rearranged its constituent words into randomly produced phrases. So far, so very strange.[13] However, one day, while searching for an electronic version of Gibbon's work to check a reference, Google returned this phrase to me: 'A voluntary society of heaven was never predicted of the very essential church.' The idea isn't in Gibbon's original, but it exactly describes the way in which the Church has been treated by its adherents. We believe ourselves to be, according to Williams, members of 'a human association dependent upon skill, agreement and goodwill', in which the major task is handing out the jobs and perpetuating the structures. In this model of the Church, ordained ministry becomes 'an idea developed by us to make things run more smoothly'.

And yet this is exactly what the Church *is not*, and what ordained ministry *cannot be*. Williams describes the reality, a reality that is both actual and aspirational, in these beautiful words:

> . . . the Church is first of all a kind of space cleared by God through Jesus in which people may become what God made them to be (God's sons and daughters), and that what we have to do about the Church is not first to organise it as a society but to inhabit it as a climate or a landscape. It is a place where we can see properly – God, God's creation, ourselves. It is a place or dimension in the universe that is in some way growing towards being the universe itself in restored relation to God. It is a place we are invited to enter, the place occupied by Christ, who is himself the climate and atmosphere of a renewed universe.

This cosmic Church is so far away from the day-to-day experience of the Church (flower rotas, PCC meetings, Gift Days) that it can make one weep. It is akin to reading Bernard Cornwell's series of novels about King Arthur.[14] Caught up in the page-turning, swash-buckling thrill of the read, you realize that Cornwell has also convincingly depicted the divine right of kings. Arthur, in his telling, was a man who could represent the nation, a man who could lead you into battle, a man for whom you could imagine yourself dying. As you think this (heroic Arthur and his heroic subjects!), unbidden the thought comes into your mind: 'Prince Charles'. The Prince of Wales is a good and serious man, with thoughtful and constructive things to say about the nature of society and our relationship with the created order, but can you imagine following him into battle? The God-touched nature of the ancient kings has dwindled down into the present-day philanthropist and amateur gardener. Likewise, the cosmic Church, the 'place where we can see God properly', becomes another voluntary association in a society where all voluntary associations are failing to keep the show on the road. Some wise priest once said to me, about the mysteries of Holy Communion, 'I have no problem in believing that the sacrament is the body and blood of Christ; believing that it's bread and wine is my trouble!' Similarly, I have no problem in believing in the Church Universal, the mystical body of the communion of saints, or in the Church Triumphant, those faithful saints in heaven; it is the Church Militant that causes me difficulty.

And yet this is the community in which we are called to see most clearly, in this life, the promise of Creation redeemed and renewed! The only explanation for the dissonance must be in the theological concept of a *proleptic* Church. Very different from a prolapsed Church (one hopes), a proleptic Church is one in which the perfect future state of the Church is treated as if it is already seen in the imperfect present state: in other words, we behave as if the future has already happened. This is the form of the church community which we see in Paul's letters, especially in 2 Corinthians, and Romans 12, a community in which the fruits of Christ's victory lead us to live in complementary forms:

> For as in one body we have many members, and not all the members have the same function, so we, who are many, are one body in Christ, and individually we are members one of another. We have gifts that differ according to the grace given to us: prophecy, in proportion to faith; ministry, in ministering; the teacher, in teaching; the exhorter, in exhortation; the giver, in generosity; the leader, in diligence; the compassionate, in cheerfulness. (Romans 12.4–8)

This differentiation of actions is for the single purpose 'that together you may with one voice glorify the God and Father of our Lord Jesus Christ' (Romans 15.6). As the Archbishop puts it, 'The energy for this searching for words and forms is created by the fact of God's gift, not by any attempt to make a human community run better; it is an energy devoted to what will *show* the inner and prior fact.'

So, we have to deal with two given facts: the Church itself, and a differentiated ministry within it (by *whom* these facts are given doesn't concern us in this instance, let's just accept the fact that this is where we start from today). Given these givens, within a proleptic Church, what is the part that ordained ministry has to play? Here the Archbishop has three images to suggest,[15] which I have adapted for the purpose of this book and my own ministry. His images are nuanced and subtle; my adaptations all begin with the same letter: that's the difference between the Archbishop and me. I will explore these images in greater detail in later chapters, but it will be useful to have an overview of the three before we proceed.

The first image is the priest as *Witness*. The Archbishop makes it clear that the Church has to be a 'responsible' community. By this he means that the Church, as it is now, as we are now, is obliged to *respond* to what went before us. 'Responsible' here does not just mean moral accountability; Williams uses it to mean both 'being obliged' and 'reacting'. In other words, the Church is not something that we have invented for ourselves: if we had, we probably wouldn't have started from here! This sense of responsibility is built in to the very nature of two fundamentals of the life of the Church: scripture and ordained ministry. Scripture is the record, agreed by the breadth and depth of the early Church, of the fullest revelation by God to his people. Ordained ministry is the means by which, through 'a network and sequence of specific relationships', the hearers of scripture today are connected to those in whom the Word and the Spirit were first at work. The priest's ministry as Witness is, at first, 'to be simply witnesses of that community's character . . . [The priest's words] connect the hearers with Christ; they make Christ contemporary with all who hear the good news.' The Witness must again and again call his community back to its foundational character, the cosmic Church, the climate of Christ. This is the reason why the Witness role is given to the person who leads the community in worship. It is in worship, with its dual focus on Word and Sacrament, that the Church can see its unworldly nature most clearly. It should be in worship that the Church is most *unlike* a voluntary society and should be most like heaven.

Which brings us to the second image: the priest as *Watchman*. In Habakkuk, the prophet is portrayed standing on fortress walls, looking out for signs of God's action:

> I will stand at my watch-post,
> and station myself on the rampart;
> I will keep watch to see what he will say to me,
> and what he will answer concerning my complaint. (Habakkuk 2.1)

In Isaiah, the watchtower is the place from which the downfall of Babylon will be seen:

> Then the watcher called out:
> 'Upon a watch-tower I stand, O Lord,
>   continually by day,
> and at my post I am stationed
>   throughout the night.
> Look, there they come, riders,
>   horsemen in pairs!'
> Then he responded,
>   'Fallen, fallen is Babylon;
> and all the images of her gods
>   lie shattered on the ground.' (Isaiah 21.8–9)

Christian priests today are called to take up a similar position, so that we may see the 'lie of the terrain' in which God has placed us. Like the Watchman on the tower, we look for riders approaching, with threat or good news: the priest 'has to tell the Church what and where it is, must be free to see what and where it is' (Williams again), which is often easier said than done (more on this later).

Third, the post-Herbertism parish priest knows that God isn't at work just within the confines of the Church, however narrowly or widely we seek to define it. Part of the priest's responsibilities is to be, therefore, a *Weaver*. Williams calls this an interpretive role, but it is not just 'someone who interprets culture to and for the Church or interprets the Church's teaching to the world outside', but rather someone who has 'the gift of helping people make sense to and of each other'. Part of the role is creative as well, bringing communities into existence: communities 'in spite of the sentimental way we sometimes think of them, don't just happen'.

Thinking unsentimentally about community leads to concrete and specific results, as Williams addressed in another speech:[16]

> . . . one of the healthiest and most constructive things that any community can ever do is to put in place some structures by which connections can be made. So that instead of a map of little voluntary enterprises, all of them seeking to respond to this or that particular problem, there is a vivid sense of common calling and common vision.

Such connections are to do with the very nature of being human: they are to do with, or ought to be to do with, 'an integral, integrated picture of human beings as they grow at every level'. This is an inclusive vision:

> Making connections, keeping the overview. Seeing voluntary and community work as more than just what I called a series of enterprises in firefighting – this is what is positive about what we are celebrating this morning. This is what I would say every town, every city, deeply needs, in order to work as a genuine human community. A picture of human value, and human good. A sense that work for the needy must never be fragmented and competitive, but must always be co-operative, imaginative, comprehensive.

For voluntary associations this connecting, weaving overview will have its origins in a myriad of places and values: it does not require a belief in God to believe in humanity. However, for the Christian priest, the leader and servant of the Christian community, the origins of the weaving will begin in the priest's role as the president of the worshipping community. Williams quotes approvingly the assertion by Dumitru Staniloae that the priest's role is to 'assemble and concentrate' the Christian people at prayer:

> . . . when Christians pray together in a way that places them in and with Christ, publicly and ritually, the one who animates and co-ordinates this is giving expression to the priestly essence of the Church; the very least we can say is that it is a coherent and intelligible sign of this fact if the president is, routinely, precisely the person who is charged with telling the Church where and what it is, in his or her daily and lifelong service.

Being a Christian priest today, therefore, begins and ends in worship. The priest is nothing and no one if not a person of prayer. This is certainly a vision to set against the corrupted busy-ness of Herbertism. We need to explore these images a little further.

7

Witness*

> . . . there can be no argument to the truth of God in Jesus Christ without witnesses . . .
>
> (Stanley Hauerwas, *With the Grain of the Universe*, 2002)

From the very beginning, the Christian community recognized the need for witnesses. Luke's history of the early Church, mediated by the later experiences of that community, tells us that appointing a witness was the task of the Church before all else. In the Acts of the Apostles, Peter's first recorded speech deals with the gap in the number of witnesses left by the betrayal and death of Judas. In the presence of the whole community of the followers of Christ (the sound and round number of 120), Peter explains his plan:

> So one of the men who have accompanied us throughout the time that the Lord Jesus went in and out among us, beginning from the baptism of John until the day when he was taken up from us – one of these must become a witness with us to his resurrection. (Acts 1.21–22)

Famously, the lot fell on Matthias. It is instructive to note the twofold distinction that Peter makes in his job specification here. Primarily, the new witness is to testify to the resurrection of Jesus. But the qualification for that witnessing to the resurrection is direct, first-hand experience of the ministry of Jesus, from baptism to ascension. To witness to the resurrection means nothing, Peter is saying, if the witness has not experienced the teaching, healing, travelling, judging, prophesying Jesus

* I am grateful to Professor Michael G. Cartwright, of the University of Indianapolis, for comments on an earlier draft of this chapter.

as well. There is a rider to this qualification: the new witness (Matthias) will become a member of a wider body: he will become a witness 'with us' to the resurrection. The body of the apostles calls a person as a witness, and it is their continuing oversight which allows the witness to remain true to that calling. What we see in the New Testament witness is essentially

> . . . an assembly of believers, a community in which the vision of the 'new heaven and the new earth' is kept alive with reference to Jesus of Nazareth, confessed as 'the Christ, God's only beloved Son, our Lord', and in prophetic witness and practice conformed to this kingdom of God.[1]

This first sense of being an apostle and a witness ended, of course, with the death of the first apostles and witnesses. If we were to apply St Peter's selection criteria for the leadership of the Church today then no one would qualify: there is no one alive who accompanied Jesus in his earthly ministry. Which is why 'apostolic' and 'witness' changed in the second generation of Christians (the former word, like 'catholic', first used by Ignatius of Antioch, *c.* AD 35–107).

> Apostleship in the sense of the original and fundamental ministry of the first witnesses and messengers died out with the death of the last apostle. Apostleship in this sense of witness and mission cannot be repeated or continued. What remains is a task and a commission. The apostolic commission is not finished, but will remain to the end of time. The apostolic task is not completed; it embraces all peoples to the ends of the earth.[2]

Who then, can we say are the successors to the apostles? Who are the witnesses for our day? Hans Küng is clear: today's apostles are to be found in the Church.

> The whole Church, not just a few individuals, is the follower of the apostles. We do, after all, confess an apostolic *Church*. The *whole* Church is the new people of God, gathered by the apostles through the preaching of the Gospel of Jesus Christ. The *whole* Church is the temple of the Spirit, built on the foundation of the apostles. The

> *whole* Church is the body of Christ, unified by the ministry of the apostles. The authorized mission of the apostles has been handed on to the Church which the apostles summoned together; the authorized ministry of the apostles has been handed on to the Church which the apostles ministered to. The Church is the successor of the apostles in obedience, and from this obedience it derives its authority.[3]

This apostolic succession is not a human invention, but the operation of the Holy Spirit within the Church, permitting spiritual authority in the name of the glorified Lord who remains sovereign over the Church and the world. Apostolic succession in this sense is applied, not just to a sequence of bishops and presbyters, but

> . . . to the whole Church in all her members. It manifests itself in manifold ways throughout the centuries and in all countries in the continuous process of baptizing and being baptized, in faith and in obedience to the apostolic testimony, in the community of worship and in the Eucharist, in the transmission of the apostolic testimony in the congregations, in the missionary preaching to the world, in the fellowship and unity with the churches of the whole world.[4]

However, there is no revelation of the supernal that cannot be domesticated, routinized or sterilized by human intervention, and apostolic succession, if elevated to a doctrine, can decay into a sterile mechanistic model of being a witness. I recall attending an ordination service at St Paul's Cathedral in the early 1990s in which the then Bishop of London explained to the congregation (who filled the entire length of the building) that at the Peace everyone in the congregation was to wait for him to exchange the Peace with the new deacons in the sanctuary, and then the new deacons would fan out through the cathedral and exchange the Peace with the people sitting in the pews. Then, and only then, were we allowed to give a sign of the Peace to our neighbours, and in this way we would show how God's peace is brought into the world by those whom he has called to ordained ministry. All very well and good, but the cathedral was full and the deacons were slow and it was well into the eucharistic prayer before the official Peace-carrying deacon reached our party on the very last rows of the nave. One of our number, devout and soon to be ordained himself, thought this ridiculous and began muttering, not-so *sotto voce*, 'Has anybody seen the Holy Spirit?' The idea that it was a transmission of touch that brought the Peace to a gathered community of worshipping Christians was neatly speared by a questioning of liturgical rebellion.

As in St Paul's, so in the wider world. If we are not careful we end up with fruitless, mechanistic models of being a witness. Endless arguments about apostolic succession and who laid hands on whom. Look at the websites of the various flavours of *episcopi vagrantes* if you want to see 'apostolic succession' in all its most depressing, train-spotting, form.* And more than that, it is, technically, superstitious; that is, it attempts to coerce the operation of the Holy Spirit through a systematic pattern of behaviour: if we just get the logistics right, then the Holy Spirit (and the accompanying spiritual authority) will follow:

> . . . the imposition of hands is only an instrument, a sacramental sign. Just as God in the Holy Spirit can baptize also through the unworthy, the sinful, and the heretical, so can He also ordain through the unworthy, the sinful, and the heretical representatives. Even ordination does not take place in the name of the ordaining minister, nor on the grounds of his own virtue, but in the name and by the virtue of Jesus Christ who has promised and sent us His spirit. The *opus operatum* [the work done] is not an *opus operatum ministri* [work done through the ministry], but an *opus operatum* of Jesus Christ.[5]

For Küng, writing within the context of the years of the Second Vatican Council, this approach to the apostolicity of the Church was a liberation from the deadened clericalism of the previous dispensation. Even so, his vision of the apostolic succession, and the witnessing function of the Church, still operated through the structures of the Church. The Church remained one holy, catholic and apostolic Church when it preserves, 'within all its members', firstly, an agreement with the witness of the apostles:

* For example, the 25-page document detailing 'The Apostolic Succession from St Peter and St Paul to Larry Wilson Johnson, First Bishop of the Anglican Church of Virginia, Presiding Bishop of the Orthodox Apostolic Anglican Church of Haiti, and of Australian Anglican Church of Virginia International Communion', available online from: <www.theanglicanchurch.net/apostolicsessionACOVA2004.doc>. Accessed 10 November 2007.

> The original and fundamental witness of the apostles is the source and norm of the Church's existence in preaching, faith and action alike, in all times and places. This witness must constantly be heard anew in the Church and allowed to bear fruit in its whole life. Apostolic succession is therefore a question of a continual and living confrontation of the Church and all its members with this apostolic witness: apostolic succession is fulfilled when this witness is heard, respected, believed, confessed and followed.[6]

This agreement is expressed through a continuation in the apostolic ministry, which is, fundamentally, a servant ministry:

> The Church can only be certain of its apostolic mission and authority if it is a serving Church. Apostolicity is never an unchallenged possession, a secure piece of property which the Church has at its disposal. Apostolicity can never mean power through which the Church might rule. It is not a question of others submitting to the Church; the Church must itself submit by accepting the authority of the apostles and of the Church's and the apostles' Lord.[7]

Edward Schillebeeckx built on the insights of Vatican II which had so motivated Küng, in his 1981 book *Ministry: A Case for Change*. Here, Schillebeeckx is concerned to press the specifically New Testament apostolicity of the Church:

> The apostolicity of the Christian community always implies the apostolic communication of the faith and therefore also the permanent importance of the foundation document in which the 'gospel of Jesus' is related in kerygmatic form: the New Testament read against the horizon of understanding of what is called the 'Old Testament'.[8]

Schillebeeckx develops Küng's two criteria for apostolicity into eight, orienting them towards his chosen foundational model of the New Testament experience.

First, a Church, an ecclesial community, retains New Testament apostolicity if it retains an awareness that it is 'carrying on the cause of Jesus':

> . . . a living community is a community of believers who appropriate the cause of Jesus, i.e. the coming kingdom of God as essentially bound up with the whole of the career and ultimately the very person of Jesus, and therefore seek to maintain the story of and about Jesus in its significance for the future of all humanity.[9]

Second, a permanent importance is accorded to the New Testament, interpreted against the Old Testament as the 'foundation document' of the Church. Third, the apostolicity of a community derives, in turn, from being connected to the community of Jesus, which derives from accepting the discipleship of Jesus, which is 'to be realized again and again in new historical circumstances'. Fourth, in the life of the apostolic community today we should expect to see proclamation, liturgy and service, which are all apostolic characteristics of communities of God. Fifth, an apostolic community has a right to a minister or ministers and a right to the celebration of the Lord's Supper on the basis of Jesus's mandate, 'Do this in remembrance of me.' Sixth, separate, physical communities need to recognize their interdependence: they are clearly not 'isolated entities but bound together in love . . . a great *koinonia* or brotherly community in which mutual criticism, grounded in the gospel, must be possible if all communities are to be maintained on apostolic lines'. Seventh, the ministry which belongs to a community of right is not a ministry of status but service, and is therefore a gift of the Holy Spirit. 'Suffering solidarity with the poor and insignificant is an essential mark of the apostolicity of ministry, since it is an apostolic mark of the whole community of Jesus.' Eighth and finally, there can never be any decisive, final theoretical formulation of these marks of apostolicity. Rather, apostolicity is expressed and explored in 'a mutually critical correlation (which must be both theoretical and practical) between what the New Testament churches did and what the Christian communities do now'.[10]

Both Schillebeeckx and Küng are Roman Catholic theologians working in the aftermath of the Second Vatican Council. It might be thought, then, that their work, insight and agenda would be particular to their tradition. And yet, on the question of the Church's witnessing vocation, there is an interesting convergence of thought between these post-Conciliar scholars and theologians who have emerged from the Reformation tradition. The most important work on the Church's vocation to witness in recent years has come from John Howard Yoder (1927–1997), a Mennonite, pacifist and ethicist, and his pupil Stanley Hauerwas (b. 1940), originally a United Methodist, but who more recently identifies himself as an Episcopalian.

In 2001 Hauerwas was invited to give the Gifford Lectures at St Andrew's University. Endowed by Adam, Lord Gifford in 1885, the lectures are intended to explore the idea that:

> . . . the true knowledge of God, that is, of the Being, Nature, and Attributes of the Infinite, of the All, of the First and the Only Cause, that is, the One and Only Substance and Being, . . . is the means of man's highest well-being, and the security of his upward progress . . .[11]

Gifford wanted a series of lectures on 'natural theology'; that is, 'knowledge of God obtainable by human reason alone without the aid of revelation'.[12] Specifically, lecturers are instructed to treat natural theology as a science; that is, 'without reference to or reliance upon any supposed special exceptional or so-called miraculous revelation'.[13] For those familiar with his work and thought, it will not be surprising that Hauerwas refused to play this game. For him, natural theology undertaken by Christians 'simply names how Christian convictions work to describe all that is as God's good creation'.[14] In other words, there is no such thing as a 'natural theology' which clears the ground to allow a specifically Christian understanding of the implications of 'natural theology' to be explored. For Hauerwas, and this is his relevance to our discussion, Christian witness comes *before* every other form of discourse. Hauerwas is emphatic, and thrilling, in his insistence on this point:

> If what Christians believe about God and the world could be known without witnesses, then we would have evidence that what Christians believe about God and the world is not true. All that is, all that is creation, is a witness to the One alone who is capable of moving the sun and the stars as well as our hearts. If we and the world existed by necessity, then no witnesses, no story of creation, would be required. But God did not have to create, much less redeem; yet we have it on good authority that God has created and redeemed. Creation and redemption constitute the story necessary for us to know who we are. Such knowledge comes only through the telling of this story.[15]

To be a Christian witness is, therefore, *both* to tell the story about all that there is *and* to recognize the need to tell the story. In fact, recognizing the need is the greater part of the witness, for it is the part that runs so *against* the prevailing story of our time and culture (this is all that there is, and existence and human will are just brute facts that cannot and need not be explained) and at the same time runs *with* the grain of the universe (the fundamental nature of creation brought into being by the Christian, triune God).

If Christian witness is such a fundamental part of both being a Christian and part of Creation, then obviously the question of how such a witness is expressed also becomes important:

> To be a witness does not mean that Christians are in the business of calling attention to ourselves but that we are witnesses to the One who has made our lives possible. Witness, at least the witness to which Christians are called, is, after all, about God and God's relation to all that is.[16]

This is a witness about God, and therefore is a witness about truth. Which will be a difficult task in times in which competing 'truth claims' are managed by relativizing them into no more than personal preference, and of no more importance than other personal preferences, like favourite colour or usual coffee. Here Hauerwas, showing the influence of his Mennonite teacher, quotes Yoder:

> It is within these [relativist/pluralist] skins that we need to restore whatever our claims are. Since for some even the phrase 'truth claims' evokes echoes of theocratic compulsion or of pretensions to infallibility, let us use the more biblical phrases 'witness' and 'proclamation' as naming forms of communication which do not coerce the hearer.[17]

Yoder and Hauerwas have in mind Paul's teaching in Romans:

> 'Everyone who calls on the name of the Lord shall be saved.' But how are they to call on one in whom they have not believed? And how are they to believe in one of whom they have never heard? And how are they to hear without someone to proclaim him? (Romans 10.13f.)

This is the missional foundation of apostolic succession, what Yoder calls the 'missionary instrumentalities': we know for we have heard, and, in turn, we are to bring others into the knowledge of the love of God in Christ Jesus.

So we need to unpick two connected themes: the form of witness and the content of Christian witness. We will come to its form in a moment, but first let us look at the message rather than the medium.

I once knew of a priest in the Church of England who, on going for an interview, was completely flummoxed by a 'trick question'. Initially sympathetic, I asked what the question was. It was simply, 'What is your gospel?' This was thought to be deviously tricksy by the priest in question (who didn't get the job!). And yet the answer ought to be one that is at the forefront of the mind of any halfway competent post-Herbertian priest: 'What is your gospel?'

For me, I have been massively influenced by Michael Ramsey. I was introduced to his thought by my university chaplain (an example of witnessing in the tradition). For Ramsey, the abiding theme of his teaching, study and ministry was the glory of God. St Irenaeus taught that 'the glory of God is man fully alive, and man is fully alive when he beholds God',[18] and Archbishop Ramsey spent his life understanding how this may be so. His success is seen in the book of Ramsey's teaching, edited by Douglas Dales, called *Glory Descending: Michael Ramsey and his Writings.*

A significant scriptural passage in Ramsey's teaching is the meditation in Hebrews 2 on the relationship between Jesus seen, suffering experienced, and glory looked for:

> As it is, we do not yet see everything in subjection to them [i.e. angels], but we do see Jesus, who for a little while was made lower than the angels, now crowned with glory and honour because of the suffering of death, so that by the grace of God he might taste death for everyone. (Hebrews 2.8b–9)

This passage gets to grips with the mysterious connection between creation, suffering, redemption and ultimate glory. The writer of the letter to the Hebrews is concerned to convey the 'newness' of the Christian good news to an audience steeped in the world of the Covenant of Abraham and Moses. He has, consciously or subconsciously, found a 'witnessing strategy' in which his new ideas, insights and testimony can be communicated to a people with a particular world-view, a shared discourse. John Howard Yoder has examined the techniques and tactics used by the five New Testament writers to convey their message, and six aspects common to the witnessing strategy.[19] First, the writer is at home in the linguistic world he wishes to address; he uses its language and faces its questions. Second, he does not fit Jesus into the pre-existing cosmology of this world: Jesus does not occupy a place like one of any number of predecessors, but rather is placed in a position of lordship over and above the pre-existing cosmology. But this is lordship of a new and unusual kind, for, third, Christ's cosmic overlordship is achieved by, or expressed by, an emphasis on his human rejection and suffering. This means that, fourth, 'salvation' (however it is defined) is not achieved for the devout believer by entering into the pre-existing cosmology, but by sharing in the self-emptying, and death and resurrection of the Son. This is assured, this cosmic victory won, by, fifth, the pre-existence of the Son and his participation with the Father in creation and providence. Finally, the writer and readers 'share by faith in all that that victory means'.[20]

Michael Ramsey teases out these New Testament connections between the broken creation of pain and the new creation of Christ's victory. In *The Glory of God and the Transfiguration of Christ*, he wrote:

> The mystery of evil afflicts not only human beings but all creation too. Human suffering in the present time, the bondage of corruption in nature (Romans 8.18–21), and the fact that we do not yet see all things made subject to human rule (Hebrews 2.8) all indicate the frustration of the divine design by the fall of humanity. But by the cross and resurrection of Christ the inauguration of a new creation has begun, and this new creation will include human beings brought to sonship and glory, and nature itself renewed in union with humanity in the worship and praise of God (Romans 8.21; Hebrews 2.10). The Christian hope is therefore far more than the salvaging of individual human souls into a spiritual salvation: it is nothing less than the re-creation of the world, through the power of the resurrection of Christ.[21]

So we see, finally, that Christian witness is not about arguing people into belief. It is about loving people into the ambit of God's work. As Michael Cartwright puts it:

> . . . the primary problem confronting the Christian Church in a post-modern world is not whether Christian claims about God can be debated in credible ways with alternating accounts (*logos*) of abstract reasoning. Rather, the challenge is about *ethos* of Christian witness. Can particular Christian communities produce and sustain the kind of witness to God in which their practices of discipleship can serve as credible signs of God's reconciling work in the world?[22]

In other words, it ain't what you do, it's the way that you do it. (For remember, these are ideas emerging from Christian traditions of the Reformation: we do not have here a restatement of false 'works' salvation.) Yoder goes further, asserting that Christian witness today should take the example of the first Christians to heart:

> Instead of requesting free speech and room for one more stand in the Athenian marketplace of ideas for a new variant of already widely respected diaspora Judaism, their claim was that now the Hebrew story had widened out to include everybody; that, with the inbreaking of the messianic era, the Jewish hope in process of fulfilment was wide enough to receive all the nations and their riches.[23]

Cartwright suggests seven features or marks of this ethos of Christian witness, features which would be well marked by any diligent post-Herbertian parish priest seeking a sustainable model for parish ministry. First, witness should begin with an acceptance of the *mission* that has been entrusted to us. This should not be narrowly defined. The Church's mission is the making of new disciples of Jesus Christ, and new disciples require a new form of community. As Yoder has written:

> That men and women are called together to a new social wholeness is itself the work of God, which gives meaning to history, from which both personal conversion (whereby individuals are called into this meaning), and missionary instrumentalities are derived.[24]

A responsibility (but not the *primary* responsibility) for this new social wholeness is assigned to the priest of the community. It is not wholly the priest's responsibility, because it is not the priest's work: to use the language of our post-Conciliar theologians, it is not an *opus operatum ministri*, but an *opus operatum* of Jesus Christ. Cartwright gives a very good example of this distinction in the story of Fr Elias Chacour, parish priest for the Melkite Christian community in Ibillin, an Arab village of both Christian and Muslim Arabs. On Palm Sunday 1966, when he had been in post for less than six months, Chacour suddenly realized that his village, the community of the Church, was riven completely by suspicion, anger and enmity. Nothing he could do seemed to make a difference to the lives of his parishioners: to speak to one family risked the anger of another. On Palm Sunday, after the celebration of the Eucharist, Chacour snapped, and locked his congregation in the church. Turning to them he said:

> This morning while I celebrated this liturgy, I found someone who is able to help you. In fact, he is the only one who can work the miracle of reconciliation in this village. This person who can reconcile you is Jesus Christ, and he is here with us. We are gathered in his name, this man who rode in triumph into Jerusalem with hosannas from the people ringing in his ears. So on Christ's behalf, I say this to you: The doors of the church are locked. Either you kill each other right here in your hatred and then I will celebrate your funeral gratis, or you use this opportunity to be reconciled together before I open the doors of the church. If that reconciliation happens, Christ will truly become your Lord, and I will know I am becoming your pastor and your priest. That decision is now yours.[25]

Chacour makes it clear, to his listeners and his readers, that the 'missionary instrumentalities' that have come into place in Ibillin Church are down to Christ, and to him alone. It is in Christ's name that the Mass was celebrated. It was Christ's name that was proclaimed with loud hosannas. It is Christ who is able to effect the miracle of reconciliation. It is Christ who will be shown as Lord when the fractious villagers are reconciled to one another. Chacour functions, merely, 'on Christ's behalf', to speak the invitation, and to act, literally, as the keeper of the keys, with power to bind and to loose.

If the first mark of Christian witness is mission, then the second is similar: *the praise of God*. After being held hostage in their church, having been confronted in the starkest possible way with the consequences of their disunity, the people of Ibillin are reconciled to one another. Then, for the first time for a long time, they are able truly to praise God:

> The people even then began to sing the resurrection hymn as they streamed out the open church doors:
>
> 'Christ is risen from the dead!
> By his death he has trampled upon death
> And has given life to those
> Who are in the tomb!'
>
> All afternoon I could hear singing, ululations, happy voices and laughter. I knew this was a whole new life for Ibillin.[26]

Being brought into the new community of God's redemption and re-creation inevitably leads to joy without measure that overflows into the whole of the community's life.

The third mark is to do with *keeping time*. Christians live under the light of the resurrection, and the truth of the resurrection is that the end of history has come in the birth, life, ministry, death and resurrection of Jesus Christ. The new creation imagery of 2 Corinthians is important here: anyone who is found to be in Christ is 'a new creation: everything old has passed away; see, everything has become new!' (2 Corinthians 5.17). And that new creation is not yet completed: the earthly tent which we inhabit will be replaced by a dwelling of God's making, 'a house not made with hands, eternal in the heavens' (2 Corinthians 5.1). And even though we might 'groan' in longing for this heavenly dwelling, we know that before we come into our heavenly dwelling comes judgement:

> For all of us must appear before the judgement seat of Christ, so that each may receive recompense for what has been done in the body, whether good or evil. (2 Corinthians 5.10)

We have already seen this connection made between the promise and the fulfilment in the teaching of Michael Ramsey. It is impossible to understand Christian witness to the gospel if we aren't able to see the implications for our future selves. Palm Sunday leads to Good Friday before it comes to Easter Day.

The fourth mark is to do with *remembering God's story*, and the character of that story. It is no accident that much of the Lord's teaching to his disciples was conveyed in the form of stories: 'The kingdom of heaven may be compared to someone who sowed good seed in his field . . .' (Matthew 13.24) or 'Every one then who hears these words of mine and does them will be like a wise man who built his house upon the rock . . .' (Matthew 7.24) or 'He who has ears to hear, let him hear' (Mark 4.9; Luke 8.8; Matthew 13.9). The disciples took this narrative proclamation to heart. The first post-Ascension proclamation of the Christian good news, Peter's address to the crowds of Jerusalem at Pentecost, takes the form of a narrative in which the events of the day are explained by being interpolated into the wider events of God's saving work for the people of Israel:

> 'You that are Israelites, listen to what I have to say: Jesus of Nazareth, a man attested to you by God with deeds of power, wonders, and signs that God did through him among you, as you yourselves know – this man, handed over to you according to the definite plan and foreknowledge of God, you crucified and killed by the hands of those outside the law. But God raised him up, having freed him from death, because it was impossible for him to be held in its power.' (Acts 2.22–24)

Fr Chacour did the same thing to the recalcitrant people of his parish. Their behaviour was a scandal to Christ, because his story included the hosannas of the crowd on Palm Sunday, and their mocking cries on Good Friday.

The fifth mark is *serving God*. The Son of Man came to serve, not to be served, and those who wish to be grafted into the telling of his story need to remember that imperative. As Paul says:

> Let love be genuine; hate what is evil, hold fast to what is good; love one another with mutual affection; outdo one another in showing honour. Do not lag in zeal, be ardent in spirit, serve the Lord. Rejoice in hope, be patient in suffering, persevere in prayer. Con-

> tribute to the needs of the saints; extend hospitality to strangers. (Romans 12.9–12)

And it won't be enough to have done all these things: they will have had to be undertaken for the right reason:

> . . . do not pronounce judgement before the time, before the Lord comes, who will bring to light the things now hidden in darkness and will disclose the purposes of the heart. Then each one will receive commendation from God. (1 Corinthians 4.5)

Perhaps curiously, the next mark of Christian witness seems to head in an unexpected direction; not out into the world of suffering and need, but back into church. For Cartwright says that the sixth mark is *performing liturgy*. But when you think about it, you see how exactly right he is. Take the example of Palm Sunday in Ibillin. The people of the parish could not go out into their village, their wider community, singing the praises of God in how he had transformed their damaged relationships, if they had not been present at divine worship: 'witness derives its meaning from the work of the people (*leitourgia*) as displayed in their public gatherings for worship'.[27] Because Christian worship began in the Holy Land, it was associated from the earliest days with memories of Jesus's life and ministry. It was 'stational', moving from significant place to significant place: here in Bethlehem we remember Jesus's birth, here in Nazareth we remember his family life, here in Capernaum we remember his teaching and his healing, here in Jerusalem we remember his passion and death. So, from the very beginning, Christian worship was intimately bound up with a remembering and a retelling and a re-presentation of God's saving actions in Christ Jesus: '. . . when Christians gather for worship, what they are doing is nothing less than bearing witness to what God has done and is doing in human history'.[28]

The final mark of Christian witness can also be illustrated by Fr Chacour's experience. It is *exercising authority*. Although Chacour gave the invitation to reconciliation on behalf of Christ, he still gave it. It is false humility to act as if no authority at all goes with the office and work of a priest in the Church of God. We have tried pretending that for some time now, believing that all that is needed is a little more niceness.

Occasionally, the exercise of authority might require the binding and loosing of the keys, such as was done by Chacour on that Palm Sunday.

> By refusing to let the congregation leave until they had reconciled with each other, Fr Chacour bound them to confront their responsibility for living in ways that nullify their witness to the gospel. When he invited them to go forth into the world rejoicing in their newly reconciled relationship with one another, he set them free to live lives of obedience.[29]

Very much more often, authority is exercised in other, more subtle ways. Michael Cartwright relates another story of Fr Chacour which illustrates this subtler authority. In 2000, one of the students of Fr Chacour's school, the Mar Elias Educational Institutions, was killed by the Israeli Defence Force in the intifadah. There was no possibility that he had been involved in violence: the boy was a leader in the 'Seeds of Peace', an inter-faith group of pupils, which worked hard to find common ground with young people on both sides of the Israeli–Palestinian conflict. A memorial service was held for him at Mar Elias, and wreaths would be placed at the memorial for all those who have been killed in the years of conflict: a memorial with two curved, facing stone walls. On one is carved, in Hebrew, 'To the martyrs of the Palestinian people'; on the other, in Arabic, 'To the martyrs of the Jewish people'.

At the moment of the wreath-laying, the Israeli education minister stepped forward to lay the wreath beneath the wall for the Jewish dead. Fr Chacour stopped him, and directed him to lay his wreath under the memorial to the Arab dead. The Arab official followed, his wreath placed for the martyrs of the Jewish people: 'What could have been a cause for taking offence was turned into an occasion for sowing seeds of reconciliation.'[30]

Chacour exercised a different sort of authority from that normally expected by the word, the authority of a host. This is a fundamental mark of what constitutes a Christian community, an eighth mark of Christian witness, *hospitality*. Chacour, in acting as host, ensured that guests at the ceremony were allowed to know what was expected of them, so that their behaviour and what they had to offer the gathering was accepted in the right spirit. This is the authority seen in the Messianic banquet:

> 'But when you are invited, go and sit down at the lowest place, so that when your host comes, he may say to you, "Friend, move up higher"; then you will be honoured in the presence of all who sit at the table with you. For all who exalt themselves will be humbled, and those who humble themselves will be exalted.' (Luke 14.10f.)

And it is an authority of hospitality which we are expected to take on for ourselves. The early Church took Jesus's instruction very seriously:

> 'When you give a luncheon or a dinner, do not invite your friends or your brothers or your relatives or rich neighbours, in case they may invite you in return, and you would be repaid. But when you give a banquet, invite the poor, the crippled, the lame, and the blind. And you will be blessed, because they cannot repay you, for you will be repaid at the resurrection of the righteous.' (Luke 14.12–14)

The culture of the time, Gentile and Hebrew, had the household as its basis. The Christian gospel reconstituted this household, forming the separate kinship households into a single household of God:

> This expanded and transformed household was responsible for imitating God's hospitable and gracious character. God's household represented the welcome of the Gentiles into the inheritance together with Israel (Ephesians 2.19), and relations within this new household explicitly transcended ethnic boundaries.[31]

One of the central Greek words for hospitality, *philoxenia*, shows this transcending of divisions; it has as its roots *phileo*, love for kinship group, and *xenos*, stranger: 'Because *philoxenia* includes the word for stranger, hospitality's orientation towards strangers is also more apparent in Greek than in English.'[32] Furthermore, hospitality is not an optional extra for Christians, an expression among many other possible expressions, of the Christian faith. Rather it is at the heart of Christian self-understanding. We are shown how Jesus practised hospitality to welcome the marginal and the outcast; we are exhorted to be hospitable in turn, for in doing so we show hospitality to Christ. Christ is both host and guest: 'Christians offered hospitality in grateful response to God's generosity and as an expression of welcome to Christ "who for your sake was a stranger".'[33]

Eight marks to being a witness to the transforming and healing power of God: eight marks to show the Church's participation in 'the re-creation of the world, through the power of the resurrection of Christ'. Christian praxis should be oriented, in its entirety, towards this goal. It is in recalling this witnessing, loving, serving ministry that the post-Herbertism priest remains true to an apostolic calling, a calling which is authenticated by the living of it. There is a 'cash value' in living like this. As John Howard Yoder puts it:

> To know the Lamb who was slain was worthy to receive power not only enables his disciples to face martyrdom when they must; it also encourages them to go about their daily crafts and trades, to do their duties as parents and neighbours, without being driven by cosmic doubt. Even before the broken world can be made whole by the Second Coming, the witnesses to the first coming – through the very fact that they proclaim Christ above the powers, the Son above the angels – are enabled to go on proleptically in the redemption of creation. Only in this evangelical Christology can be found a truly transformationist approach to culture. We still do not *see* that the world has been set straight. We still have no *proof* that right is right. We have still not found a bridge or a way to leap from historical uncertainty to some other more solid base that would oblige people to believe or make our own believing sure. As it is, we do not see everything in subjection to him. *But we do see Jesus*, revealing the grace of God by tasting death for everyone.[34]

8

Watchman

Had'st thou but lived, though stripp'd of power,
A watchman on the lonely tower,
Thy thrilling trump had roused the land,
When fraud or danger were at hand . . .
(Marmion, 1808)

One autumn I found myself rewatching Peter Jackson's *Lord of the Rings* in my lunch hour. Gradually I was drawn in, and half an hour (very occasionally!) became an hour when I could have profitably been visiting, filing, sermon writing, planning, form-filling. I finished the final film on 1 November, overwhelmed once more by the breadth of Tolkien's vision and the skilfulness of Jackson's film-making.

The next day was All Souls', and with it a Requiem Eucharist. I realized that *Lord of the Rings*, book and films, is about, on one level, the cost of death and the waste of life. What sacrifices can we bear, and in what cause? What lasting effect does the slaughter of the previous age have upon our own? Can the unheroic hero Frodo, who has suffered so greatly, and seen so much destruction, ever find rest and redemption? I realized that this was a story written in middle- and late-age by a man who, as a callow lieutenant, had fought in the trenches of the Somme. And yet, Tolkien had been able to describe the healing of death in a memorable image: 'The grey rain-curtain turned all to silver glass and was rolled back, and he beheld white shores and beyond them a far green country under a swift sunrise.'[1] Jackson transposed this description into a speech by the wise and powerful Gandalf, made in the middle of a battle in which violent death was a certainty. The transposition was inspired, for Gandalf's speech did not offer cheap comfort; the costliness of the experiences lived through and described by Tolkien prevents that. This is a truer, deeper resonating understanding of life and death. My sermon on All Souls' night used Tolkien's experiences and Jackson's creative depiction of Tolkien's work to present my congregation with the Christian hope through and over death. A member of the congregation came up to me afterwards and confided that she had never really understood such hope before it had been presented to her in the imagery of Tolkien and Jackson.

So, on one level my lunchtime viewing was a waste of time. For the Time and Motion outsider it might seem to have been a self-indulgent distraction from the core responsibilities of my job. Perhaps. But sometimes what is seen as 'waste of time' is actually fallow ground becoming fruitful.

The Archbishop of Canterbury in his lecture on 'The Christian Priest Today' makes much of this apparent time-wasting. He calls it making sense of the landscape in which the priest conducts his ministry. There is an explicit precedent for this role in the scriptural tradition, and the Archbishop draws the attention of his listeners to Habakkuk and Ezekiel: in this role, the priest is to act as Watchman.

In Habakkuk 2, the prophet tells how he has been set at the watchpost by the Lord, upon the rampart. Habakkuk makes clear that what he will see is what the Lord wants to tell him: 'I will keep watch to see what he will say to me, and what he will answer concerning my complaint' (Habakkuk 2.1b). The events seen by the prophet will be interpreted as the word of God to him, and an answer to his complaint. God will reveal his purpose to the prophet (and thus to the wider community of Israel) through the events the prophet will see.

In Ezekiel, the prophet is lifted up in the Spirit of the Lord to act as a sentinel. At first, it seems that this sentinel role is a traditional, verbal one:

> Mortal, I have made you a sentinel for the house of Israel; whenever you hear a word from my mouth, you shall give them warning from me. (Ezekiel 3.17)

The prophet has the responsibility to pass on the verbal admonitions of the Lord. However, towards the end of the book, the role of the sentinel is explained. If the sentinel sees a sword coming upon the land of Israel, he is to warn the people. This is not just a practical, military role: as the Lord warns: 'If any who hear the sound of the trumpet do not take warning, and the sword comes and takes them away, their blood shall be upon their own heads' (Ezekiel 33.4). The people shall not just be killed, but judgement is upon them as well. The Lord then applies the role, in analogy, to the prophet: 'If you warn the wicked to turn from their ways, and they do not turn from their ways, the wicked shall die in their iniquity, but you will have saved your life' (Ezekiel 33.9).

Let's press this image of the priest as Watchman a little further. Let us consider what the image says of the position and *dis*position of the priest. Imagine a city with a Watchman on its walls. In the city below the walls, life goes on: markets are held, goods made, bought, sold; meals prepared and eaten. It is clear that not everyone can be a Watchman. If everyone in the city were to be appointed a sentinel at the same time, then life would come grinding to a halt. If everyone were watching then no one could be buying, selling, teaching, learning, living. It is not possible to live the life of the city, a civilized life, on the city walls. Life goes on in the city below; people live their lives, trusting the Watchman to see the approaching army or tornado or whatever. There should be only one Watchman per vantage point.

Similarly, it is not possible to be a Watchman in the marketplace, in the public library or in the private home:* the Watchman must stand in the high and liminal places, on the edges of city life, so as to be able to see what is *beyond* the city, to be able to see what threatens or promises the city.

These are all characteristics of position; what about disposition? Disposition is a matter of attitude and discernment. The Watchman needs to believe there is something worth watching for: a Watchman who believes that no army could possibly attack the city from his watching place actually becomes the weakest point in the city's defences. The Watchman also needs to be able to judge what it is he sees: is that cloud on the horizon rain or the dust from horsemen, is it a camel train or a raiding party? The Watchman also needs to know what not to notice. Not every sign of life or activity is significant.

* This is not to say that there is no place for any kind of surveying in the public places of the city, but the person who fulfils that role is a *policeman* and not a watchman, and a policeman is a rather different role. Similarly, the person who stands on the city walls and watches the city inside is also not a watchman, but rather a *prison guard*. These roles might be necessary, but they are not our concern for the moment.

When we transfer this (somewhat over-elaborated) metaphor to church life, we see that the priest as Watchman needs to be able to read the signs of the times. He needs to be able to understand what is significant, what is changing, what is unfolding in the times and culture in which he finds himself, and in which his community lives. He needs to be engaged with, but not overwhelmed by, the sheer volume of events that unfold in our culture, especially with its tendency to value unmediated novelty. As Rowan Williams puts it, the best priest-watchmen 'in this and other eras are, it seems to me, those who have known how to read the surface and the depths, but have had no great interest in the shallows'.[2]

This is a tricky thing to achieve as a member of a stubbornly anti-intellectual body such as the Church of England. Judith Maltby puts it well:

> It isn't hard to find preachers and pastors, liberal or conservative, high or low, Protestant or Catholic, expressing the view that feeling matters more than thinking; spirituality more than theology. In this assessment the heart always trumps the head . . . Anti-intellectualism is one of the ecumenical success stories of modern Christianity. We all subscribe.
>
> In the Church of England it is commonplace to hear the view that theological inquiry at worst destroys faith, at best is inferior to uncritical acceptance – as though the life of faith was chiefly about an uncritical, emotional assent to a set of propositions about God that can only get muddled and muddied by thinking about it.[3]

Despite this anti-intellectualism (or perhaps because of it), for a priest to be a meaningful witness to the reality of the Church's past experience of Christ at work, then he will need to be a diligent student of the present in which the Church finds herself. He has to be able to answer the conspectus questions: Where are we? What are the big stories of our day? What are the assumptions of our time and culture? Like a mountain guard, the priest today needs to be able to discern the tiny trembles of snowflakes that precipitate the cataclysmic avalanche. What are the signs of change in our time? Where can we discern God's purpose being enacted?

And this requires cultural literacy.

If this is uncontentious for you, if this is a simple statement of the patently obvious, then you might like to skip to the next section (from p. 120, in which I set out a modern theologian's 'three fundamentals' of cultural theology). If, on the other hand, cultural literacy in a priest seems a novel or threatening idea, then read on. You will need to set aside any inherited cultural reluctance in dealing with ideas, because the study of culture is nothing less than the study of ideas, and the philosophers of ideas take no prisoners in their work. Even so, to have a grounding in the theory of culture and cultural literacy is crucial to habilitating Herbertism.

The priest should be able to read cultural artefacts, because in them he can see what people really value. Samuel Butler's novel *Erewhon* (1872) gives us a satirical depiction of this. Butler, the son of a parson and grandson of a bishop, had broken with his family over his conviction of the truth of Darwin's *On the Origin of Species*. He emigrated to New Zealand, and made his fortune sheep-farming. Returning to England, and disappointed by the hypocrisies of Victorian society, he wrote *Erewhon* ('nowhere' rearranged, to make the obvious point). In it, the hero wanders into a European-like civilization in the interior of the New Zealand islands. Life is both like and unlike England. The hero, Higgs, gradually realizes the central place of the Musical Banks to Erewhonian society. On a visit to one of the grand, impressive buildings which houses a branch of the Musical Banks, he realizes that the currency of the Bank is:

> . . . supposed to be *the* system, and . . . in which all monetary transactions should be carried on; and as far as I could see, all who wished to be considered respectable, kept a larger or smaller balance at these banks . . . [but] . . . the amount so kept had no direct commercial value in the outside world; I am sure that the managers and cashiers of the Musical Banks were not paid in their own currency. Mr Nosnibor used to go to these banks, or rather to the great mother bank of the city, sometimes, but not very often. He was a pillar of one of the other kind of banks, though he appeared to hold some minor office also in the musical ones. The ladies generally went alone; as indeed was the case in most families, except on state occasions.[4]

The Musical Banks are the cathedrals and churches of Erewhonian society: the desire to be respectable was stronger than the usefulness and meaning of the Banks. The *real* currency, the real business, happened somewhere else. Here Butler takes Jesus's injunction in the Sermon on the Mount and asks what would a society look like in which the treasures of earth and the treasures of heaven were much more clearly distinguished. Like Higgs, the priest as Watchman needs to be able to read the inconsistencies and hypocrisies of a society's cultural values in order to see what is truly important, not just what is said to be or thought to be important.

Before we unpack what cultural literacy might mean, it would be good to register a dissenting opinion. Pope Benedict XVI has a characteristically firm idea of what the Church and its people require of her priests: 'The faithful expect only one thing from priests: that they be specialists in promoting the encounter between man and God.'[5] This means that 'there is absolutely no need for the priest to know all the latest, changing currents of thought; what the faithful expect from him is that he be a witness to the eternal wisdom contained in the revealed word'. In other words, 'the priest is not asked to be an expert in economics, construction or politics. He is expected to be an expert in the spiritual life.'[6] This might seem to be an assertion of an older, restricted expertise for the priests of the Church, a conservative revision of 'rendering unto Caesar'. But Benedict XVI is too good a theologian to fall into that trap. In one of the innovations of his pontificate, the Pope has instituted regular Q&A sessions with various groupings within the Church. He has met the priests of the diocese of Rome twice now, and in the session held in the summer of 2007 he responded to a question about his beliefs on the human side of the priesthood. The Pope's response was clear:

> Catholicism, somewhat simplistically, has always been considered the religion of the great '*et et*': not of great forms of exclusivism but of synthesis . . . we cannot always live in exalted meditation; perhaps a Saint on the last step of his earthly pilgrimage could reach this point, but we normally live with our feet on the ground and our eyes turned to Heaven. Both these things are given to us by the Lord and therefore loving human things, loving the beauties of this earth, is not only very human but also very Christian and truly Catholic . . . this

> aspect is also part of a good and truly Catholic pastoral care: living in the '*et et*'; living the humanity and humanism of the human being, all the gifts which the Lord has lavished upon us and which we have developed; and at the same time, not forgetting God, because ultimately, the great light comes from God and then it is only from him that comes the light which gives joy to all these aspects of the things that exist.[7]

Even a dissenting opinion can be tempered by the great *et et*.

The starting point for any consideration of the priest's role as an observer and interpreter of culture has to begin with H. Richard Niebuhr's *Christ and Culture*, published in 1951.[8] This was the definitive book on the subject, and remains the definitive book: as someone once said, books by theologians don't remain in print, and they certainly don't remain in print for 50 years. It is, in short, a classic, which means that it 'is a work of genius that a later culture must take into account once that work has had a chance to leave its marks'.[9] No wonder, as Glen Stassen has said, *Christ and Culture*:

> . . . is studied in graduate and undergraduate classes; it is required reading in courses in colleges, universities, and seminaries. It is used primarily not to introduce the theology of H. Richard Niebuhr, but to introduce a systematized representation of the various dominant forms of Christian belief. Often it serves as a basic text in the systematic study of Christian ethics, but more probably just as frequently as an orientation to Christian theology more generally.[10]

Niebuhr's book had its origins in a lecture series given at Austin Presbyterian Theological Seminary in Texas in the autumn of 1949. (It is worth bearing in mind the political and social context in which Niebuhr was working at the time of the original lectures and in the preparation of the book for publication in 1951. We'll see the importance of context in the criticisms made of the book in later years.)

In the book Niebuhr presents a problem (the 'enduring problem') and five typologies with which the problem may be addressed. The problem is the relationship of what Niebuhr variously, and imprecisely, calls the 'relations of Christianity and civilization' or 'exponents of a Christian civilization and the non-Christian defenders of a wholly secularized society' or 'the problem of human culture'.[11] Niebuhr eventually settles on the polarity which gives the book its title: 'Culture' on the one hand, 'Christ' on the other.* Recognizing that in a work of typology, definitions are vital, Niebuhr sets out to give a working definition of his two terms. There is nothing definitive about his definitions: both sections of the opening chapter are tentatively titled 'toward a definition of . . .'. Even so, for many of Niebuhr's later critics the definitions are part of the weakness of this thesis.

To begin with, simply, Niebuhr looks to define 'Christ' by defining 'Christian': a Christian is someone:

> . . . who counts himself as belonging to that community of men for whom Jesus Christ – his life, words, deeds, and destiny – is of supreme importance as the key to the understanding of themselves and their world, the main source of the knowledge of God and man, good and evil, the constant companion of the conscience, and the expected deliverer from evil.[12]

So far, so comprehensive, it might seem. But Niebuhr recognizes that there has been an innumerable variety in the working out and the living of this definition. Even so, he asserts that these workings out all have their origins in the single expression of who Jesus Christ was:

> . . . this Jesus Christ is a definite person, one and the same whether he appears as a man of flesh and blood or as risen Lord. He can never be confused with a Socrates, a Plato or an Aristotle, a Gautama, a Confucius, or a Mohammed, or even with an Amos or Isaiah . . . But there always remain the original portraits with which all later pictures may be compared and by which caricatures may be corrected. And in these original portraits he is recognizably one and the same.[13]

(Which seems to beg the question somewhat.) For Niebuhr, this fundamental unity in the original portraits of Christ can be seen most clearly in an examination of his various virtues. It is not enough, for Niebuhr,

---

* In the interests of strict accuracy, the book should have been titled, as we shall see, *Christ and/or/instead/because of/above Culture*.

to say with religious liberalism that Jesus is love, for all the expressions of Jesus's love are directed to and through God the Father: 'Jesus Christ's love of men was not merely an illustration of universal benevolence but a decisive act of divine *Agape*.' In other words, the only adequate way of describing Jesus's possession and expression of the virtue of love is to say that 'his love was that of the Son of God'.[14] Similarly, although Jesus may be said to be an exemplar of hope (in eschatological interpretations), radical obedience (existentialist), faith and faithfulness (orthodox Protestantism), humility (monasticism), the Christ of the New Testament, for Niebuhr, may possess these virtues but he isn't defined by them:

> . . . each of them [these virtues] is expressed in his conduct and teaching in a manner that seems extreme and disproportionate to secular, cultural wisdom. But he practises none of them and requires none of them of his followers otherwise than in relation to God.[15]

Each of the virtues may be understood as 'due to that unique devotion to God and to that single-hearted trust in Him which can be symbolized by no other figure of speech so well as by the one which calls him Son of God'.[16]

For Niebuhr there are two parts to the question of finding meaning in Christ. First, belief in Christ means belief in God, 'to be related to the One to whom he [Christ] undeviatingly points'. Second, and in the opposite direction, because Christ is the Son of God, so completely immersed in the perfect will of the Father, he becomes the 'moral mediator of the Father's will towards men'.[17] Thus there is a double moral movement, 'with men toward God, with God toward men; from the world to the Other, from the Other to the world'. Christ is 'mediatorial not median . . . He exists rather as the focusing point in the continuous alternation of movements from God to man and man to God.'[18]

Niebuhr then moves to a consideration of the other half of the problem: how does one define 'culture' so as to be able to usefully and accurately measure it against the given definition of Christ?

Curiously, having stated that he wants to work towards a theologian's definition of culture (which will of necessity be a layman's definition, as a theologian is not a 'professional anthropologist'[19] – an interesting enough assumption) – he then goes on to say that his theologian's definition will be without theological interpretation (as the theological interpretation is precisely that which is at dispute among the Christians).

Niebuhr begins his definition of culture negatively, saying that it cannot be identified with any particular society, and especially modern Western culture. From here he again negatively refuses to distinguish between 'culture' and 'civilization'. For Niebuhr, culture is 'that total process of human activity and that total result of such activity'. It is the layer of artifice placed upon the natural environment, and 'comprises language, habits, ideas, beliefs, customs, social organization, inherited artefacts, technical processes, and values'.[20] In other words, culture is everything we do and every way we do it: a river is nature, a canal is culture.[21] This might not be a helpful definition.

Having done the groundwork, Niebuhr then sets out five types, possible answers to the enduring problem, and answers which have had varying support and success over the Christian millennia. The five types can be defined, following Timothy Gorringe, as Oppositional, Conformist, Synthetic, Dualist and Conversionist;[22] or, more memorably, and following Niebuhr himself, as 'Christ against Culture', 'The Christ of Culture', 'Christ above Culture', 'Christ and Culture in Paradox', and 'Christ the Transformer of Culture' (with the emphasis on, in most cases, the prepositions).* With each type, Niebuhr gives an outline of its familial resemblances, some exemplars from scripture and Christian history, and some critiques of its weaknesses (the thoroughness or otherwise of these critiques has led to some of the greatest reservations expressed about the impartiality of the whole process). It is important to outline Niebuhr's five types as they are the basis of all later theological understandings of culture, even if they have been, in many ways, superseded.

The first type described is 'Christ against Culture', what Yoder later glossed as 'radical tension'. Here the apparent New Testament contrast between 'the Church' and 'the World' is emphasized, with true followers

* Interestingly Stassen, Yeager and Yoder's critique of Niebuhr included a previously unpublished essay dating from the years immediately before *Christ and Culture* was written in which Niebuhr was beginning to delineate these heuristic typologies (H. Richard Niebuhr, 'Types of Christian Ethics', pp. 15–29). There the categories are the New Law Type (Christ against Culture); the Natural Law Type (Christ of Culture: the Accommodationist Type); the Median Types – the Architectonic Type (Christ above Culture); the Oscillatory Type (Christ and Culture in Paradox); the Conversionist Type (Christ Transforming Culture).

of Christ called to remove themselves from a corrupt and corrupting culture. The world is rejected and a new order is to be followed. Individual exemplars of this attitude are Tertullian and Tolstoy: group exemplars include early monasticism, Mennonites (to the later ire of John Howard Yoder) and, to a lesser extent, the Society of Friends.

The second type, 'Christ of Culture', describes the way in which Christ has been proclaimed as the embodiment of all that is noble and desirable in humanity and human culture: in this type Jesus is also the 'Messiah of their society, the fulfiller of its hopes and aspirations, the perfecter of its true faith, the source of its holiest spirit'.[23] Historical exemplars of this attitude include the Christian Gnostics Basilides and Valentinus, Peter Abelard, and the eighteenth-century rationalists such as John Locke and Immanuel Kant. The group exemplar is best represented by the 'Cultural Protestantism' of nineteenth-century Germany (and Niebuhr presents a defence of culture faith which was countercultural for his times).

These first two types are the extremes of Niebuhr's typology. He assigns the last three to a median type, in which there is a common goal 'to maintain the great differences between the two principles and in undertaking to hold them together in some unity', what he calls 'the church of the centre'.[24]

The third type, 'Christ above Culture', refuses to accept the polarities of the first type and the simple accommodationism of the second. Instead its proponents approach the problem not as if it were a simple either/or but a more nuanced both/and. There is a synthesis between Christ and culture, analogous to the synthesis between the dual natures in Christ himself. The synthesist 'affirms both Christ and culture [as] one who knows that the Christ who requires his loyalty is greater and more complex in character than the easier reconciliations [Type 1] envisage'. The same is true for the synthesist's relationship to culture: 'Both divine and human in its origin, both holy and sinful, a realm of both necessity and freedom, and one to which both reason and revelation apply.'[25] Historically, synthesis is represented by the early apologists such as Justin Martyr and Clement of Alexandria, but most completely by Aquinas. Hence, the group exemplar is the fullness of the Catholic tradition.

The next solution to the problem, 'Christ and Culture in Paradox', Niebuhr labels 'dualist': not in the sense of a Manichean reading of the relationship between the material and spiritual worlds, but in the sense of wanting to provide a both/and answer to the problem. Niebuhr identifies proponents as dualists for the way they recognize the reality of both law and grace, wrath and mercy, revelation and reason, time and eternity. Despite (or because of?) recognizing the fallen nature of culture, as a product of man's fallen nature, these dualist Christians recognized as well that they need to live within both realities: law and grace, wrath and mercy, and so on. The dualist:

> . . . is under the law, and yet not under law but grace; he is a sinner, and yet righteous; he believes, as a doubter; he has assurance of salvation, yet walks along the knife-edge of insecurity. In Christ all things have become new, and yet everything remains as it was from the beginning.[26]

This is a tension, but it is a creative and an affirming tension, for the dualist asserts that this world is the world we have and the world made, in its origins by God:

> . . . the dualist knows that he belongs to that culture and cannot get out of it, that God sustains him in it and by it; for if God in His grace did not sustain the world in its sin it would not exist for a moment.[27]

Individual and group exemplars of this type are Martin Luther and the Lutheran Christians. But this is not an ultimately convincing solution to the problem, for, as Niebuhr did not point out, but should have, paradoxes are contradictions you like, and a solution cannot be ultimately based upon preferences.

The final type, 'Christ the Transformer of Culture', is Niebuhr's preferred solution to the problem; what John Howard Yoder has called the synthesis of syntheses. The 'conversionist' (according to Gorringe) is the clear-eyed realist. He recognizes the implications of creation, atonement and redemption, and the possibility that culture may have some part to play in humankind moving from sinful self-centredness to Christ-centredness. Niebuhr claims Augustine ('without the anti-Pelagian treatises'[28]), John Calvin, and (bizarrely) F. D. Maurice as examples of this type. The conversionist is seen 'not to reject the cultural tradition he has inherited, but to transvalue it, to redirect, reinvigorate and regenerate it'.[29]

After more than 50 years of citations and the status of 'classic' accorded to the book in the theological faculties and seminaries of North America, and despite the frequent and increasing assertions of Niebuhr's disciples of the timelessness of his work, it is probably true to say that the continuing usefulness of *Christ and Culture* (as opposed to its continuing status as a classic representative of its time and culture), has been fatally damaged in recent years. Niebuhr's critics have pointed out at least five weaknesses in his work, one contextual and four structural.

Christ and Culture's status as a timeless classic ignores the very particular political, social and economic context in which Niebuhr was working. This is not Niebuhr's fault. The very first line of the book places the problem within Niebuhr's own time and culture: 'A many-sided debate about the relations of Christianity and civilization is being carried on *in our time*.'[30] That time was in the immediate aftermath of the Second World War.

> After the debacle of Nazism, the Holocaust, fascism, the horrors of World War II, the rapidly rising threat of international communism, and the danger of the bomb, American and British cultural leaders were engaged in intense debates over the future of Western civilization. Was there any way of strengthening its moral base so that it could meet the challenges of the technological age?[31]

For Niebuhr, the problem seemed to be, generally, how society could work for toleration in the face of totalitarianism; and, specifically, what part would Christianity play in this post-war rebuilding? In the forefront of his mind were the cultured despisers of Christianity, personified by Gibbon, who believed in the eighteenth and the twentieth century that Christians were 'animated by a contempt for their present existence and by a just confidence in immortality'.[32] It is possible, therefore, that the definitions Niebuhr supplied for his argument, and the very argument itself, might have been skewed by his underlying motives. If your intention is to use Christianity to effect the healing of the nations, then won't your description of Christianity's interaction with its culture tend to the proscriptive?

The four structural problems with Niebuhr's argument begin with the very obvious observation that Niebuhr's personal preferences, despite his protests of contingency and provisionality in his definitions, are clearly exposed in the way in which he evaluates his types:

> . . . behind this posture of humble non-normative objectivity, it will become clear to any careful reader that Niebuhr has so organised his presentation as to indicate a definite preference for 'transformation'.[33]

This, of course, is only really an issue if you have a different preference yourself (as Yoder most certainly did).

However, the next three structural problems are more serious, and they were most clearly described by Yoder himself in an essay written in 1958 and which circulated for many years as a *samizdat* photocopied document. The essay was finally published in 1996 to an understandably hostile reception from the true Niebuhrites. James M. Gustafson, in his preface to the fiftieth anniversary edition of *Christ and Culture*, says this:

> John Howard Yoder . . . for years circulated versions of a critique of *Christ and Culture* which is laced with more *ad hominem* arguments and fortified with more gratuitous footnotes than anything I ever read by scholars in the field of Christian ethics. This paper has been published, but I have not had access to it – perhaps fortunately.[34]

Despite Gustafson's hissy fit, there is actually very little *ad hominem* hostility to Yoder's critique (he does, as we have noted, show some pique at Niebuhr's misconstruing of the contribution made by Mennonites to wider culture). Instead he describes three different ways in which Niebuhr's thesis is fatally weak.

First, there is a weakness in terminology. Yoder points out that Niebuhr's definition of 'culture' is so broad as to be unfalsifiable, and yet at the same time culture is both monolithic and autonomous: monolithic in that it is impossible for Niebuhr to imagine that someone might reject some part of culture, affirm other parts of culture and seek to transform yet another part; autonomous in that Niebuhr's argument requires culture to be defined in absolute opposition to Christ: 'It is independent of Jesus Christ in the orders of both being and knowing . . . Christ can critique or "convert" those values, but their validity stands prior to his criticisms of it.'[35]

Second, there is a weakness of logical circularity in Niebuhr's approach. He defines his five types; he selects examples from Christian history to illustrate his types (exemplars who might have been surprised to discover the use to which they were being put). He then criticizes his exemplars for inconsistencies in their working out of the type, and applies that criticism to the type as a whole. So, for example, Tertullian is an exemplar for the 'Christ against Culture' type, and yet Tertullian is criticized both for his embracing of Latin literary culture and at the same time for his rejection of Latin philosophical culture. The exemplars become straw men which become weapons against the types which fail to solve the problem. As Yoder says, '*Christ and Culture* has regularly led its readers to make too much of the normative rigidity of the five-type model.'[36]

The third weakness is a theological one: how Niebuhr understands and defines Christ. For Niebuhr, according to Yoder, Christ is primarily a moralist, insistent upon orienting himself and his community of disciples away from the world and towards God: Jesus 'does not condemn culture because it is particularly sinful, nor does he condemn aspects of culture because these portions of it are more sinful than others; in fact he does not condemn it at all. He simply "points away from it" towards something else incomparably more important.'[37] And yet when this picture is compared with the portrait of Christ in the New Testament we can see how inadequate it is:

> Niebuhr's portrait of Christ ignores his teaching, his example, his call to discipleship, his promise of the Spirit, his atoning death and resurrection, and his Great Commission to his disciples. Niebuhr's view of Christ has no place for the Lordship of Christ and the community of disciples who live under that Lordship in joyous anticipation of the full coming of the reign of God. Niebuhr does not speak of the church as an alternative polity, a renewed community or a new cultural influence.[38]

So where do we go from here? The text which has determined the dialogue between Christianity and culture for 50 years no longer seems to be able to function in the way in which we might want it or need it to. There is another place to look, one which has been cleverly rediscovered by Tim Gorringe: we need to go back to the future.

In 1926 Karl Barth gave a lecture to the Congress of the Continental Association for Home Missions in Amsterdam. It was later published as 'Church and Culture'.[39] For Barth, the most significant part of his title was the word 'and': for 'the small but very significant word *and* in our title assumes a relationship between Church and culture'.[40] As Barth has already considered the 'theological inner aspect of the Church' it seems reasonable to assume a 'theological inner aspect' for culture as well. Barth acknowledges that it is possible to define culture untheologically (Niebuhr's 'without theological interpretation'?), and cites a couple of definitions of culture and civilization from the *Religion in Geschichte und Gegenwart* encyclopaedia (first edition, 1909–13), which would have satisfied Niebuhr: 'the sum of the aims proceeding from human activity and in turn stimulating human activity'.[41] Although this might have satisfied Niebuhr as a working definition of culture, for Barth it is entirely unacceptable: 'If such formulations were to be accepted as determinative and all-inclusive, then the Church could speak only negatively and polemically on the significance of culture. The two entities would not only exist on different levels, but on mutually exclusive levels, as truth and error.'[42]

For Barth, the fundamental purpose of the Church is to confront the individual believer and his community with the judgement presence of the Word of God: '. . . as a sinner undisturbed in the dream of my likeness to God, I could deceive myself about myself. But the Word of God fixes the limit for man as such and thereby defines him . . . The Word confronts man with the problem of his existence.'[43] This problem is existential, for humanity exists 'as soul *and* body, spirit *and* nature, subject *and* object, inwardly *and* outwardly, *judged* on the synthesis of both these elements'. And yet, the existential synthesis is exactly what humanity lacks. This is the reason why Christian preaching 'has met every culture, however supposedly rich and mature, with ultimate, sharp scepticism'.[44] But this is to deny the true nature of both humanity and culture, for 'culture means humanity' and both are the product of, and only meaningful in relationship with, the Word of God: 'culture is the promise originally given to man of what he is to become'.[45]

Gorringe develops this approach further, with three fundamentals for any theology of culture (note the refusal to follow Niebuhr's atheological supposition). First, the doctrine of the Incarnation is the non-negotiable grounding of any theology of culture:

> The 'Word'– teaching, doctrine, story, narrative, reason or cause – became *flesh*, not as an adventure, an avatar, a brief encounter, but as an account of how it might be possible to talk about God in a world where the powerful wash their hands of inconvenient decisions and the poor are crucified, and where there is nothing whatsoever, no knowledge and no revelation, which is not mediated by the body.[46]

'Flesh' means culture, as John the Evangelist goes on to flesh out in some detail (pun intended): 'food, the world of symbols, the way in which we cherish bodies'.[47] 'Culture' as a word and as a concept had its origins in agriculture: the cultivation of the fields and the cultivation of minds was a conceptual connection made as early as Cicero, if not sooner. Francis Bacon referred, in an earthy metaphor, to 'the culture and manurance of minds'.[48] Culture is enfleshed, and any consideration of enfleshment has to take into account the Incarnation.

Second, the 'sharp scepticism' of Barth's phrase introduces a prophetic edge to the Church's engagement with culture: 'no culture embodies the kingdom', and every culture has its dark side. It is impossible to celebrate the culture of Christian Europe without addressing its role in the Holocaust or African slavery: 'The agenda of Christian theology cannot be set by Western guilt, nevertheless there is a bland ignoring of those facts which borders on indecency.'[49] Even so, it is possible that God will work through the culture in which the particular church finds itself set, and so 'culture takes its place among the earthly signs by which the Church must make God's goodness, his friendship for men, visible to itself and the world'. In other words, the coming of the kingdom will not be effected by any particular cultural achievement, but the Church should be 'alert for the signs which, perhaps in many cultural achievements, announce the kingdom approaches'.[50]

The third fundamental grounding for a theology of culture is a development of this second. Along with a prophetic watchfulness, the Church should be aware of the eschatological implications to be found in culture. Everything is under judgement, and ultimately, everything will be subject to judgement. All is to be seen under the light of eternity and as part of God's working out of the tasks of redemption. The Church should always remember this: the Church 'simply takes death too seriously for true humanity possibly to be anything more or anything other than a hope of the resurrection of the dead'. 'See, I am making all things new' (Revelation 21.5) has to be the biblical underpinning of this theology of culture.

With the promise of Revelation behind it, the Church confronts culture:

> Not with an undervaluation of cultural achievement, but with the highest possibly [*sic*] evaluation of the goal for which it sees all cultural activity striving. Not in pessimism, but in boundless hope. Not as a spoilsport, but in the knowledge that art and science, business and politics, techniques and education are really a game . . . the significance of which lies not in its attainable goals but in what it signifies.[51]

So, if the priest is to act as a Watchman, as a discerner and interpreter of culture, he must take these three fundamentals into account: nothing can be understood outside or beside the Incarnation; all culture has its dark side, yet God is able to work his purposes out through culture; and ultimately, all will be renewed, Church and culture, individual and community.

Which brings us to the Archbishop's third of three images, the parish priest as Weaver.

9
Weaver

What is a community? Consider these four newspaper reports:

> 'In the broadest sense, community involvement is how a company interacts with the communities in which it operates,' says Hannah Jones, Nike's head of corporate responsibility. 'For us, it's the 800,000 workers in our supply chain.'

> . . . if the intelligence community is to be believed, the breeding grounds have spread ominously within our own boundaries.

> The school community should take more interest in the behaviour of adults who are neither employees nor members of the school. If we find an adult taking drugs within the community we will ask them to leave.

> . . . the British Army Rumour Service at arrse.co.uk, prides itself on being 'The unofficial British Army community website'.[1]

All four reports are taken from the British national press in the summer of 2007. In those three months newspapers used the word 'community' more than 3,000 times. In fact, the word was used so often that Lexis-Nexis, the newspaper database, is unable to give an accurate count, which is a shame, because there are a lot of communities out there; along with the business community, the intelligence community,* the

---

* HIGGINS: It'd have to be somebody in the community. TURNER: Community? HIGGINS: Intelligence field. TURNER: [soft laugh] 'Community!' [then to Higgins] Jesus, you guys are kind to yourselves. 'Community!' (From *Three Days of the Condor*, written by Lorenzo Semple, Jr and David Rayfiel, directed by Sydney Pollack, Paramount Pictures, 1975).

school and army communities in the reports above, we also find mention of the 'gay', the 'Muslim', the 'sporting' and even (surprisingly?) the 'criminal' community. What can all these communities possibly signify?

As Rowan Williams has pointed out, 'communities, in spite of the sentimental way we sometimes think of them, don't just happen. They need nurture, they need to be *woven* into unity.'[2] In order to think intelligently and unsentimentally about community, we need some help. We can find that help in the life and work of another German theologian, Dietrich Bonhoeffer.

Born to a prosperous upper-middle-class family in Breslau in 1906, Bonhoeffer moved with his family to Berlin when his father, Karl Bonhoeffer, became professor of psychiatry and nervous diseases at the University of Berlin in 1912. An exceptionally bright boy, with gifts in sport and music, Bonhoeffer's family at first assumed that he would follow his father into psychiatry. He surprised them, and himself, by wanting to become a theologian: the family were no more than 'cultural Christians' and Bonhoeffer's family experience of Christianity mostly came from the telling of exemplary tales from the scriptures by his mother. Later on, this academic drive to theology drew him into a vocation as a Lutheran minister. Only much later, paradoxically, did he accept the need to become a Christian as well (the meaning of which we will explore below).

Bonhoeffer studied at Tübingen and the University of Berlin, and produced his doctoral thesis in 1927, subsequently published to no attention at all in 1930: it was only after the war and Bonhoeffer's death that Karl Barth described *Sanctorum Communio: A Theological Study of the Sociology of the Church* as a 'theological miracle'.[3]

Bonhoeffer's first published book is still relatively overlooked (in favour of his monumental *Ethics*, the revolutionary *Cost of Discipleship*, and the profoundly moving *Letters and Papers from Prison*). Even so, some scholars in recent years have argued that the outline of Bonhoeffer's theology and ministry begins with the argument of this book: if we want to understand what Bonhoeffer attempted and what he represents today, then we should read *Sanctorum Communio*. It is particularly relevant to our task, as in the book Bonhoeffer begins 'exploring the nature and vocation of the church within the wider context of human sociality and historical concreteness'.[4]

In his study of what the communion of the saints actually means, Bonhoeffer begins with an exploration of what it means to talk about a 'person'. Where do 'persons' exist? He is very clear on this:

> Every concept of community is essentially related to a concept of person. It is impossible to say what constitutes community without asking what constitutes a person . . . *The concepts of person, community and God* are inseparably and essentially interrelated. A concept of God is always conceived in relation to a concept of person and a concept of a community of persons. Whatever one thinks of a concept of God, it is done in relation to person and community of persons.[5]

Bonhoeffer expressed this aphoristically when he said '. . . the Christian concept of the person is really exhibited only in sociality . . .'[6] This is a crucial word to understanding Bonhoeffer's concept of community. The *Oxford English Dictionary* can take us some of the way:

> *Sociality*: 1. a. The state or quality of being social; social intercourse or companionship with one's fellows, or the enjoyment of this. 2. The action or fact on the part of individuals of forming a society or of associating together; the disposition, impulse, or tendency to do this.[7]

There is, of course, a lot more to the word in Bonhoeffer's understanding than this, a richness and complexity that has been ably drawn out by Clifford Green. In order to understand Bonhoeffer's ideas about 'sociality', and thus to be able to understand something about 'community', we have to realize that we are performing *theological anthropology*, says Green. In other words, we are walking and thinking in that narrow space where what we say about humanity depends upon what we say about God, which in turn depends upon what we think about humanity. This is inescapable, because Christian words about God, Christian theology, can only be spoken in the light of the Incarnation, in which we have learnt that:

> God's being is not in transcendent isolation and absence. God is free for humanity in our history; that is, in the light of Jesus Christ, God

> is revealed as present to us in the world – God's being is being-in-relation-to-us. This is the meaning of the incarnation: God with us, and God for us.[8]

Nicholas Lash explains this interconnection very well. He says:

> The Church is a people, an assembly of men and women. Therefore, we will not think sensibly about the Church unless we think sensibly about the kinds of things human beings are. Moreover, human beings are creatures, constituents of the world of which they form a part. Therefore, we will not think sensibly about human beings unless we think sensibly about the world which God creates.[9]

Because of the self-revelation of God in relation to humanity through the person and saving actions of Jesus Christ, the very nature of being human has been changed: we are fundamentally people in relationship – with each other and with God. 'To be human is to be a person before God, and in relation to God. The relation of individual persons to each other, and the relations between human communities of persons, has this theological understanding of God and human existence at its core.'[10]

This has a deep impact on the meaning of community. Bonhoeffer said that it is impossible for any human, social, community to truly exist apart from the community of God:

> Inherent in the Christian concept of God that we know through revelation in Christ, but ultimately through Christ's church-community, is that community of God and social community belong together . . . Thus we are saying that direct community with God also demands direct human community, that the latter is absolutely necessary as the corollary to community with God, and that it is no coincidence that Genesis 2.18 reads: 'It is not good that the human being [*Mensch*] should be alone'.[11]

In other words, it is impossible to be a Christian apart from community: the relational nature of being human means that if we are to be fully human, by being drawn into relationship with God, then, at *one and the same time*, we are being drawn into relationship with others.

This is something more than the basic huddling instinct. It is not, Bonhoeffer says, the result of mere impulse. The formation and continued functioning of the community has to be an act of conscious will:

> When men are brought together by sheer impulses it is not possible to speak of human society. The impulses of imitation, subordination, sociability, and in particular of hunger and sexuality, man has in common with the animals. Specifically human community is present only when conscious human spirit is at work, that is, when community is based on purposive acts of will. Human community does not necessarily arise from such acts of will, but it has its being in them.[12]

The question then arises, whose community, whose will? In other words, what is the *ethical component* of Bonhoeffer's theology of community? He says something about the way we should behave – towards ourselves, towards others and towards God. What will be the basis for this? Theoretically, the ethical component should be simple: human community functions best when it is completely subordinated to the will of God.

> To be in community with God obviously means, first of all, the absolute identity of purpose of the divine and human wills, within the relation of the creative to the created (i.e. obedient) will – in other words, in the relation of ruling and serving.[13]

But Bonhoeffer is also a realist. He recognizes that such an 'absolute identity of purpose' is no easy thing to achieve this side of the Fall:

> . . . since every person is created with a uniquely individual character, tension between wills cannot be avoided even in the community of love. With this concession we already recognize that strife as such is by no means as a result of the fall but arises from a common love of God. The will of every individual strives to attain the single goal of serving the divine will, that is, serving the community in its own way.[14]

Which reminds me of the speech given by the vice-principal of my theological college at his farewell dinner. He touched on his relationship with another member of staff, which had been notoriously rocky, but finished by saying: 'Even so, Joan and I both sought to serve God, she in her way, and I in His'!

Bonhoeffer gives us two concepts to correct against this imposition of the human will in place of God's will. First of all he emphasizes the importance of 'responsibility', which is the translation for the German *Verantwortlichkeit*. This means so much more than merely being answerable or accountable. For Bonhoeffer, *Verantwortlichkeit* was the constant encountering of one ethical agent against another: we achieve maturity as human beings when we realize that the boundaries and limitations of our will are defined against the boundaries and limitations of another's will. Here we see an echo in the Archbishop of Canterbury's lecture on 'The Christian Priest Today', in which Dr Williams describes the Church as being the '"responsible" community, answering to what is there before it',[15] called into being by the witness of the scriptures and ordained ministry. In other words, for Bonhoeffer and for Christian communities, 'responsibility' allows us to find out who we are when we find the limits of our will and our scope for autonomy.

The second idea is that of *Stellvertretung*. This means, literally, 'standing in the place of another', but it has a much deeper resonance than a simple translation like 'proxy' or 'deputy' can convey. For Bonhoeffer, the 'vicarious representation' of Jesus's actions (his passion and death) are means by which God takes human culpability seriously, and by which sin is punished and overcome. Humanity can only abandon ethical responsibility for ourselves in the face of this loving offer by God:

> Through the Christian principle of vicarious representative action the new humanity is made whole and sustained. This principle gives Christian basic-relations their substantive uniqueness . . . [and] unites the new humanity with Christ, but also links its membership to each other in community.[16]

Christ's free, self-giving and other-loving actions are the basis of this new community. Bonhoeffer says that it has (or should have) two modes of being, 'being-with-each-other' and 'being-for-each-other', each depending on the other. Bonhoeffer traces an expression of the former in the work of Martin Luther, most beautifully in the latter's *Fourteen Consolations*:

> Therefore, when we feel pain, when we suffer, when we die, let us turn to this, firmly believing and certain that it is not we alone, but Christ and the church who are in pain and are suffering and dying with us . . . We set out upon the road of suffering and death accompanied by the entire church.[17]

'Being-with-each-other' cannot happen without 'being-for-each-other': 'Since I as a Christian cannot live without the church, since I owe my life to the church and now belong to it, so my merits are also no longer my own, but belong to the church.'[18] Bonhoeffer points us to scriptures to understand this: Christ is the measure and standard of our conduct. In John 13.15 we are told: 'For I have set you an example, that you also should do as I have done to you', and in 1 John 3.10:

> The children of God and the children of the devil are revealed in this way: all who do not do what is right are not from God, nor are those who do not love their brothers and sisters.

He sets out the Pauline teaching on the unified Body of Christ:

> For just as the body is one and has many members, and all the members of the body, though many, are one body, so it is with Christ. (1 Corinthians 12.12)

and that one unified Body is differentiated and interconnecting:

> For as in one body we have many members, and not all the members have the same function, so we, who are many, are one body in Christ, and individually we are members one of another. We have gifts that differ according to the grace given to us: prophecy, in proportion to faith; ministry, in ministering; the teacher, in teaching; the exhorter, in exhortation; the giver, in generosity; the leader, in diligence; the compassionate, in cheerfulness. (Romans 12.4ff.)

And in doing so, we show the power of the love of Christ.

So, throughout *Sanctorum Communio*, Bonhoeffer has argued that the Church, the holy community called into being by God, is not a human society like all other human societies, a disparate group of people with something (or one thing) in common, who have gathered together to advance general interest in the something/one thing, and who, in the memorable phrase of Rowan Williams, become 'a chaotic mass trying to apportion jobs'.[19] Rather, the Church is the place in which human beings subject themselves to the 'ethical other', God and fellow humans, and in which we find ourselves under the rule of serving and being served, through mutual love:

> Community with God is not an individualistic possibility, but is actual and real in the community of God's creatures with each other; to serve and love God is simultaneously to serve and love God's creatures, one's fellow human beings. Community with God is simultaneously the community of co-humanity.[20]

It is all summed up in Bonhoeffer's memorable phrase: the Church is *Christus als Gemeinde existerend*, Christ existing as community.[21] And from this we can say that 'the word of the Church to the world is the word of Christ spoken with the same authority as words spoken during his earthly life'.[22]

Sanctorum Communio is a dense book which handles its material – scriptural, theological and philosophical – with dazzling skill. It was quite unlike anything else that was coming out of the German Church in the between-war years, and so it is not surprising that it was so overlooked then. It could also have been dismissed as the demonstration work of a very young man, one without experience in university or parish life. And yet, in the work Bonhoeffer showed his ability to find the memorable phrase, and in his subsequent ministry he showed how serious he was in following this path.

Bonhoeffer continued his work as a theologian, but he also began to work as a pastor: in the German church in Barcelona, as a catechist in the proletarian parishes of Berlin, as a student chaplain, as pastor to the German churches of east and south-east London. In each place he attempted to gather around him and to minister to a community of believers. Eventually, in 1935, he was called back from London to a Germany and a Church in crisis. The Nazi seizure of power in early 1933 (the *Machtergreifung*) led to deep divisions within German society. There were some who welcomed the simple, strong leadership, based upon national pride and identity, which the Nazis promised. Others feared, even at this early stage, the loss of important parts of German self-understanding in an onslaught of national self-worship. The divisions convulsed the churches in Germany as much as in wider society. The Lutheran Church was also subject to the Nazi *Gleichschaltung* (the euphemistically entitled 'co-ordination' actions of the new government), in which any possible opposition or dissent, within trade unionism, political parties, school and university educational institutions, was forcefully (and sometimes forcibly) removed. The Lutheran Church was split between the so-called 'German Christians', who recognized the authority of the (Nazi-imposed) National Bishop, Ludwig Müller, and the ministers of the Pastors' Emergency League (the *Pfarrernotbund*), who went on to form the Confessing Church. The new church movement needed pastors, and so illegal *ad hoc* seminaries were formed: Bonhoeffer, as the ablest young theologian of the Church, was invited back from London to become director of the seminary for Brandenburg and Pomerania.

In an old school house in the out-of-the-way town of Finkenwalde, Bonhoeffer and 23 students took up residence in the summer of 1935. The seminary was able to last just over two years, until it was raided and closed down by the Gestapo. Bonhoeffer had very firm ideas on how the seminary was to be organized: he visited English theological colleges in his last weeks in London, and even made a tour of Anglican monastic communities. He brought with him some very un-Lutheran ideas:

> The programme for the day began and ended with two long services. In the morning the service was followed by half an hour's meditation, an exercise that was not interrupted by the circumstances of the removal, though packing cases and youth hostel bunks were the only furniture. The services did not take place in church but round the ordinary dinner-table. They invariably began with a Psalm and a hymn specially chosen for the day. There followed a lesson from the Old Testament, a set verse from a hymn (sung daily for several weeks), a New Testament lesson, a period of extempore prayer and the recital of the Lord's Prayer. Each service concluded with another set verse from a hymn. Readings from the Psalms and the Scripture took the form of a lectio continua, for preference without any omissions. In structure this very much resembled Anglican evensong. Bonhoeffer

> believed that this sequence of readings and prayers was the most natural and suitable form of service for theologians.[23]

Life in the seminary was basic. The library was mostly Bonhoeffer's own (lost when the institution was shut down); letters were sent out to the Lutheran parishes of the surrounding countryside, and the 'ordinands' humble request' produced a startling amount of practical support (from church congregations which had never previously been required to support the training of their ministers). Eberhard Bethge, one of the ordinands, and later Bonhoeffer's friend and biographer, recalls that the humble request produced a live pig, which required collecting from the nearest railway station![24]

The seminary lasted until September 1937: before the year's end, 27 students had been arrested by the Gestapo and imprisoned.[25] Even so, in existence for such a short time, it had two great lasting legacies. First, it was the place in which Bonhoeffer first delivered the lecture series which became his great work, *Discipleship*.[26] Second, when the seminary was suppressed, Bonhoeffer was encouraged to write down an account of the experiment and experience that was Finkenwalde. He did so, and *Life Together* was published in 1938. Surprisingly, despite the times in which it was published, it was a popular and critical success, the best received and best selling of Bonhoeffer's books published in his lifetime. Overshadowed now somewhat by the three posthumous 'greats', *Life Together*[27] deserves to be better known and wider read, as it is one of the most important of Bonhoeffer's legacies for the Church*:

> When he [Bonhoeffer] wrote his account of his community-sustained spiritual life in the Finkenwalde seminary, he was not reminiscing about an agreeable, idyllic experience of a like-minded group of dedicated seminarians. He intended to share with others this experience, with its joys and trials, its mutual support and enduring friendships, that it might serve as a model for forming moral leaders and for the creation of new forms of church community throughout Germany.[28]

* Bonhoeffer himself thought that *Life Together* would be his definitive work: he referred to the book, somewhat jokingly, as his 'swan-song' (Bethge, *Dietrich Bonhoeffer*, p. 582).

The book, like the life in the seminary, is divided into five sections: 'Community'; 'The Day Together'; 'The Day Alone'; 'Service' and 'Confession and the Lord's Supper'. It is worth examining each of these sections in turn.

'Community'

Very often, the Christian community is regarded as, at best, a necessary burden in being a Christian: we all have crosses to bear, and mine is other Christians. This was not so for Bonhoeffer. The dominant theme for both the book written and the life lived is set in the book's lines: 'How very good and pleasant it is when kindred live together in unity!' (Psalm 133.1).

> Christian community means community through Jesus Christ and in Jesus Christ. There is no Christian community that is more than this, and none that is less than this. Whether it be a brief, single encounter or the daily community of many years, Christian community is solely this. We belong to one another only through and in Jesus Christ.[29]

There are three ways in which this is worked out. First, Christians need each other for Christ's sake; second, Christians are only able to encounter each other through Christ; third, Christians encounter Christ and each other in a looping movement that passes from eternity, through this world of time and back to eternity ('We who live here in community with Christ will one day be with Christ in eternal community'[30]). We see in this the radical Christocentric nature of Bonhoeffer's community: Christ is the Mediator. Often when that title is used of Jesus of Nazareth it refers to Christ's role as go-between for God the Father and humanity: Christ is the intercessor and friend of sinners, and no one can come to the Father except by him. Bonhoeffer means this and more: for him, Christ as Mediator means that no one can encounter *anyone else* except through Christ: he is the Mediator for person-to-person as well as person-to-God relationships: 'I have community with others and will continue to have it only through Jesus Christ . . .' Elsewhere Bonhoeffer says, in relation to the difference between spiritual and emotional love: 'Spiritual love . . . comes from

Jesus Christ; it serves him alone. It knows that it has no direct access to other persons. Christ stands between me and others.'[31] So, for Bonhoeffer, Christian community should be thought of as 'life together under the Word':[32] a position that implies both hierarchy (a submission to Christ's judgement) and protection (gathered under his loving arms). Here we can see how Bonhoeffer the theologian has become Bonhoeffer the Christian.

'The Day Together'

This 'life together under the Word' is enacted in the second section of the book, 'The Day Together', which describes the community at worship. It is not from lack of imagination that Bonhoeffer begins, rests and ends the community's communal activity in worship. This is the purpose of a Christian community, its *raison d'être*. The daily life of the Christian community should begin and end in worship: 'the first thought and first word of the day belong to God', and evening prayer should be the last activity of the day, so that '[w]hen night falls, the true light of God's Word shines brighter for the community of faith'.[33] Bonhoeffer has very clear ideas about the way in which community worship should be structured, the parts which long, continuous readings from scripture, the Psalter and unison hymn singing should play, as well as a stability of leadership. All these things will help the community to avoid 'mere reverie' and to participate in the 'holy, divine reality'.[34] The divine reality is experienced also in the work undertaken by members of the community, and the table fellowship they will share:

> The breaking of bread together has a festive quality. In the midst of the working day given to us again and again, it is a reminder that God rested after God's work, and that the Sabbath is the meaning and the goal of the week with its toil.[35]

'The Day Alone'

But Bonhoeffer did not think that the individual's life in the community should be entirely communal. He did not advocate an Orwellian deprivation of privacy or individual reflection. He recognized the need, both a human need and a need of service performed to God, for silence in an individual's day; time alone, in 'down-time'. This is foundational for the well-being of both individual and community:

> Whoever cannot be alone should beware of community. Whoever cannot stand being in community should beware of being alone.[36]

This duality was built into the pattern of the day in Finkenwalde. Green has pointed out the reverberation from one mode to the other:

> The pattern of daily life for the college included worship, study of the Bible, meditation, prayer, lectures, sermon practice, meals and recreation. Some of these belonged to the 'day together', others to the 'day alone'. Here we see the counterpoint of community and individual persons . . .[37]

This duality was designed to avoid the fantasies that so often accompany experiments in community living:

> Community is not an escape route for those unable to cope with life on their own, or for those who desire to bury bad experiences of their past with help from the companionship of gracious people.[38]

Bonhoeffer condemns this, emphatically, as 'wishful dreaming':

> Every human idealized image that is brought into the Christian community is a hindrance to genuine community and must be broken up so that genuine community can survive.[39]

Bonhoeffer condemns those who place a dream of Christian community before the reality, a reality which must be lived under the protection and judgement of the Word of God: 'those who dream of this idealized community . . . [live] as if they have to create the Christian community, as if their visionary ideal binds the people together'.[40] In actual fact, Christian community is God's work, and the task of his people is to be clear-eyed and realistic enough to recognize that fact and to get out of God's way as he goes about building upon the foundation of every Christian community, Jesus Christ.

It is in this time spent alone, in personal prayer with the words of scripture, that the Christian disciple discovers the hardest and most necessary task: intercessory prayer. And it is not just intercessory prayer for the community, or for those Christians with whom the individual agrees or likes. Bonhoeffer makes clear that prayer is for friends and enemies:

> A Christian community either lives by the intercessory prayers of its members for one another, or the community will be destroyed. I can no longer condemn or hate other Christians for whom I pray, no matter how much trouble they cause me. In intercessory prayer the face that may have been strange and intolerable to me is transformed into the face of one for whom Christ died, the face of a pardoned sinner. That is a blessed discovery for the Christian who is beginning to offer intercessory prayer for others.[41]

'Service'

And yet, for all this, Bonhoeffer was a realist, one of the few in the German Church of his day. He knew that if we rely on human will then any Christian community will fail. He begins his section on service with Luke's report of the dissension among the disciples as to who should be greatest in the kingdom of heaven: 'No Christian community ever comes together without this argument appearing as a seed of discord.'[42] As soon as Christians come together they begin to classify and judge and condemn each other.* There is only one solution to this dynamic, which begins so naturally and so inevitably. That solution is service.

Service begins by simply refusing to verbalize the 'odorous comparisons': the Epistle of James tells us this (James 3.3ff.). Once we refuse to speak the comparison, we begin to refuse to play the harmful game of jockeying for position and status and power.[43] Then we can begin to see in our brothers and sisters opportunities to serve them, and in serving them, serve God.

The true, humble service of one Christian sinner to another takes three forms. First, be prepared simply to listen to your brother or sister:

---

* Rather like George Bernard Shaw's comment in the preface to *Pygmalion* (1912): 'It is impossible for an Englishman to open his mouth without making some other Englishman hate or despise him.' Which was a fine thing for an Irishman to say.

'We do God's work for our brothers or sisters when we learn to listen to them.'[44] Anyone who is not prepared to surrender this time to the other members of the Christian community is not prepared to surrender the time to God. Second, be prepared to live in 'active helpfulness . . . [where] nobody is too good for the lowest service. Those who worry about the loss of time entailed by such small, external acts of helpfulness are usually taking their own work too seriously.'[45]* Third, Christian service is expressed by forbearance: Galatians tells us, 'Bear one another's burdens, and in this way you will fulfil the law of Christ' (Galatians 6.2). For Bonhoeffer, forbearance is an expression of the mutuality of the Christian community, the interconnectedness of the Body of Christ. The strong and the weak, the healthy and the sick, the learned and the ignorant, the dedicated and the slack, should all seek ways in which each may help in the building up of the other. Even sinners should be forgiven daily.[46]

'Confession and the Lord's Supper'

Bonhoeffer believed that one of the pernicious effects of sin and sinfulness is to drive human beings into isolation: 'Those who remain alone with their evil are left utterly alone.'[47] Confession is a means of overcoming this isolation, and it works in four related ways: it is a breakthrough to community (transferring the burden of the sin from the individual to the community); a breakthrough to the cross (marking the confessing sinner with the humiliation of his sin and drawing him to the 'promise and glory of such humiliation'[48]); a breakthrough to new life ('Everything has become new', 2 Corinthians 5.17, Bonhoeffer quotes approvingly); and a breakthrough to assurance (if we are able to confess our sins to another sinful Christian, how much more meaningful does the forgiveness of the sinless and ever-loving God become?). Bonhoeffer makes it clear that confession works most effectively, that is, is most effectively a medium for God's grace, when it deals with 'concrete sins' rather than a general and unspecific sense of sinfulness:

* I'd like to interject a caveat into this precept (or, in other words, disagree): it will only work when there is a recognition of mutual accountability. Often what happens in parish Christian communities is that the priest's time is regarded as a public resource available to all; and, if we get him moving tables or unblocking drains, then that is a reminder for him to be humble.

'Jesus dealt with people whose sins were obvious, with tax collectors and prostitutes. They knew why they needed forgiveness, and they received it as forgiveness of their specific sins . . . it is in confessing these particular sins that we receive the forgiveness of all our sins, both known and unknown.'[49] So confession can become, in the words of Kelly and Nelson, 'a unique way for Christians vicariously to experience the cross of Jesus Christ as they themselves, with some pain, contribute to their deliverance from the sins that could tear a community apart'.[50]

Confession is an appropriate preparation for participating in the Lord's Supper. All malice and envy and wickedness are to be set aside so that the feast may be celebrated, in the resurrection presence of Jesus (1 Corinthians 5.8): 'What takes place in the Christian community [is] in the power of the present Jesus Christ.' Once reconciled to one another in their reconciliation to God, the Christian community is then able to receive

> . . . the gift of Jesus Christ's body and blood, therein receiving forgiveness, new life and salvation. New community with God and one another is given to it . . . Here joy in Christ and Christ's community is complete. The life together of Christians under the Word has reached its fulfilment in the sacrament.[51]

The source of all life within the community is the person of Jesus Christ: it is only in seeking to follow Christ that the building-blocks of the community's life together can find expression:

> Such commitment to Jesus Christ opens up a number of elementary Christian concepts: community, solitude, service, Scripture reading, prayer, intercession, meditation, the ability to listen, forgiveness, confession and the forgiveness of sins, Christians' breaking of bread together, the celebration of the Lord's Supper in the church of Christ, as well as the hope of breaking bread together eternally.[52]

Which seems an admirable summary of Bonhoeffer's concept of Christian community (in the particularity of Finkenwalde, and in general).

It will have been noted that again and again in *Life Together* we see Bonhoeffer's abiding commitment to the person and authority of Jesus Christ: it is Jesus Christ who is the leader and authority of the community. In fact, it almost seems from Bonhoeffer's description that apart from Jesus Christ, a Christian community is a leaderless community: it is wrong for one person to act as confessor to all the community, because that would place an unnecessary burden upon the shoulders of the confessor, which may lead to 'the exercise of spiritual tyranny over souls'.[53] Although Bonhoeffer mentions 'head of the house' (*hausvater*), he only does so once, and in the context of the person offering extemporaneous prayer at evening prayer.[54] If we accept that Bonhoeffer's description of Christian community is a valid one for parish ministry, then where does that leave the parish priest, as *hausvater* or Weaver?

The first point to make is that although the seminary in Finkenwalde might appear to be a leaderless community from the description in *Life Together*, in practice it was anything but. Eberhard Bethge's memoir of Bonhoeffer shows the reality. Bonhoeffer, we are told, 'did not look kindly on attempts to evade [the necessary] daily routine'. His capacity for hard work and 'his ability to interrupt work for play without ever falling behind sometimes made him unjust towards others who were toiling night and day in preparation for some examination'. His manner, like his preaching style, was 'startlingly direct'.[55] And yet, most of Bonhoeffer's leadership was modelled by example:

> A request arrived from the kitchen for help with the washing-up but there were no immediate volunteers. Without saying a word Bonhoeffer arose from the table, disappeared into the kitchen and refused admission to those who hastened to follow suit. Later, when he rejoined the students on the beach, he made no comment. And in Finkenwalde many a student was to discover with shame that someone else had made his bed in the big dormitory.[56]

Bonhoeffer's role as *hausvater* enabled the Finkenwalde community to begin the transformation from a collection of individuals to a community. Bonhoeffer was the pump-primer, allowing the community to place itself, penultimately and ultimately (to use a favourite Bonhoeffer motif), under the authority of Christ.

We find confirmation of the importance of this role in the experiences of Vincent Donovan as a missionary priest in the early 1960s in Tanganyika (now Tanzania). Donovan followed in the footsteps of scores, if not hundreds, of European Christian priests before him. The

Christian churches had been evangelizing in East Africa for 100 years, and, on the face of it, their achievements were great. They had helped to stamp out slavery; through preaching, teaching, political pressure, and, when all else failed, buying the slaves from the slavers and giving them their freedom. They had helped set up an impressive system of Western-style schools: buildings, compounds, curriculum and examinations. They had taught and baptized, and confirmed, married and celebrated the Eucharist, heard confessions and buried the people of East Africa. A great achievement indeed.

But Donovan found a puzzling thing. Despite all this effort, goodwill, thoughtful and prayerful action, Christianity had not *caught* in Tanganyika. By independence, in 1961, there was only one African bishop in the diocese of Tanganyika; there were no African clergy at all in the diocese of Nairobi. In a letter to a bishop in May 1966 Donovan wrote: 'The best way to describe realistically the state of this Christian mission is the number zero . . . up until this date no Catholic child, on leaving school, has continued to practise his religion, and there is no indication that any of the present students will do so.'[57] Donovan realized that the previous approaches to evangelizing East Africa were doomed to failure, and a different method was needed: the story of how he stumbled into the new method is immensely moving and exciting, and the book he wrote as a result of his experience has become a modern-day classic: *Christianity Rediscovered: An Epistle from the Masai* (1978).

His subtitle is a significant one, for Donovan discovered that there was something in the Masai's approach to religion, and Christianity in particular, which could profitably be reflected and acted upon by the prosperous and complacent churches of the West. He saw that the Masai operated as a community: a real community, and not a lip-service community that the churches in the West have become. 'A community, a group like this, will act as a unit, accepting you or rejecting you together. I found out that change, deep meaningful change, like the acceptance of a hopeful, expectant world vision, does not take place in one individual at a time. Groups adopt changes as groups, or they do not adopt them at all.'[58]

Donovan came away from his time in East Africa with a burning desire to see how God works with communities: not organizations, nor groups, nor collections of individuals, but communities, for a community is 'a group of people . . . so vitally interrelated that their very fate is in the hands of others in the community'.[59] He had realized that at the centre of every Masai community was a single man, who was able to gather the community around him. He wouldn't necessarily be the most educated man in the village, he wouldn't be the richest man, but he 'had the talent and the ability to call these people – this community – together, and to hold them together'[60]:

> . . . he would be the focal point of the whole community, the one who would enable the community to act, whether in worship or in service. He would be the animator of the individual members of the community, enabling them to make their various contributions, enabling the preacher to preach, and the teacher to teach and the pray-er to pray and the prophet to prophesy. He would be the necessary sign of unity that exists among them. He would be their link with the outside, the sign of their union with the outside, universal church. He would be their priest . . . His job in a very real way is to enable that community to function.[61]

Part of that community functioning is in worship: as we have seen, Rowan Williams quotes approvingly the Romanian theologian Dumitru Staniloae, who said that 'the priest's role was to "assemble and concentrate" the Christian people at prayer'.[62]

But weaving, building a 'differentiated unity', does not stop with presiding at worship.[63] Paul tells the church in Corinth that although Christ's ministry is that of reconciliation, he has entrusted that ministry to his Church (2 Corinthians 5.18f.). This reconciliation may take many different forms, perhaps as many forms as there are individual Christian communities and individual priests, but all forms will share a sense of making connections between people who may otherwise feel themselves to be disconnected. This is what Williams calls 'the gift of helping people make sense to and of each other'.

In case anybody thinks that this calling of priest as Weaver sounds a little vague, or comfortable, or prissy (a kind of 'knit-your-own-Christianity' ministry), Williams points out exactly how difficult and demanding it is and will be. If the priest is to help 'people make sense to and of each other', occasionally that will be making sense of alienation or threat. When people feel threatened or alienated, then they can be at their most volatile. Making the connections between separated people means, following Bonhoeffer, showing the connections between people who have been initially separated from Christ, making Christ known, in the mission statement of the Archbishop's Cathedral.[64] This is something more than a sentimental 'I'm OK, you're OK, Jesus is OK' introduction. Encountering Jesus Christ means encountering not only the healing and absolving Jesus, but also the judging and dying Jesus. Occasionally the word of Jesus to his disciples is a word of rebuke; occasionally the parish priest may be the means of speaking that rebuke. Encountering Jesus means meeting him in his birth, and his refugee status, in the poverty of his adult life, in the deeply demanding content of his teaching, and the (properly) awful circumstances of his passion and his death. It means a puzzling meeting with the gardener outside an empty tomb, and not quite getting, not quite understanding, what the power of the resurrection means to either Christ himself or to his followers. It is the task of the parish priest (among others) to prepare people to meet Jesus in all these places, just as they are, 'without one plea', and without the barriers and defences and rationalizations that human beings use to protect themselves from what is real and important.* As Williams says, acknowledging the boldness of his formulation: 'the priest sometimes has to speak not only as parent to the prodigal son, but as parent to the elder brother who can only see his brother's forgiveness as his own humiliation and loss'.

And helping people to divest themselves of these unnecessary defences, or to recognize their unaccustomed relations, can be a painful process: 'To be yourself a place where lines of force intersect, where diverse interests and passions converge is one of the hardest aspects of that dimension of priestly life which is about living in the fantasies and expectations of others.'

* A memorable scene from a modern comedy of manners: MICHAEL: I don't know anyone who could get through the day without two or three juicy rationalizations. They're more important than sex. SAM: Ah, come on. Nothing's more important than sex. MICHAEL: Oh yeah? Ever gone a week without a rationalization? (*The Big Chill*, written by Lawrence Kasdan and Barbara Benedek, directed by Lawrence Kasdan, Columbia Pictures, 1983.)

Part 3

THE KGH METHOD

So far we have attempted to do three things in our project to kill George Herbert. We have examined the historical legacy of Herbert's short ministry, and the much longer and much more effective posthumous publicity campaign which was based on the short ministry. We have seen how Herbert's example (wrongly and inaccurately remembered) was both cause and expression of the Church of England's search for authenticity and authority. We looked at the way in which Herbert's example was followed and developed in the ministry of his successors through the eighteenth, nineteenth and twentieth centuries. We saw how the example began to break down in the twentieth century, and how it was finally exhausted in the hitherto overlooked ministry of Nick Stacey in Woolwich. Thus our survey has been *historical.*

Along with the historical story of Herbert's example, we have examined the personal cost of Herbertism, borne by its unwitting victims, the sincere clergy of the Church of England. Our survey became *psychological.*

Setting Herbertism to one side we have found the beginnings of a better model, based upon a lecture given by Rowan Williams, and finding expression in a mnemonic of the three Ws of Witness, Watchman and Weaver. We have seen ways in which witnessing, watching and weaving have been important themes in the work, teaching and lives of such diverse people as Michael Ramsey, Fr Elias Chacour, Stanley Hauerwas, John Howard Yoder, Benedict XVI and Dietrich Bonhoeffer. We have found, I hope, a better, stronger, more sustainable, more honest (scripturally and psychologically) place from which to proceed. Our survey finished as *theological.*

It remains to flesh out the skeleton of these three Ws into a practical methodology, which will maintain with integrity the ordination charge placed upon clergy. I call this method KGH ('Killing George Herbert'), to remind me every day that I must resist a phantasm of parochial ministry and instead seek the truth, a pattern that is sustainable and authentic.

The method is divided into five different sections, but I hope that it will be seen that they relate to one another as a whole. I don't mean to advocate a series of techniques by which the overworked parish priest might 'manage' his or her work, and be justified by competence. Each section presupposes that knowledge is a fundamental quality for a priest's life and ministry. In KGH, knowledge will set you, if not free, then certainly freer.

The five sections cover self-knowledge, parish-knowledge, and skills-knowledge. The first three areas, I will argue, are non-negotiable, essential to the honesty and authenticity which KGH seeks to express. The fourth and fifth areas are means by which such honesty can be achieved. All five are necessary foundations for this approach to parish ministry, five pillars to support the building. Just as I demarcated the Archbishop's subtle theologizing on the nature of the Christian priest today by applying three identical lettered labels, I have also given each of these pillars a title beginning with the same letter.

The first pillar is *Rule*: in other words, know who you are, and what rule you will live under. It is important to work out, exploring with the help of another, wiser and more experienced priest if necessary, what will be important to you in your life and ministry, and for those important things to be systematically and explicitly expressed in the form of a rule of life.

The second pillar is *Role*: in other words, know what you are for. This is an important distinction from the first pillar, a distinction that is frequently overlooked or even not recognized as existing in the first place by frantic clergy attempting to keep the show on the road and the balls in the air. However, we will see the importance of the distinction, and a simple way in which to express the differences between the two.

The third pillar is *Responsibility*: in other words, know who you are set over. One of the unintended consequences of Herbertism has been the tendency to use a 'one size fits all' approach to parochial ministry, as if the only thing that every parish or every church community needs is Herbertian ubiquity and affirmation from its parish priest. KGH, on the other hand, recognizes that ministry happens in context, and only in context. How does the KGH priest identify the context in which he will minister?

The fourth pillar, and the first of the protective skills, is *Reckoning*: in other words, know how to make decisions. This might seem to be simple: all the best decision-making is collaborative. People will only abide by decisions made if they have had a share in the decision-making process; and, after all, we are desperate to get away from the 'father knows best' model of previous years. However, it will be seen that the advocates of collaborative decision-making, which has its origins in social psychology studies of businesses in the 1970s, identified a series of different models for making decisions, and we will see that different situations require different ways for deciding things.

The fundamental truth of parish life is this: any decision made will annoy somebody. Therefore, the final pillar is *Reconciling*: in other words, know how to manage conflict. Herbertism managed conflict by pretending that it didn't exist, or, if it did, behaving as if it didn't.* KGH, on the other hand, has to face conflict, not 'manage' it. The origins of any conflict, the 'presenting principles', may be sincerely held opinions by the quarrellers. But such presenting principles can also be accompanied by psychological baggage unrelated directly to the disputed matter, and it is this unspoken, unexpressed baggage that ramps up the intensity of the dispute. We might not necessarily grow through conflict, but we can certainly die by it.

You may think that the subtitle of this book indicates an extreme attitude to innovation and novelty: 'radical' often is a synonym for 'overthrowing everything that has gone before'. Not so: 'radical' means returning to the roots, and perhaps examining those roots in a slightly more reflective way than they have been treated before. We don't do these things because we have always done these things: we do these things in this way because these things done in this way demonstrate where we have come from, how we want to be in the journey and perhaps the place to which we are travelling. Not much of what I will say in the following short section is new (as in novel); you might feel that you have already read something, thought something, even practised something, akin to what I advise. If so, then, like the Athenians and with St Paul, I say 'Good for you' (Acts 17.22–31). However, part of the purpose of KGH is to make these old ways explicit, so that people

* If you don't believe me, then re-read chapter 18 of *The Country Parson*, and imagine how the advice of 'The Parson in Sentinel' has been applied to the parish life of your experience.

10

Know who you are: Rule

> A man and his small son went for a walk that took them past the parish church. They saw the vicar, wearing a cassock, putting up some notices. 'Daddy,' asked the small boy, 'what is that man for?'
>
> (Michael Hocking, *A Handbook of Parish Work*, 1984)

Michael Hocking begins his how-to book on being a priest with this question, and his answer involves the full range of Herbertism. The boy's question was and is a valid one, but Hocking's answer was and is not the solution; it is part of the lingering problem of Herbertism.* So what would a KGH answer to the question be? We can put it quite simply: a priest is there to be religious.

This is not necessarily a fatuous answer, even though it might be a counter-cultural and unpopular assertion. How many times have you heard the following said, proclaimed even, in a tone of some pride: 'I am not a religious person, but I am spiritual'? In his book *Spiritual, but not Religious: Understanding Unchurched America*, Robert Fuller described how perhaps one in five of Americans, about half of those who are 'unchurched', identify themselves as 'spiritual but not religious'. It is an interesting distinction to make, and open to potential confusion, for 'spiritual' and 'religious' both have much the same meaning: 'Both connote belief in a Higher Power of some kind. Both also imply a desire to connect, or enter into a more intense relationship, with this Higher Power. And, finally, both connote interest in rituals, practices, and daily moral behaviors that foster such a connection or relationship.'[1] But 'spiritual' people, often describing themselves as 'seekers' to eager sociologists, make a clear distinction between what they do and what the religious do: 'Seekers often say that "being religious" is for people

* Have a look at his 'Top Twenty Priorities' on pp. 23–5 for a good checklist of Herbertism at work.

who are worried about death, while "being spiritual" is for those who want to get the most out of life.[2] This is a 'lifestyle choice' for people who are opposed to organized religion (and we all know how preferable disorganized religion is to modern sensibilities!). In common thought today, 'religion' means systematic oppression, and 'to be religious' means to live as an unspiritual and unthinking follower of outmoded dogma, subject to the process by which, according to Abraham Maslow, spirituality becomes a 'set of habits, behaviours, dogmas, forms [which then in turn becomes] . . . entirely legalistic and bureaucratic, conventional, empty, and in the true meaning of the word, antireligious'.[3] But religion can also be worse than this; more than a desiccated dogma, it can be positively poisonous. Gore Vidal expresses the idea with his characteristic vigour:

> From a barbaric Bronze Age text known as the Old Testament, three anti-human religions have evolved – Judaism, Christianity, and Islam. These are sky-god religions . . . The sky-god is a jealous god, of course. He requires total obedience from everyone on earth, as he is not just in place for one tribe, but for all creation. Those who would reject him must be converted or killed for their own good. Ultimately, totalitarianism is the only sort of politics that can truly serve the sky-god's purpose.[4]

This, of course, is not the definition of 'religion' which I wish to claim for KGH, and yet I assert that a KGH priest must be religious.

'Religion', as an idea and as a word, has a 'doubtful etymology' according to the *Oxford English Dictionary*. A popular explanation for the word, one which is often made as an unsupported sermon assertion, is that the word 'religion' comes from living under a rule ('which is why monks and nuns, who live under the rule of their founder, are often known as "religious"'). There is something more about this understanding that I would wish to affirm, but unfortunately, like many folk definitions, 'religion' coming from 'rule' ain't necessarily so. Professional etymologists used to follow Cicero in thinking that 'religion' derived from the Latin *relegĕre*, meaning to read over again. But, according to the *OED*, later authors believe the word is more likely derived from *religāre*, meaning 'to bind'. It therefore has connections with 'ligature', a form of binding, or 'ligament', the tissues which keep the bones of the body together. Religion, in this sense, is that which binds, connects, holds together; it prevents the dissolution that comes from things falling apart.

This sense of 'religion' is famously and familiarly expressed in the old Irish prayer *Faeth Fiada* ('The Deer's Cry', c. AD 700?). 'The Deer's Cry' is a form of prayer known as a *lorica*, named after the Latin for 'body armour'. The word was applied, later and metaphorically, to a type of prayer, 'a prayer or statement of faith to be recited for protection, arming oneself for spiritual or physical battle'.[5] *Faeth Fiada* is more commonly known as 'St Patrick's Breastplate', particularly in the translation by Cecil Frances Alexander:

> I bind unto myself today
> The strong Name of the Trinity,
> By invocation of the same,
> The Three in One, and One in Three.[6]

So, with this etymology and hymnody in mind, we can see that to say that you are a 'religious person' means something more than Vidal's surrender to Bronze Age morality, or Maslow's succumbing to bureaucratic behaviours. Surprisingly, perhaps, the *OED* gets it about right. Religion is:

> Recognition on the part of man of some higher unseen power as having control of his destiny, and as being entitled to obedience, reverence, and worship; the general mental and moral attitude resulting from this belief, with reference to its effect upon the individual or the community; personal or general acceptance of this feeling as a standard of spiritual and practical life.[7]

In other words, religion is a response to an objective encounter (something out there) which requires an ethical response (something we do) and impacts upon what we think and how we behave as individuals and within a larger group. To be a religious person means to be someone who seeks to live under a binding protection, someone who recognizes that life is fraught with danger for those who live in isolation. In other words, yes, religion is a crutch; but who's to say that you're not limping?

We have seen, in the first section of this book, that to live as a parish priest in the Church of England today is to live, as never before, in a time of change. Perhaps more than any other institution, the Church has been affected by society's rapid changes in technology, mobility, wealth creation and morality. The Church and its ministry was predicated on stability, authority, deference, inequality of education (between clergy and congregation), and financial independence (of both clergy from parishes and parishes from national structures). These values have been undercut, almost removed, by the dynamics of change, even within the period of my ordained ministry. It is no longer possible to live an ordained life and exercise an ordained ministry on unspoken assumptions and implicit expectations. Our society is content for individuals to sacrifice themselves for ideals which it no longer values itself, but in that sacrificial living it demands accountability and transparency.

Furthermore, the prevailing social ethic of our time is 'You go, girl!' Living for the present whim, the passing fancy, is the acme: I can do whatever I want to do, as long as it doesn't harm anybody else; there is no value in discipline or self-denial, which lead inevitably to repression and psychological damage.

There is an antidote to this for the KGH priest, which is to accept the discipline of living under a Rule of Life. A Rule of Life can help priest and people mutually to understand the nature of the role and calling of the priest today. A Rule of Life, and the willing submission of the priest to live *sub regula*, is a profound witness to a proper Christian understanding of the relationship between God and his creation, and to take a stand against self-gratification.

In the spate of 'How to be a priest' books of the last ten or so years, the idea of a Rule of Life has often been mentioned, in some books more explicitly than in others. For example, Stephen Conway asserts, very firmly: 'I strongly recommend that all of us, therefore, make a rule of life . . . which sees the worship of the church as an integral part of our own spiritual diet and not separate from it . . .'[8] Malcolm Grundy similarly makes the connection between prayer, worship and a rule of life: '. . . at the heart of every priest, as of every Christian person, there needs to be a worked-out pattern which enables prayers to be said. The time-honoured way of achieving this is by developing a Rule of Life.'[9] Chris Edmondson, in a book of 'environmental pastoral theology',*

* Which is what I call those books which explore an environment in which a priest's ministry might be exercised. You know the sort of thing: a priest might do this, with these people, in these ways.

never mentions the phrase 'Rule of Life', as far as I can tell. Even so, he gets very close to the concept, in an unsystematic and unthreateningly evangelical way, by listing fourteen different strategies for 'taking care of ourselves': 'Review every three months or so, preferably with someone else, what has been effective in ministry and what has not, so energies can be put into the appropriate areas – what is essential, what is not, what is getting missed out.'[10] He then unhelpfully suggests that these strategies might be approached in a 'pick'n'mix' fashion!

Most of these discussions about how to develop and follow a Rule of Life for today's priests derive from one source, Harold Miller's 1983 Grove Booklet, *Finding a Personal Rule of Life.*[11] Miller describes how his interest in what he calls 'Rule' developed when he was a tutor at St John's College, Nottingham:

> The problem was that very few people knew where to start in talking about their spiritual lives, and the concept of setting goals for spiritual growth appeared to be very new – and the thing which helped me to enable them to begin to explore in a fresh way was the age old idea of 'Rule' . . .[12]

Miller's booklet wasn't a new formulation of the idea of 'Rule': he acknowledges his debt to a much older work. Martin Thornton, a parish priest for many years in the Diocese of Truro, wrote two exceptional books in the 1950s. One, *Pastoral Theology*, is still occasionally read and cited in books on the subject.[13] The other, *Christian Proficiency*,[14] published 50 years ago, seems to have all but disappeared (other than as a footnote in Miller's booklet), which is a shame, because Thornton has a lot of encouraging things to say to a Church more often in need of evangelization than evangelism.* Thornton calls the goal of this evangelization 'Christian proficiency'; that is, encouraging people to move on from a beginner's faith to being able to 'play a really creative, efficient part in the Church's work'.[15] Living as a 'Regular Christian' – that is, being a Christian under a Rule of Life – plays a vital part in this project. If you can find a copy, it is well worth a read.

* A distinction, valid in my own mind if nowhere else, which points out the difference between strengthening and deepening the faith of those who are already believers (evangelization) before going out to get more disciples (evangelism).

From all these writers, and from my own experience as a Herbertian and post-Herbertian parish priest, I think we can state four broad considerations necessary for devising a Rule of Life: four rules for a Rule.

1. A Rule of Life is not a collection of rules

The first is to say simply, firmly and repeatedly, that a Rule of Life is not a list of things to do. This is a common error, and one which Thornton clearly refutes: the proper name for this spiritual discipline is a *Rule* (singular) of Life, not (as in Richard Templar's pop-business psychology books[16]), the *Rules* (plural) of Life, Work, Business, Parenting, whatever. This is an important point. A Rule of Life is a process or a system, not a legal code; or, better, it is more about an attitude, an orientation, than it is about codifying all the different things we ought to be doing – in other words, in the words of the old saw, it is more about *being* than *doing*:

> . . . Rule is a help and not a hindrance, something liberating not restrictive, expansive not burdensome, in accord with the freedom of the Christian spirit and absolutely opposed to 'legalism'. It is *always* the means to an end and *never* an end in itself.[17]

If you decide to accept a Rule of Life for yourself then you will be saying, in effect, 'I believe that God has plans for me: I am to become the person God has intended me to be all along. I think that this calling is best expressed by adopting a fundamental orientation to my life: my life as a whole – actions, behaviours, attitudes. If I have got that wrong, and my actions, behaviours and attitudes are taking me away from the person God wants me to be, then I will amend them accordingly, for actions better suited to the person God is calling me to be.'

2. A Rule of Life is not just another thing to do

A Rule of Life is not an invitation to burden yourself with more responsibilities, is not a slippery slope on the road to Pelagianism, and is not contrary to Article 11 of the Thirty Nine Articles:* 'We are accounted

* A friend of mine once told me: 'I'm thinking of starting a new church confraternity, called *AXIA*, the Article 11 Association. Members would agree to show their commitment to

righteous before God, only for the merit of our Lord and Saviour Jesus Christ by faith, and not for our own works or deservings.' That is to say, in short and forcefully, a Rule of Life is not about (deadening) routine.

This is the mistake made by Malcolm Grundy and Felicity Lawson. Grundy begins his discussion with a confession: 'I have a perpetual fear of a life like that of the Revd Patrick Brontë, who retired to bed at the same time every evening, pausing halfway up the stairs to rewind the grandfather clock!'[18] Lawson worries that most books on the spiritual life, and the rules of life recommended by them, are written by and intended for those who thrive on such a routine: '[d]eveloping a basic rule of life and sticking to it is easier for those who enjoy routine than for those who don't'. Those who don't enjoy routine will be 'made to feel a failure before they have even begun!'[19]

But this has nothing to do with a Rule of Life properly understood. Do the people who find routine such a trial choose to eat their meals at random times and in random places? A bowl of cereal at dinner, roast chicken for breakfast? Do they wake up in the morning and debate with themselves whether or not they will wash and dress that day? Do they decide at the last minute whether to use the prayers for a funeral or prayers for a wedding when conducting a service at the crematorium, as routinely using the words of the committal at a funeral can be so trying? Of course not.* Even for the most flibbertigibbet of clergy, routine has some part in their lives. As Thornton says, a Rule of Life properly understood and followed becomes not so much routine as unobtrusive: 'This is the real meaning of the word Regular: a Christian who has no need to worry over much about duty, or about what he ought to do next, because an orderly integrated prayer-life has become part of him.'[20] In other words, a Rule of Life is not a routine, or actions that have to be grimly undertaken and completed. It is not a burden to be borne, but (again) an attitude to be embraced. Miller concurs: 'embracing' a Rule of Life: '. . . warms up the cold feeling of the word "Rule", and points towards a loving and wholehearted acceptance of the Lord's

---

Article 11 [of the Thirty Nine Articles of Religion] by agreeing to devote a significant and increasing proportion of their time to things they do badly, and agreeing not to try to do better! All licensed ministers in the C of E would have automatic membership.'

* Although we do all know clergy in whom such whimsical behaviour has appeared – but then we have recognized it as being evidence of the final stages of a nervous breakdown and not the expression of their spontaneous nature!

pattern and discipline for us as individuals, born of grace and freedom and not of punishment and law.'

3. A Rule of Life is not there to help you do things better

A Rule of Life is not a strategy for managing priestly life more proficiently, according to some master plan of personal and professional development. Such a master plan is important (although not as important as our present church culture seems to insist on making it), but it does not find its expression in a Rule of Life. Malcolm Grundy is unhelpful when he says 'A rule is a measure – in modern language, a reviewable achievement – of how you are progressing.'[21] Not so: a Rule of Life is about the person you are called to become, not the achievements you hope to attain.

Think of it this way: in your Rule of Life you decide that attendance at corporate worship (Morning Prayer, Evening Prayer, the Holy Eucharist, whatever) will be a part of your daily life. You write it down and pin it up on your noticeboard. You begin to attend corporate worship every day. Some weeks you make seven out of seven, some weeks you make four out of seven. Some weeks you make one. What do you do? Feed the data into a spreadsheet, so that your computer can draw a pretty chart? What does the chart measure, other than the simple empirical fact of attendance at daily worship? Does it measure that you are a better priest, a more prayerful priest, a more spiritual priest, a priest more likely to be going somewhere? Of course it measures none of these things, it is nothing more than bald statistics. The purpose of a Rule is to deepen prayer life, not to keep score of a series of targets, and so is wholly opposed to the Church's creeping managerialism!

Why not manage without a Rule at all then? Martin Thornton puts it this way:

> . . . one of two things is bound to happen. The scrupulous or even conscientious person will tend to discount his own weakness (which is pride) and take on far too much. He will never satisfy his own conscience, pray himself to a standstill, or into chronic aridity, and confront Holy Saturday with nothing more creative than a nervous breakdown (which will doubtless be called religious mania). The lax

> person, and I fear this the more likely alternative, will simply slip back into a dull and dormant mediocrity.[22]

So we can say further, for two reasons, that any breach of your Rule of Life should not be seen as a sin, but rather as a 'fault'. First, following a Rule of Life must not provide us with an opportunity for more sinning: there is more than enough opportunity for sinning in human life as it is! Second, to concentrate on breaches of the Rule as if they were sins might allow the KGH priest to camouflage his or her own, real, sins. How much easier it is to say that you have sinned by not spending twenty minutes in quiet time each day this week than it is to say you have indulged in the greater sin of Messiahism (see p. 159 below).

4. A Rule of Life is not something you invent/apply/adjust yourself

Miller's little booklet, which has proved to be so influential, has one great flaw: it allows a Rule to be drawn up which is an entirely individual thing – the flaw is in the title, 'finding a *personal* rule of life'. Certainly at one point he remarks that writing your rule 'if at all possible, should be done with someone else',[23] but elsewhere the assumption is firmly upon the individual's own needs and objectives.[24]

This is not something of which St Benedict, the writer of the first great rule of life, approved. In the first chapter of the Rule of St Benedict he condemns in forthright terms those monks known as sarabaites 'who have not been tested by a rule, as gold is tested in a furnace, not been taught by experience, but are like soft lead . . . they shut themselves up in their own sheepfolds, not those of the Lord; and their law consists in yielding to their desires: what they like or choose they call holy . . .'[25] So, best not to be a sarabaite!

As Thornton puts it: 'Rule is essentially corporate significance, and I very much doubt if, according to Catholic tradition, a person who lived to his own Rule alone and without everyone else knowing anything about it would really be entitled to the designation "Regular".'[26]

At the very least your own Rule of Life should be something devised in consultation with a spiritual director. Even better would be assuming a Rule common to one of the Church's societies or confraternities (and not necessarily just the *AXIA*!), and contextualizing it for your own particular needs and circumstances. There is sometimes a conflict, a dangerous 'wishful dreaming' as Bonhoeffer called it, between an individual's need to find God and the reassurance of salvation within a community, and the healthy running of a community itself (see page 135). Even so, a Rule of Life such as that compiled by Benedict, and lived for the last 1,500 years by the most disparate communities and individuals, has something to commend itself:

> Benedict understood that it is not the community that saves, but rather God's grace working through very fallible human beings (and in many other ways). His *Rule* describes a middle way between desperate isolation and the headlong rush into community, because it is grounded in Christ's teaching and practical experience.[27]

There is a humane system of checks and balances in any community rule which has survived for this great length of time. Living within a common Rule is a practical expression of the individual's need for support and fellowship. It also asserts, visibly, that there is no such thing as the isolated Christian.

What is my Rule of Life?

What does this look like when worked out in a practical example? What will be my own Rule of Life? What kind of priest am I called to become? Simply, how would I answer the child's question: 'Daddy, what is that man for?'?

My attempts to answer that question eventually centred on resisting two particular pressures in my own life and ministry: anti-intellectualism and the denigration of prayer. That the former is present in the life of the Church will be obvious to any thinking person; the latter might be surprising.

The success of anti-intellectualism (see Judith Maltby's acerbic comment on page 108) is not due just to a suspicion of things of the mind: it is also the product of the elevation of emotions above all other values: 'What I *think* is just what I think. What I *feel* is real.' I recall a curate I knew who refused to participate in continuing ministerial education because it was all 'academic theology' ('academic' here being a synonym for 'useless, time-wasting'), but who, when asked what was the heart of his gospel, foundered, and could only eventually answer, 'I suppose, to love people.' Frank Viola, a leading exponent of the house church movement in America, has produced a book in which anti-intellectualism becomes the defining New Testament marker of an authentic church. He quotes approvingly: 'We cannot obtain anything in our New Testament as the result of human study, research, or reason. It is all the Holy Spirit's *revelation* of Jesus Christ.'[28] Mr Viola would not approve of this book.

The denigration of prayer is an interesting phenomenon, and one which is almost entirely subjective: there are very few empirical studies on the place of prayer within parish ministry. Douglas Turton and Leslie Francis have attempted to measure the place of prayer within the life of parish clergy, and they found that a life of prayer:

> . . . may, however, be difficult to sustain in a busy and pressurized round of parish ministry and may be dulled by the repeated experiences of unanswered prayer and of fractured relationships with the divine. Ordination itself is no guarantee that the belief system supporting the practice of prayer will be positively sustained throughout ministry. It may well be the case that for clergy, 'it is their profession to pray', but it may also be the case that this aspect of the profession is particularly difficult to support and to sustain.[29]

We are told, and we tell ourselves, that prayer is foundational to our whole way of living: we should, as Paul tells us, 'devote yourselves to prayer, keeping alert in it with thanksgiving' (Colossians 4.2). But then we don't. We are suspicious of those who pray. They are God-botherers; they don't perform any useful function; it's wasting time. Two examples: a priest admonished by her churchwarden for advertising a weekly morning prayer service in the parish magazine – she should have checked with the warden before introducing this innovation; another priest, who used to say morning prayer surrounded by church cleaners, ostentatiously shuffling their feet, waiting for him to get out of the way before the real, important business of the church was allowed to begin. Prayer, it seems, is a specialized, fringe activity for the Church: we have other things to be getting on with.

Bearing these two pressures in mind, the question remains, 'Daddy, what is that man for?' I think the best (or most succinct) answer comes from another Benedict, Pope Benedict XVI. His description of the laity's expectation of their priests to be 'specialists in promoting the encounter between man and God'[30] is a compelling one. How should one go about this? Where might we find exemplars in promoting this encounter with God?

Which is why, when I looked to draw up a Rule of Life afresh, a Rule of Life which would no longer be complicit with Herbertism, I realized I needed a Rule which allowed, encouraged and fostered both prayer and study. I was therefore naturally drawn to the discipline of the Dominicans, the Order of Preachers. For 800 years the Dominicans have based their individual and community life upon four pillars of *Prayer*, *Study*, *Community* and the *Ministry*. This is a pattern of life which has borne immense fruit in the most difficult and trying circumstances, and, more impressively, has kept the Dominicans true to their foundational calling in times of comfort and prosperity.

The Dominican rule can possibly be summed up in a famous phrase of that great Dominican scholar, Thomas Aquinas. The purpose of the Dominican life, said Thomas, is 'to contemplate and to share the fruits of your contemplation'.[31] But, more impressively, as Fr Donald Goergen OP has put it:

> Deep within the Dominican spirit lies an urge toward integration, balance. Dominican spirituality is an integrative, integrating, integral spirituality.[32]

That sounds like something the KGH priest, so split for so long in attempting to placate Herbertism, should go for.

Thus, my Rule of Life, emulating this Dominican integrative pattern, begins in *Prayer*, the deliberate systematic exposing of myself, ego, desires and will, to the loving chastisement of God. It continues in *Study*, of God and the application of the insights and testimony of previous faithful Christians to my own situation. It continues in *Community*, which here means something more than a co-incident group of like-minded, like-professioned, like-housed individuals. It means that I must allow the judgement of the wider Christian community, PCC, spiritual director, diocese, confessor, upon my living. And it finds an external expression in *Ministry*, in which what I think God might require of me is measured against what other people, inside and outside the Church, think God might be providing through me.

Prayer

I am unable to do anything without it being grounded in prayer, but, more importantly, I am unable to *be* anything without being grounded in prayer. Allowing myself to be open to God is the means by which I become myself, the person created, redeemed and loved by him. Therefore my day, like my life, should begin and end in prayerful waiting on his presence. I must remember, however, that

> Prayer is more
> Than an order of words, the conscious occupation
> Of the praying mind, or the sound of the voice praying.[33]

Prayer must become a fundamental attitude of my living.

This is, of course, in order to become a Christian. It is only by being open to God that we have a chance of knowing God and knowing his purposes for us. But prayer, as the fundamental attitude of my living, is also in order to relinquish being a Messiah. For Eugene Peterson, prayer is the only possible antidote to that great weakness of ministry and ministers, 'messiahism'. Pastors, he says, colluding with people's fear of God, and desiring to be loved,

> . . . enter into the practice of messiah: we will do the work of God for God, fix people up, tell them what to do, conspire in finding the shortcuts by which the long journey to the Cross can be bypassed since we all have such crowded schedules right now. People love us when we do this. It is flattering to be put in the place of God. It feels wonderful to be treated in this godlike way. And it is work we are generally quite good at.[34]

Prayer reminds me that I am not the Messiah, *and that's how it should be.*

Study

Study is not the purpose of my life but the instrument by which I may, under God's grace and guidance, achieve that purpose. I study in order to make myself 'useful to the souls of my neighbours'.[35] To study is to contemplate God's purposes for his people and the working out of those purposes in creation, society and the lives of individuals. My study, therefore, will not, and must not, be limited to the scriptures and ecclesiastical subjects. The action of the Holy Spirit is not restricted to the parts of our world which we set aside for him. A knowledge of the breadth of society and the human learning is an appropriate skill for a Christian minister. As we have seen Rowan Williams note above: 'Those who have preached most effectively in this and other eras are, it seems to me, those who have known how to read the surface and the depths, but have had no great interest in the shallows.'[36] However, scripture is properly the chief of my studies, for in scripture we see the clearest historical revelation of God's action in the world, and his principal self-revelation in the man and Lord, Jesus Christ.

Study reminds me that it is my responsibility *to give the Holy Spirit something to work with.*

Community

The centre of my working week is Sunday morning at the Gathering of the eucharistic community. Everything I do is to prepare myself to say, 'The Lord be with you', for it is at that point that the community of believers, the Church, allows itself to be formed. I am placed in the privileged position to be part of a church community while not 'of' it: the parish priest in the Church of England must never be reduced to chaplain of an enclosed community: 'Welcome . . . to our way of doing things.' I have the responsibility to represent God to the community, and the community to God, but also the differing parts of the community to itself, never allowing one part to feel itself superior to or the victim of another. I am 'the person who is charged with telling the Church where and what it is, in [my] daily and lifelong service'.[37] This has always been a perilous undertaking, and it is especially so in our times, when the willingness to hear words spoken in authority has almost completely decayed away: 'To be yourself a place where lines of force intersect, where diverse interests and passions converge, is one of the hardest aspects of that dimension of priestly life which is about living in the fantasies and expectations of others.'[38] The inevitability of this crushing intersection is the reason why God has not called me to be alone; I am called into being within multiple layers of community: family, friends, Church, society. I will not live in one to the exclusion of others, for that would be to choose, according to my own impaired judgement, the place in which God wants me to be me.

Community reminds me that God saw that it was not good for the man to be alone, and that *we are called to salvation together.*

Ministry

The purpose of my life is to make Christ known to his people. My words, actions, prayers and thoughts must be centred on this task: this is the 'cure of souls', my own as much as the parish. We live in a day and culture in which the basic facts of the Christian faith are unknown to the majority of people, inside and outside the Church. The words, unhistorically but truthfully in spirit, attributed to St Francis, apply: 'Preach the gospel at all times. Use words if necessary.' It follows from this that the formal sermon on Sunday morning, despite its pre-eminent place in the breaking of the Word in the midst of the gathered community of believers, cannot be the only form of evangelism I undertake. I don't mean that the KGH priest is a great subscriber to evangelistic exercises, schemes or programmes. KGH evangelism has precious little to do with the pernicious aspects of the 'church growth' movement. Rather, the KGH priest recognizes the truth of what Antoine de Saint-Exupéry, author of *The Little Prince*, said: 'If you want to build a ship, don't summon people to buy wood, prepare tools, distribute jobs and organize the work, rather teach people the yearning for the wide, boundless ocean.'[39]

Ministry reminds me that it is my task to co-operate with God in nurturing this yearning for the wide, boundless love of the Divine which is within and before them.

Such is my Rule of Life (I reproduce it in more detailed form in the Appendix). It is temporary and contingent, as all rules of life should be. It will do for the moment, and, when necessary, it will be relinquished for another, more fitting for God's purposes for me then. For the moment, though, it helps me distinguish between who I am, and what I am for, the tasks I am required to undertake. This latter aspect, the role of the KGH priest, is what we must examine now.

11

Know what you are for: Role

> Like all Christians, clergy are accountable to God. Yet to be called into fellowship with Christ is to be called into fellowship with one another, and there is a mutual accountability that comes with being a member of the Body of Christ. Anyone holding office within the Church is part of a network of mutual responsibilities, and it is unhelpful if those responsibilities are unclear and ill-defined.
>
> (*Summary Review of Clergy Terms of Service*, 2004, §27)

As I was leaving theological college in the early 1990s it was just becoming fashionable for newly ordained curates to negotiate a job description with their training incumbents. This would enable the curate to know the expectations that would be placed upon them, and the training incumbent to know what needed still to be covered in the curate's remaining training. It also would prevent, it was hoped, 'occasional offices exploitation' (eight funerals a week down at the local crematorium). We were all bright-eyed, bushy-tailed, enthusiastic about this, and absorbed the different models of job description for the different types of title parish we might go into. The training incumbents themselves were invited to a short conference at our college, during which they were introduced to the changes in theological training since they had been ordained by Thomas Cranmer. All would be well.

Until a friend of mine, to be ordained to a seaside parish in a northern diocese, asked his incumbent if they might talk about his job description. 'Job description? Simple!' his incumbent replied. 'It's five words. You. Do. What. I. Say.'

Would that count as responsibilities being 'unclear and ill-defined'?

Of course the usual situation faced by Herbertian clergy is that their responsibilities are the opposite: clear and clearly defined, and mutually contradictory. We want a priest who is always available, who is always on the end of the telephone, who is always out visiting, who is good with old people, good with young people, brings new families into church, looks after the old families of the church community, makes the church grow, keeps the church the same, preaches well, is the first to arrive and the last to leave, keeps a happy family, attends every meeting, and so on, until the last syllable of recorded time. One survey of the coping strategies of parish clergy asked its respondents a question about expectations:

> What are the expectations of pastors? That we exercise 'responsible stewardship' of our lives, take care of ourselves, and 'model sanity' for our congregants . . . or that we pour ourselves out in the Lord's service, serve 'sacrificially' and without counting the cost to ourselves, our health, and our families, work harder and longer without ever, ever, ever being lazy or giving up?[1]

'You. Do. What. I. Say' is preferable to what is actually at work here; 'You. Do. What. I. *Think*. You. Should. Be. Doing.'

> Clergy deal with issues such as rigid bureaucratic structures, poor administrative support, budgetary and financial problems, and a never-ending list of demands from parishioners. Combine these with expectations of facilitating congregational growth, starting new programs, visiting sick congregants, not to mention the handling of weddings, funerals, and baptisms, and the family reactions that often emerge around these events. In looking at this list of pressures, it becomes clear that there is bound to be an interactional effect as the clergy person attempts to respond to these forces.[2]

When the nature of the parish-based life is spelt out like this, you can see the wisdom of the Summary Review of the *Clergy Terms of Service* in making the expectations of the role clear and well defined.

Which leads to the question: Whose expectations?

There is a pressure point operating here. The simple answer to the question would be that the priest is there is fulfil the expectations of the people among whom he has been set to minister and the expectations of the bishop who set him there, and with whom he shares the 'cure of souls'. However, the financial independence of the clergy, independence from both diocesan structures and present-day parishioners, has gone. It is the living who pay for the church now, and the living have a tendency to wonder if they are getting value for their money. But the measurements of value when it comes to parochial ministry are either crude or nebulous, and are sometimes both: crude, because frequently they boil down to simple numerical counts of parishioners (the Electoral Roll and Usual Sunday Attendance)*; nebulous, because people realize instinctively that a 'successful' ministry cannot be just quantified, but who is to say what the intangible priorities should be? This is particularly difficult when it is reduced to money. As Guy Wilkinson wisely puts it:

> Clergy can be squeezed both by the wider diocesan systems, which increasingly look to parishes to contribute at least the cost of providing them with a priest; and by the PCC which is encouraged by such an approach to see the vicar as 'theirs'— the one whom they have paid for and by extension whom they employ.[3]

And it isn't just priests in the Church of England who face this pinching. According to Fr George Morelli, a clinical psychologist and a priest of the Antiochian Orthodox Church of North America,

> Orthodox clergy face the same chronic stress events as the general population. In addition they have the events common to a hierarchal church: the episcopacy (from above) and a parish council (from below) both often presuming they have control over the priest.

Which resulted, in one example given by Morelli, in the following contradiction:

> The bishop asked that all parishes in his diocese perform a certain liturgical practice. When I did it, some in the parish complained and he told them they were right. He never even supported or backed me up.[4]

---

* In the summer of 2008, the appointment of a new suffragan bishop was announced by his diocese with the proud boast that he had increased the membership of his parish church to more than 900 people in the ten years he had been incumbent. In other words, this man is an empirical success.

John Davey summarized this as 'role overload':

> Unlike other professions there is no clear distinction between the priest's work role and non-work role. Having too much to do – quantitative work overload – or being underqualified – qualitative work overload – is now endemic within the clerical profession.[5]

So, it is important that the KGH priest should have a clear idea of what he or she is responsible for; in other words, what their role is to be. It doesn't matter whether we call this a 'job description' or 'role expectations', the important thing is to remember that whatever we call it, it is *not* just a grander, more formal version of a 'to do' list. We saw in the previous chapter how often a Rule of Life is confused with a list of things the priest is expected to do and the sort of person the priest is expected to be. You might therefore think that this is the chapter in which we list the things that the priest is supposed to do. Not so. As John Truscott says, 'Most churches muddle a job description with a list of tasks to carry out.'[6] No job description should be a list of jobs to do: if it becomes that, then it is no more use in managing expectations, energy and abilities, and no better at furthering the kingdom than 'You. Do. What. I. Say.'

The simplest and clearest way to work this out is to ensure that the job description is written out, having been agreed between the relevant parties. This is a solution that has been made unavoidable by the requirements of the *Ecclesiastical Offices (Terms of Service)* legislation.

A proper job description, as opposed to a written 'You. Do. What. I. Say.', should fall into two main sections. The first section is simply the name and conditions of the job. For clergy in the Church of England this first section will be provided, after the implementation of Common Tenure, by the statement of 'Particulars of Office'. The diocese will provide a written statement which will set out:

- The title of the office to which the office holder has been appointed.
- The date on which the appointment took place.
- Entitlement to stipend, fees and reimbursement of expenses.
- Whether the appointment is part-time, and, if so, the amount of the stipend . . . and hours of work.
- Terms and conditions relating to rest periods and public holidays;

for example, specifying a maximum number of Sundays on which leave may be taken, or specifying dates on which rest periods or annual leave may not be taken.

- Incapacity for work due to sickness or injury, including provision for sick pay.
- The right, if working full-time, to receive a stipend of not less than the national minimum stipend pension provision.
- The person or body to whom the housing in which they are required to live for the better performance of their duties belongs . . . and . . . the terms of occupation.
- The length of notice required to give in order to terminate the appointment.
- The body to be treated as the respondent in any proceedings brought before an employment tribunal.[7]

This is all information that a priest has had before, or been entitled to have. The new thing is that under the previous regime the information has not been collated into a single document. Now it will be the responsibility of a designated person within the diocesan secretariat to provide a newly appointed Common Tenured priest with this information within a short period after taking up their new post. It is a useful starting point for the job description, and you may be surprised how few people in parishes understand the terms and conditions under which clergy have (not) been employed: in one parish in which I worked, a churchwarden expressed his surprise when I moved my formal day off to a Saturday, 'because I thought you already got Saturday off'.

The second section of the job description should contain, John Truscott advises, the answers to three simple questions:

1. *Why* am I doing this job?
2. *Who* do I relate to in doing this job?
3. *What* am I responsible for?

Be careful in answering these questions, and note well the order in which they are presented: the first two questions aren't just preliminaries, they are important too. As Truscott says, too many job descriptions prepared for church workers think that Question 3 is the only one that needs answering.[8]

1. *Why* am I doing this job?

There is no need to rewrite your Rule of Life for this section. It can be short, concise, punchy even. It will be the basis of your work and the reason why you have a function: think of it as the practical distillation of your Rule of Life, blended with the purpose, values and mission statement of your church. Give it some time, thought and prayer: it needs to be got right. Depending upon the awareness and culture of your particular church community, it may be the most difficult three bullet points you write in your whole life: 'This may be the first time the purpose has been defined, and may require some hard thinking . . . There will be real value in having to think this through.'[9]

You may want to use the Ordinal as the basis for this section, or the words of the institution service from your own diocese. Bishop John Vernon Taylor wrote the following prayer for institution services in the Diocese of Winchester when he was Bishop there:

> Almighty God, our heavenly father, fill the heart of your servant N . . . with eager love in caring for your people; joy in affirming all that is good in this community; courage in challenging all that is mean and destructive; and unceasing thankfulness in celebrating your Holy Mysteries among them. Give him vision for his preaching, faithfulness for his teaching, diligence for his visiting, sympathy for his counselling, compassion in declaring your pardon for the penitent and the peace that passes understanding for his daily walk with Christ, in whose name we pray. Amen.[10]

Be careful that you don't incorporate too much Herbertism though. Resist the temptation and pressure to define your purpose as if you were a combination of the Archangel Gabriel, the Second Coming, and old Mr Bracewell, that lovely vicar we had in the 1950s. Go easy on jargon and clichés. If you replicate the usual 'to know Jesus and make Jesus known' tropes, or use 'ministry' as noun, verb and adjective, you are just showing that you haven't really thought this through.

'Why am I doing this job?' is about *context of purpose*: how do you fit in with the expressed purpose of the church community in which you will work?

2. *Who* do I relate to in doing this job?

As we saw in the writing and ministry of Dietrich Bonhoeffer, the Christian life is all about relationship (mediated, according to Bonhoeffer, through the person and saving actions of Jesus Christ). So, when it comes to answering this question it would be accurate, in the strictest sense, by saying simply, 'Jesus Christ'. Accurate, but less than entirely constructive. You might be doing the Lord's work, but who does he want you to do it with?

It is helpful to answer the question by considering three dimensions: ascending (who are you responsible to?); descending (who are you responsible for?); and laterally (with whom should you be liaising?).* These three dimensions are not necessarily about supervision and authority (although that will come into it in certain circumstances). For example, in some parishes the incumbent may have the assistance of a secretary, and be responsible for the training of a curate. Both those relationships are aspects of the descending dimension, but the incumbent may have to answer to the PCC as the legal employer of the secretary, and the bishop and his officers as those overseeing the pastoral and professional formation of the curate. Considering the nature of your relationships in three dimensions encourages the KGH priest to see ministry taking place within a network of relationships; both more complex than the traditional 'I stand here in the pecking order' model, and more rewarding.

This is how Truscott suggests the relationships question might be answered:

> The incumbent is responsible to the Bishop of (diocese) with whom (s)he shares the 'cure of souls' within the parish. (S)he acts as the leader of the church staff team, works in close liaison with the Church Wardens and is ex-officio chairman of the Parochial Church Council. (S)he is a member of the deanery chapter and synod and of the local fraternal. *(Add other links which may also exist: e.g. chair of governors of a church school, trainer of a curate.)*[11]

---

* And let's leave aside any pretence that the Church is not a hierarchical organization: it is, and no amount of calling bishops by their Christian names will remove that fact. Remember, collegiality in a hierarchical organization is an irregularly declining verb (p. 53).

Again, none of this is earth-shattering or paradigm-breaking: all it does is set out clearly, and in writing, with whom the parish priest is expected to work. For some parishioners, seeing the context of parochial ministry will be an education.

So, in summary, 'Who do I relate to in doing this job?' is about *context of relationship*: with whom will you be working, and what are their responsibilities and expectations?

3. *What* am I responsible for?

The task is unlimited; resources to undertake the task are not: the realization of the chapter retreat (p. 50) holds – once the sermons have been written and the services planned, and the youth group supervised, and the funerals taken and the wedding couples prepared, there are still 5,000 people out there who could be visited. If you allow yourself to be driven by Herbertism, *the job never ends*. And, worse than that, allowing yourself to set infinity as your quota of work will prevent you from accomplishing very much at all. Merlin Mann, writer of the *43Folders* blog, talks about this as 'opportunity costs': 'the things you COULD do are infinite, while your time and attention are FINITE. Opportunity cost means: if I do "this", I necessarily can't do "that", "that", "that", and "OMG, THAT!"'[12] Well, that's fine for Merlin Mann, you might say, but I am prepared for my day to be interrupted by all sorts of activities, and new projects. I thrive on rapid and violent changes of gear: I have learned how to multi-task. You may very well think so, but the sad fact is that there is no such thing as multi-tasking.

In business studies in recent years (and business contains its own profoundly influential 'How to' subculture) there has been an interesting reaction *against* the prevailing culture of multi-tasking. Before, books would encourage their readers to manage multiple responsibilities and projects, giving tips on how to apportion time, energy and attention between conflicting demands. All it needed was for time to be managed. A new generation of writers, including Dave Allen (of the *Getting Things Done* book and cult), Merlin Mann, and Dave Crenshaw (*The Myth of Multitasking*), repudiate both the desirability and the possibility of multi-tasking.[13] Crenshaw is most explicit. The subtitle of his book states the thesis: *How 'Doing It All' Gets Nothing Done*. He denies the existence of the ability to multi-task. Instead, he says that people who think they are multi-tasking are, in reality, *switch-tasking* – moving from one task to another and back again, sometimes so quickly they don't even realize they are doing it. Switch-tasking is the mental equivalent of the economic impact of 'switching costs', where a company changes from one supplier or subcontractor to another: changing the way a company engages with the world outside the company has a direct, measurable economic cost. Every interruption is a drain of time, attention and energy: every interruption, and the attention paid to that interruption, is a step away from accomplishing the infinite quota. As Crenshaw says: 'Saying that you are a good multitasker is the same as saying you're good at using a less effective method to get things done.'[14] This is the irony: the more a Herbertian priest *attempts* to complete the infinite quota, the less able he or she is to complete a finite part of it.

John Truscott, in his example job description for a minister in a larger church, limits the responsibilities to ten, deliberately spread over a number of distinct areas: spirituality; vision; teaching/preaching; public worship; developing others; decision-making; parish, deanery and diocese; care of self.[15] He acknowledges that some people will think that the first and the last area don't belong in a job description, but we know that to be an expression of latent Herbertism: if the parish priest can't model a balanced and integrated discipleship to his or her parish, then no amount of running around will compensate.

When you draw up your own list of responsibilities, it is imperative that this is done in collaboration with responsible representatives of the parish: your churchwardens, a ministry leadership team (if you are part of one), the Standing Committee of the PCC. Your responsibilities are the point in which your ministry intersects with the needs of your parish – needs perceived and identified by you, in collaboration with the ministry leadership team and the PCC: trust the wisdom of those 'on the ground', but also trust the wisdom of your judgement. In order for their expectations to be addressed (reasonable ones fulfilled, unreasonable ones challenged), you need to engage in a dialogue with the representatives. This also has a tactical advantage. Once the job description is agreed, it can then be presented to the wider parish as the decision of a team of people, and not the personal ultimatum of an individual priest (who ought to have known that nice Mr Bracewell from the 1950s never thought to have anything so selfish as a job description!). In the dialogue you will need to ask how can the priorities of the parish, as identified by the churchwarden, ministry leadership team, PCC, be best expressed in terms of the three Ws of Watchman, Witness, Weaver? In other words, what am I *uniquely* qualified (as priest in this place) to accomplish?

There is an important appendix to the list of responsibilities. John Truscott adds a list of exclusions: what tasks are *not* expected to be a priority for the priest? Truscott suggests, using the example of an incumbent in a large church with a staff team, that these should not be a priority: 'routine administration of the church and parish; routine visiting and pastoral care which can be carried out by others; areas of ministry in which (s)he is not specifically gifted and where work can be delegated to others; areas of ministry not felt to be priorities at a given time'.[16] It is not just the large church with a staff team which deserves such a list of exclusions. Clergy responsible for multi-parish rural benefices also have a responsibility not to perpetuate obsolete ideas about the ubiquity of the parish priest: you can no longer afford to be the vicar of 'The Village Pub' of Barnsley. People need to be encouraged in the ideals and necessity of all-member ministry, the responsibilities that come with being baptized, and they won't be able to hear that encouragement if every minor and routine task is undertaken for them by the Herbertian parish priest.

So, then, to answer the question 'What am I responsible for?' is about *context of resources*; what will you be able to bring to fulfil the tasks you have decided to undertake?

There are two other important pieces of information that need to be on any agreed job description: two dates. The first will be the date on which it was agreed, between incumbent and PCC. This is a guarantee that the job description has been discussed, circulated and agreed by the widest appropriate circle of people. There is absolutely no use in a job description which has been concocted by a priest and the churchwardens, and never emerges into the wider world. The unspoken, implicit tyranny of 'You. Do. What. I. *Think*. You. Should. Be. Doing.' will then still be in operation. The second date is the date on which the job description will be reviewed, using the same process by which it was drawn up in the first place. You might not think this to be necessary. After all, once you have agreed to pray, to visit, to preach and teach, why will it be necessary to alter it? This is the problem. If your job description is limited to bromides, then of course it will never need changing:

apple pie and motherhood remain apple pie and motherhood for as long as we have apples and mothers.

But think of this: what if your job description included something like: 'To begin, lead, resource and build up a weekly Toddlers' Service'? After eighteen months hard, concentrated (non-multi-tasking) work, the Toddlers' Service is up and running; there is a regular and growing core of members, a community of young mothers (and some young fathers), who are spending more time together before and after the service. Now is the time to begin to encourage the parents to contribute to the running of the service: telling a story, leading a song, helping to set out and clear away, preparing crafts to do. In other words, now is the time to begin to prepare for your withdrawal from the day-to-day running of the group, and to nurture a leadership group that will succeed you. When that is in place, then the job description needs to be changed. What was appropriate then ('To begin, lead, resource and build up a weekly Toddlers' Service') is no longer appropriate: you need to have something different ('To oversee the continuing development of the Toddlers' Service'). My point is, without the review date on the job description it would be very easy for the job you actually do, and the job you agreed to do, to drift apart until the job description bears no relation at all to the day-to-day, week-to-week work you undertake. Once that happens, your work has become unclear and ill-defined, and 'You. Do. What. I. Think. You. Should. Be. Doing' is in play once more.

Review the job description. It doesn't have to happen frequently, but it should happen regularly. You will be part of a Ministerial Review programme from the diocese (a requirement of the *Ecclesiastical Offices (Terms of Service)* legislation). Why not make that the opportunity to review in a parish-oriented direction as well?

12

Know who you are set over: Responsibility

> When we go back to the first records of the Church we find neither a Ministry which called people into association with it, nor an undifferentiated fellowship which delegated powers to a Ministry: but we find a complete Church, with the Apostolate accepted as its focus of administration and authority.
>
> (William Temple, Speech to the Canterbury Convocation, 5 May 1943)

Ministry happens in context, and only in context. That context, for Christian ministry, is the Christian community. For a minister to exercise ministry, he will need to know his context, he will need to understand his community.

I don't mean by this that he will have to read carefully the parish profile, compiled by a wishful PCC looking for that elusive combination of Archangel, Messiah and Mr Bracewell, which we identified in the previous chapter. Such parish profiles are interesting and useful documents, and should be closely studied by any priest applying for a new position. But they are less interesting for what they say than for what they don't say. 'We would like the new incumbent to help rebuild our youth work': what happened to *debuild* the youth work? 'We would like the new incumbent to make ministry among the unchurched a priority': why was ministry among the churched the priority up to now? 'We would like our new incumbent to foster a "fresh expression" initiative': this may be nothing more than a Homeric desire – 'Hmm, shiny new church toys. Must have!'*

For the KGH priest to understand his Christian community, he will have to learn to see the community as a whole. To do this, the insights of *systems theory* will be vital.

* 'Homeric', as in Simpson, not as in epic Greek poetry.

Systems theory developed from the needs of biological science to explain the complexity of the ways in which organisms related to one another in ecosystems. It was first formulated in the work of the Austrian-Canadian biologist Ludwig von Bertalanffy.[1] It was soon seen that von Bertalanffy's theories could be transferred to different areas of human study: just as a biological organism can only really be understood in terms of the interaction of its parts, human society can be better understood as the interaction of all its members: 'The central idea of systems analysis is based on an analogy with biology: just as the heart, lungs, and blood function as a whole, so do the components of social and political systems. When one component changes or comes under stress, the other components will adjust to compensate.'[2] In short, things are greater than the sum of their parts.

Does this sound familiar? It is nothing new: it is present, using a different language, imagery and conceptual framework, in the New Testament. Walter Wink, in his series examining the 'powers' of the New Testament, shows how the cultures of the ancient Near East, from within which the first Christians emerged, assumed a hugely complex network of human relationships in which and through which certain powers operated: powers which personified (occasionally anthropomorphized) 'the determining forces of physical, psychic and social existence'.[3] These powers (rulers, authorities, principalities, thrones, dominions, angels and so on, in the New Testament metaphors), have two aspects: an internal, spiritual one, by which the power receives its legitimacy and credibility – its moral 'heft' as it were; and an external one, by which the power is expressed within a social group through the actions of political, legal and social conformity. In other words, the way things are done was caused by the interiority of the system, and this interiority was described and justified by the means of 'symbolic projection'.

What does this mean for parish life? Simply, that the KGH priest will take the scriptural imagery of the Body of Christ (from 1 Corinthians 12.12–27 and elsewhere) very seriously indeed, and not just as a justification for giving different people different jobs to do. As Herrington, Creech and Taylor put it:

> Our congregations are living systems. We are emotionally wired together with our brothers and sisters in the family of God (Romans

> 12.3–21). Our behaviour and choices affect each other in ways of which we are often unaware.[4]

One way to conceptualize this living system is to use Wink's imagery of the 'Angel of the Church', derived from Revelation 2–3. There we find Christ instructing a letter to be written to each of the Churches of the Christian diaspora, except that each letter is addressed to 'Angel' of that Church, and therefore it would appear 'that the angel is not something separate from the congregation, but must somehow represent it as a totality. Through the angel, the community seems to step forth as a single collective entity . . . it is more than a mere personification of the church, [but is] the actual spirituality of the congregation as a single entity.'[5]

So, to describe the community, the KGH priest can identify the angel of that community. Wink suggests six areas of study:

- The *built environment* (what architectural and furnishing artefacts does the community choose to surround itself with?)*;
- The *sociology* of the congregation (class, income, educational attainment, social expectations, even the location of the church building within the physical community, are all important in this);
- The *polity* of the congregation (not just the Canons and Church Representation Rules of the Church of England, but the real polity – when the PCC meeting in the church hall is followed by the *real* PCC meeting in the car park afterwards, who has called the second meeting and who is present for it?);
- The way in which the *conflict* is handled (which is so important we will spend a chapter on it below);
- The way in which the congregation *worships* (is the worship merely the warm-up for the serious business of coffee afterwards; what within the service is emphasized or neglected?);
- The congregation's *self-perception* (usefully supplied by the most recent parish profile).

---

* As Stanley Hauerwas once said (to Princeton Theological Seminary, no less!): 'How many of you worship in a church with an American flag? I am sorry to tell you your salvation is in doubt.' (Hauerwas, 'Why Did Jesus Have to Die?')

Gently teasing out the realities of these six factors will allow the KGH priest to know something about the Angel of her church, and go some way to addressing the Angel's personality and vocation: 'Real change must . . . affect not just the visible forms an institution takes, but somehow alter the spirit, the core essence, of the entity as a whole.'[6] How is this to be done? Wink is clear: 'The angel must be constrained to change by a higher power, one capable of transforming the choices of individuals in the congregation while fundamentally altering the group spirit or group culture as well.'[7] This higher power, as in the Revelation of John, is the Son of Man, but Christ will operate, can only operate, says Wink, through a human intermediary: the minister of the congregation, the angel to the angel. Change requires, Wink says:

> . . . that we sit quite still until we have discerned the angel and have been caught up in a vision of what it could become if it were alive to the divine presence . . . As we continue to rehearse this vision and to act confidently on the basis of it, our own demeanour will be experienced by others as invitation rather than demand. And lived visions are contagious.[8]

Which all goes to show how central, vital, fundamental the KGH priest's public vocation to be a person of prayer really is.

Even so, living out the vision, and modelling the invitation to follow it, is something that will, sooner or later, require the KGH priest to dabble his toes in the dangerous waters of leadership.

Leadership: the most commonly used and least understood word bandied about in church circles today. Every parish wants 'leadership', just as every politician wants to introduce 'change', and every pop musician wants 'respect'. It sometimes seems that the Anglican Church is based on the fourfold structure of Scripture, Tradition, Reason and Leadership: and we have already seen wherein the authority of that leadership abides (see page 6).

This is very dangerous ground. If we are not careful, we will fall back into the worst danger of Herbertism: 'Messiahism' (see p. 159 above).

John Adair has collated the top ten attributes valued by the chief executives of a range of successful businesses. This is what makes a successful leader: the ability to take decisions; leadership; moral integrity; enthusiasm; imagination; willingness to work hard; analytical ability;

understanding others; ability to spot opportunities; ability to meet unpleasant situations.[9] Seemingly an unassailable list of qualities: which church community would quibble if their priest were able to personify all these virtues?

Of course, it is more complicated than that. The Archbishop of Canterbury, in a heartfelt article for *The Times*, wrote:

> Often people demand 'moral leadership' from religious figures. Confession time: like others, I suspect, my heart sometimes sinks when I hear this, and I think, cynically, that it's just about people wanting religious leaders to tell them that they're right.[10]

This is the ecclesiastical version of the philosophy of Alexandre Ledru-Rollin, minister of the interior in the French government of 1848. As trouble enveloped the Second Republic, Ledru-Rollin is alleged to have declared: 'There go my people, I must find out where they are going so I can lead them.'[11]

There is a real suspicion within church circles of the concept of leadership when expressed in this 'great person' mode, a suspicion which comes from two directions. First, it is an idea contaminated by its use in the world of business (look at the adverts in the back of journals like *The Economist* for courses offered by the business schools of the world on 'leadership', or the shelves of airport bookstalls selling the latest solution to the leadership problem for international business travellers): there is a 'reasonable wish to manage the church at many levels', Wesley Carr puts it, 'without . . . selling out to the secular themes of management techniques'.[12] Simultaneously, too much of secular, business talk about leadership functions in a 'great person' mode, which smacks too much of the old idea of 'Father says . . .' 'Leadership' is shorthand for 'telling people what to do', and is therefore to be heartily resisted.

Of course it is right that 'leadership' within the Church should not be the same as 'leadership' within secular business. Charles Handy points out the dangers, if not the impossibility, of imposing this mode within a church community.[13] But this doesn't mean that the idea of leadership is by definition impossibly tainted for church use. Elizabeth Welch draws out the biblical grounding of an understanding of church leadership which is creative: 'Leadership in the church has its foundation in our understanding and interpretation of God and God's purposes for the world. The most creative church leadership is that which is deeply rooted within the life of God.'[14] David Brown, in a pamphlet for the Foundation for Church Leadership, asserts that 'leadership' is implicit in Christian revelation, as can be seen in the thoroughly biblical and pastoral collections of ideas he says should be associated with church leadership:

> . . . confidence of the led; ability to enlist willing co-operation; sympathy to the needs of the led; loyalty; consistency/trustworthiness; clarity of thought and communication; ability to listen; willingness to change one's mind; cheerfulness and enthusiasm; largeness of heart; willingness to take responsibility for mistakes; absence of self-seeking, jealousy and resentment; good personal knowledge of the led and concern for their welfare; self-control and consistency; tact and consideration; being transparently straightforward; moral courage; professional knowledge and competence; humour; sense of justice; determination; approachability; team-player . . .[15]

All these qualities place leadership firmly against the old model of the lonely Messiah: it has no place in the future of Christian leadership:

> Leadership, in seeking to draw a community into creative harmony and purpose, is intrinsically pro-teamworking and therefore to an extent counter-individualist, and will routinely face indifference within the Anglican setting.[16]

But, Brown goes on to say, it is not just indifference to the idea of leadership within the Church of England. Often the structures of the Church themselves, both inherited and newly devised, actively militate against the expression of a true form of leadership, which he calls 'unrobed friendship'. This idea derives from his experience of working under the leadership of an admiral of the Royal Navy:

> Aside from his essential professionalism the admiral's particular hallmarks were friendliness and humility. It was as though he regarded 'rank' as an encumbrance. Except on the more formal occasions, he removed it like a robe and related to people as an ordinary human

> being. We all felt valued and respected regardless of rank or role, and were drawn into his circle of friendship.[17]

This 'unrobed friendship' is almost impossible to find, according to Brown, in today's Church:

> The imaginings and activities of clergy and parishes cannot be stimulated, inspired and led from an 'office' or a committee; it has to be a 'person', and one who identifies and engages closely with them. Yet the Church's systems have tended increasingly to relieve bishops of significant components of their engagement with clergy: spiritual and professional nurture, training, parish appointments, pastoral care, encouragement and ministerial development, counselling, active involvement when things get difficult and in a small number of cases, discipline.[18]

Perhaps we might think, in a rare case of 'the grass is greener on someone else's church lawn', this is a structural problem of an old, formal, institutional, (dying?) church? Surely this is a matter in which we can learn from the powerful, prosperous and growing churches of the new evangelical movement? Not so. Michael Spencer, a Baptist minister, school pastor and post-evangelical commentator, says this about the place of leadership within American evangelicalism:

> Evangelicals constantly talk about leadership, basically because they have very little ability to lead, aside from either natural charisma, or manipulation. Actual servant leadership, which Jesus commanded and modelled, requires such an amazing investment in the lives of people that most people don't even want to climb that hill, and in large churches it's impossible to do anyway.[19]

We obviously do not want to build our ministry on foundations of natural charisma or manipulation. We want to see what we can take from the model of Jesus's ministry to apply to our own, just as the Ordinal instructs us to do.[20] Here John Adair is a useful guide.[21] He gives us four aspects of Jesus's leadership.

First, Jesus's leadership was expressed on a *journey*. His vocation, beginning with the beginning of his pastoral ministry in the baptism by John, was to proclaim the coming of the kingdom of God on a journey which leads from the riverside at the Jordan, through the towns and byways of Galilee, to Jerusalem for the confrontation with the power of death and evil. It is significant we are told that, following his baptism, 'the Spirit immediately drove him out into the wilderness' (Mark 1.12). It is easy to read this as meaning Jesus was sent further away from human civilization, but the wilderness he was driven into was that which lay between the River Jordan in the lowlands and Jerusalem high on the Judean hills: being driven into the wilderness was the first step to Jerusalem and his passion. So, 'a leader is the person who, in one form or other, shows the way on that common journey'.[22]

There is a shadow side to this aspect, a shadow side that was not present in Jesus, the perfect human being, but is potentially present in his imperfect human followers. A journey involves a change: a change of scenery, a change of outlook, a change of attitude. Change is difficult to accomplish because change requires us to move from somewhere in which we might have become comfortable. The journey we are required to go on with Christ is emphatically *not* about making ourselves more comfortable: 'from glory to glory' is the phrase, not 'from comfort to comfort'. The goal is transformed lives; the means to that transformation is easily resisted.

A senior priest I know of, in his more despairing moments, finds it hard to recall a single transformed life in more than 35 years ministry. The goal is the kingdom of heaven. The journey involves arguments about the flower rota. This is an understandable danger, and such loss of perspective can sometimes be the first sign of a more dangerous spiritual or psychological malaise. If the impedimenta of parish life are getting in the way, then the KGH priest has ample resources to step back, refocus and renew. Retreat, emotionally and spiritually; review; regroup. Leave the flower rota (or whatever the presenting triviality might be). If it is truly important, it won't go away. If it isn't important, then it might have resolved itself, or, better dissolved itself by the time you are prepared to return your attention to it.

Ronald A. Heifetz, who teaches on leadership and governance at Harvard Business School, has a grimly realistic view of what constitutes leadership: '. . . exercising leadership might be understood as disappointing people at a rate they can absorb'.[23] Retreat, functioning like a spiritual and emotional 'pause button', slows down the rate of absorption!

Second, Adair notes that Jesus's leadership was expressed through what we now call *teamwork*. Some disciples he called, some disciples chose him, and a motley crew it was too. But, as Adair notes, most of Jesus's disciples, at least those who followed him in the early days of his Galilean ministry and those who were close enough to him to be counted among the twelve, were men from the agricultural lands of Galilee: 'fields, orchards, vineyards, gardens and olive groves' along with the fishing grounds of the Lake itself required men to work them, and to work them in teams. Adair notes that the English word 'team' derives from the Anglo-Saxon name for the set of draught animals, hitched together by the *téam* (Old English for the rope which bound them). A team was made up of 'yoke-fellows'. No wonder Jesus promised, 'Take my yoke upon you, and learn from me; for I am gentle and humble in heart, and you will find rest for your souls' (Matthew 11.29). 'Come to me', he says, 'and I will make you a team.'

But it is important to remember that this team was not a military troop. Jesus's instruction (to some) to 'Follow me' might have been obeyed, but many disciples chose, at one point or another, not to follow him. At the last, all but one had fled, and even he, John, was at the foot of the cross to protect the women who remained faithful. We shouldn't think that the centurion, the man under authority (Matthew 8.5–13), was the model for Jesus's team (although there is an element, I like to think, of 'Wouldn't my life be easier if all my followers were like you!' in Jesus's reaction to him). Only slaves and soldiers have to obey orders on the pain of punishment: instead Jesus called his disciples 'friends' (Luke 12.4; John 15.15).

> There is no trace of hierarchy or inequality in the relation of friendship. Arguably, to be a friend stresses freedom more than to be a brother or sister, where there is a tie of 'blood'. 'My friends' suggests the companionship, camaraderie of those who work together in a common cause.[24]

But beware of creating a false intimacy with people for whom you care. This can expose the KGH priest to all the dangers of co-dependency, a psychological concept developed from addiction treatment. Fred Lehr defines co-dependency in this way:

> A set of maladaptive behaviours that a person learns to survive in an experience of great emotional pain and stress and that are passed on from generation to generation. These behaviours and their accompanying attitudes are self-defeating and result in diminished capacity. Co-dependents do not take adequate care of themselves and are far too controlled by (or controlling of) other persons' behaviours and attitudes.[25]

It is understandable when applied to alcohol, abuse of drugs (legal or illegal), and other destructive behaviour, but how can this apply to the relationship between a priest and his parish? Lehr points out, following the work of Gerald May, that a person may be addicted to subtler things: approval, being good, being helpful, being needed, popularity, worthiness, praise.[26] And furthermore, he asserts that 80 per cent of helping professionals exhibit evidence of this characteristic. Even if the figure is not as high as this, the reality certainly exists, as noted by Fraser Watts:

> Like many people in the caring profession, clergy may be meeting their own emotional needs by helping other people. They can project their own neediness onto members of the congregation, and meet their own needs vicariously while ostensibly helping other people. This can result in an unfortunate pattern of encouraging excessive dependency in the congregation to help maintain the minister's own emotional adjustment.[27]

According to Lehr there are six different co-dependent roles:[28]

- *Chief enabler* (the person who keeps the show on the road);
- *Scapegoat* ('when failure belongs to the clergy rather than the members of the congregation, volunteers can function more easily');
- *Family hero* (the example of righteousness to which all members of a congregation aspire);*
- *Lost child* (many church communities are predicated on one person being perfect, and the imperfections in that person, the clergy, cannot be acknowledged);

* Church of England clergy aren't called 'vicar' for nothing, believing and behaving things on behalf of their congregations, vicariously.

- *Rescuer* (when mistakes are made, it is the clergy who will make things right);
- *Mascot* (the clergy are the provider of comic relief for the church family).*

All these roles are the product of an incomplete emotional and psychological development in the individual, and continue through a lack of self-awareness. It is not inevitable, however, that co-dependent roles must continue for ever. We'll touch on some of the strategies useful in overcoming them in a little while.

Adair's third category for Jesus's leadership is *vision*. Jesus's ministry (at least in Mark's Gospel) begins with the clearest possible statement of that vision: 'The time is fulfilled, and the kingdom of God has come near' (Mark 1.15). The power of this vision, the radical nature of Jesus's understanding of what the 'kingdom of God' meant, Adair explains by the financial concept of 'zero-basing'. This is a method of budgeting in which all previous budgets are set aside, a line is drawn under them, and every item is newly costed according to present need, rather simply applying a percentage increase or decrease to the previous figures.† In other words, Jesus's zero-based vision says this: let us assume that the kingdom of God really has come near. What will that do to all our previously held assumptions about how life, society, culture, religion, hope and fear should be organized? What difference will the kingdom of God drawn near make to our lives? As Shaw says, the difference for Jesus and his followers was radical:

> Jesus' own vision was about the clarity of his purpose and the necessity of his early death. He had a vision about his followers; he sends them very explicitly into the world to preach the gospel. Jesus was visionary for his followers because he looked at the world and the way people live in a very different way. Achievements were not based on keeping the law but on demonstrating love.[29]

The shadow-side danger is confusion between the vision and the visionary, the tendency of spiritual projection to take place, in which the

* Think of any number of depictions of clergy in popular culture, from Ian Carmichael, Derek Nimmo, Dawn French, to any role played by Rowan Atkinson.

† Unlike the perennial methods for calculating parish share.

clergy become the holy ones, impossibly separated by an unbridgeable gulf from the laity. This is untrue, and because it is untrue, it is unsustainable; but, as it is the product of subconscious psychological dynamics, when it finally breaks down, those who were responsible for the untrue projection in the first place will react with disappointment (at best) and anger (at worst): 'I thought you were different, Vicar, but you're just the same as all those other, disappointing, hypocrites.' Fred Lehr warns clergy:

> We are not holy. We are only to serve as the conduits for God's holiness that it might flow through us on to God's people. Our role is not to save the world [Messiahism], but to empower, equip and inspire others that they may be freed and emboldened to do that blessed task.[30]

In a different environment, this is much the same sort of role as played by an international rugby coach. Scott Johnson, for a short time the coach of my beloved Welsh rugby team, said this about his job: 'Without banks a river would be just a bloody great puddle. I'm the bank.'[31] Exactly. The KGH priest's job is to remember that God is the river. We are no more than the bank. We need to get out of the way and let God flow. Mychal Judge, Roman Catholic chaplain to the New York City Fire Department, and killed in the attack on the World Trade Center in September 2001, expressed the same idea in a prayer:

> Lord, take me where You want me to go;
> Let me meet who You want me to meet;
> Tell me what You want me to say; and
> Keep me out of Your way.[32]

Fourth, Jesus's leadership was expressed in *service*. It is hardly necessary in this day and age to count the ways in which Jesus's ministry was that of a servant: surely the number of times and circumstances in which Jesus described how the values and hierarchies of the kingdom are the inverse of the world's values and hierarchies will be familiar to us all? Those who seek places of honour will lose them (Luke 14.7–14); he subverted the expectations of honour of his disciples (Matthew 20.20–28; Mark 10.35–40; Luke 22.24–27); he condemned those who sought public status and respect (Matthew 23.5–12). A less noticed emphasis can be found in a conversation he had with his disciples on the road to Capernaum:

> 'What were you arguing about on the way?' But they were silent, for on the way they had argued with one another about who was the greatest. He sat down, called the twelve, and said to them, 'Whoever wants to be first must be last of all and servant of all.' (Mark 9.33–35)

It is not 'a servant' but 'servant *of all*'. Adair believes that Jesus's servant leadership is distinguished by an 'unqualified availability',[33] but this does not mean that Jesus allowed access unlimited in time and place to people: we know this was not the case. There were times when Jesus made himself deliberately unavailable to those who might have needed him (e.g. Luke 9.18 or John 6.15): easier in a world without broadband and Mobile 3G. However, there was no qualification on the *sort of person* for whom he would be available. Pharisees, members of the council, artisans, farmers, the great and the good – yes. But also children, and women, and the mad, and the unclean, prostitutes and tax-collectors, Samaritans and Romans. 'Serving others in love is a fundamental discipline of the Christian. Servanthood teaches us to follow the example of Jesus by rejecting ego and self-promotion in favour of humbly seeking to meet the practical needs of others.'[34]

What does this mean for the KGH priest? It might help to remember that ministry is for all, and not just for the noisiest, the most demanding or the most difficult.* For 80 per cent of clergy, according to Savage and Boyd-MacMillan, 'one of the greatest stressors in their lives was that one *really* difficult person in their congregation'.[35] Savage has given us some of the possible causes of these difficult people on page 60. The inevitable consequence of dealing with difficult people is conflict; such an important part of the KGH priest's ministry and leadership, that it deserves a whole pillar to itself.

If the KGH priest recognizes the proper place of boundaries in time and place, then he or she must also recognize the proper place of

* An experienced priest once said to me that a particular parishioner in his congregation reinforced for him the reality of the 'Body of Christ' imagery of Paul: 'in this Body of Christ, she is the appendix: of no discernable purpose, but always grumbling'.

boundaries for personality. An expression of service should not mean the abnegation of the self: '. . . if selflessness arises from not being able to *be* a self, this simply enables others to be abusive or selfish in response. This is very different from selflessness that owns a self, but then puts it aside for the sake of other people.'[36]

This is where another application of systems theory can help, developed from the work of Murray Bowen.[37] Bowen taught that a person develops into maturity by gradually learning that he is something (someone?) different from his mother; this is called separation–individuation. 'The human infant moves from early stages of being fused, symbiosis with the mother, to separating from the primary caregiver, to becoming a separate, distinct self.'[38] Crudely, just as a child is weaned from its mother's milk, the child is weaned psychologically. If this process happens successfully and healthily, then a successful and healthy adult is the result, someone who finds no difficulty in defining themselves separately from others, and yet is not threatened by the proximity (physical or emotional) of those around them. Or, more succinctly: 'Differentiation is the ability to remain connected in relationship to significant people while choosing not to allow our behaviour and our reactions to be determined by them.'[39] But if the process doesn't happen successfully, if childhood trauma (physical or emotional) interferes, then the person remains in a state of emotional immaturity: there is insufficient differentiation between the individual's identity and the world outside.

> The ultimate outcome of such situations is a predisposition for diminished self-esteem and repeated attempts as adults to find an 'ideal parent' in their own children or partners – or parishioners in the case of clergy. The emotionally vulnerable spiritual leader, craving admiration and appreciation, may minister to an ever-expanding workload of needy, bereaved, and troubled congregants . . .[40]

However, do not despair. KGH priests, because they place quiet prayer so centrally in their life and ministry, and regard self-awareness, not as self-absorption but as a necessary tool for ministry, are able to 'change the script' that might have caused such diminished self-esteem. As Savage and Boyd-MacMillan put it, 'Our own effort and self-awareness [can be] empowered and guided by the Holy Spirit'[41] in the renewing of identity and relationship.

There are many good guides to this process of individuation.[42] The KGH priest will seek opportunities for learning more. In the meanwhile, she will endeavour to set clear boundaries:

- I will be leader, but you must want to be led.
- I am responsible for my own feelings and my own decisions. I am not responsible for yours.
- If we disagree, then we disagree. We can still work together.
- I will help us articulate a vision, but you must then want to speak it, and act upon it.
- If our vision is reduced to 'keeping the show' on the road, or 'the vicar being nice to those of us who bother to turn up', then you must be prepared for me to find other means of expressing my vocation as a Christian minister, other forums for me to explore what it means to be a Christian disciple.
- I am not a 'professional' Christian; I am an amateur at this. I am doing it, not for money, nor status, nor power, but for the love of it (for the love of him). Don't think that I can carry your need for holiness as well as my own. Let's carry them together.

It might seem from all this that the antidote to Messianic Leadership is to encourage collaborative working at all levels within the Church. All we need to do is encourage people to work together, with no one individual possessing the 'final say'. However, we will see in the next pillar that the solution is not so simple.

13

Know how to make decisions: Reckoning

> The clergy should promote collaborative ministry across the whole range of church life and activity. It is important to recognize and affirm lay ministry that already exists and to encourage new ministries, both lay and ordained. The clergy should be ready to assist others in discerning and fulfilling their vocation and to acknowledge and respect the range of experience amongst the church membership.
>
> (*Guidelines for the Professional Conduct of the Clergy*, 2003)

It may not be a surprise to you, but the concept of 'collaborative ministry' has little or no presence in Herbert's *The Country Parson*. Anglican irony aside, the truth is actually the exact opposite: the country parson is antithetical to anything which we might regard as collaboration. The title of chapter 20 should give us some clue: 'The Parson in God's Stead'. Herbert is not kidding here:

> The Country Parson is in God's stead to his Parish, and dischargeth God what he can of his promises. Wherefore there is nothing done either well or ill, whereof he is not the rewarder, or punisher . . . *both in rewarding virtue, and in punishing vice, the Parson endeavoureth to be in God's stead, knowing that Country people are drawn, or led by sense, more than by faith, by present rewards, or punishments, more than by future.*[1]

And so it remained for many, many generations of ministry (as we saw in 'Death to Herbertism' above). The parson in God's stead was the ecclesiology of the Church of England and was 'declared to be the true inheritance of the early church and the ministerial arrangements could therefore be regarded as the guarantee of Anglican authority'.[2] What this meant in practice was that 'congregations in the 1970s were those who, on the whole, were expecting to be dependent on a godly man set apart who was given to them by the Bishop, and with whom [they] had to deal on his terms'.[3]

But things were changing. The work of theologians such as Ramsey, Allen, Barry, Robinson, Küng, Schillebeeckx, Boff, Suenens, Möltmann and Zizioulas[4] began to be regarded by the official teaching of the Church. In Venice, in 1976, the Anglican–Roman Catholic International Commission (ARCIC I) published a short statement on authority in the Church. In it, we find the first official explorations of the 'mutual responsibility and interdependence' of all those who exercise ministerial authority. Authority is a network within the service of the Church, not just a chain of command. Furthermore:

> Ordained ministers commissioned to discern these insights [a deeper understanding of the Gospel] and give authoritative expression to them, are part of the community [*koinonia*], sharing its quest for understanding the gospel in obedience to Christ and receptive to the needs and concerns of all.[5]

This is radically different from Herbert's 'God in the parish', and the training and formation of parish priests which produced 'God in the parish' could no longer cope with a distributed authority and a mutual interdependence. The Church of England needed a new pattern of training its ministers, so, as always, she commissioned a report.

The *fons et origo* of the official role that collaborative ministry would play in the Church of England was an Occasional Paper produced by the Advisory Council on the Church's Ministry in 1987 (two years before I began training). In *ACCM 22*,[6] the 'ordained ministry which the Church of England requires' was examined from (almost) first theological principles. The new pattern of training for the contemporary understanding of ordained ministry would require every ordinand 'to be prepared to work in a collaborative manner, to achieve appropriate networks of communication and to be personally capable of building up interrelations'.[7] Collaborative Ministry (CM) had arrived.

From an Occasional Paper, the idea and culture of collaborative ministry grew and grew, until the whole of the Church's thinking about ministry was expressed under its shade. Andrew Bowden and Michael West noted in 2000 that the number of dioceses with local ministry schemes (formal implementations of CM) had grown from three to eighteen in seven years: 'Most dioceses are persuaded that God is calling his church to a collaborative model of ministry where clergy and laity work together to bring about the transfiguration of the world which we believe to be his will.'[8]

Look at the way in which CM functions as the organizing principle in, for example, the report produced by the 'Pastoral Strategy Review Group' of Brighton and Hove Deaneries in the Diocese of Chichester (2003). Here we read that the purpose of the report is:

> . . . to establish the framework by which every church community will be under the leadership and guidance of an ordained minister whose role will be to act as shepherd to that community of faith whilst working alongside lay members enabling them to exercise their ministerial role. (§1.2)

The ordained minister is to ensure the equal distribution of the ministry of the whole Church: 'Within each church community it is essential that the tasks of ministry are shared between lay and ordained ministers' (§3.4.3). And, like Greenwood, this is seen as the joyful overthrowing of old oppressions:

> . . . leadership has to value and affirm the ministry of all the people of God. It must be collaborative ministry among lay and ordained colleagues. We firmly believe that there is no place for authoritarian or dictatorial concepts in the Church of England today, if there ever was a place for it. (§3.8.2–3.8.3)[9]

CM is now, officially, the way the Church of England does ministry. The Ministry Division of the Archbishop's Council said, in 2003:

> We make proposals to provide high-quality training for the clergy that will equip them to offer vibrant and collaborative spiritual leadership and to empower a vocationally motivated laity – and, thereby, to promote and serve God's mission in the world.[10]

It has become part of the *Guidelines for the Professional Conduct of the Clergy*;[11] the new Ecclesiastical Terms of Service legislation, passing through Synod and Parliament as I write, requires the Archbishops' Council to issue directions on 'procedures for enabling the capability of an office holder to perform the duties of his or her office'.[12] Such capability procedures will be designed

> . . . to help people to improve and to deal with problems of poor performance before they become too serious to be remedied. It is about ensuring that people have been made fully aware of what is required of them. Proper resources need to be made available in order to give people the opportunity – through training, counselling and other means – to equip themselves to improve their performance (where this is necessary) and to realize their full potential.[13]

And, as we have seen, CM is certainly something that is required of its ministers in today's Church of England. It is the model of an ultra-modern minister.

The trouble is, CM is not very clearly defined. We all recognize collaboration when we see it, but we have great difficulty in defining it. The contributors to a MODEM book, presumably people who are experts in adapting models of ministry to the new orthodoxy, also found difficulties with definition: 'Collaboration is an ambiguous term . . .' and '. . . collaborative ministry – a much talked about subject but rarely are we advised exactly how this collaboration is supposed to work!'[14]

Wesley Carr, one of the early explorers of new patterns in *The Priest-like Task* (1985), now seems to have an entertainingly dyspeptic view of collaboration culture. Those who were formed by this new paradigm:

> . . . brought an avowed collaborative model of ministry. Although the precise meaning varied, it seems chiefly to mean reducing any sense of difference between, for example, lay and ordained. Within the church's activity the differences are minimised. For example, some advocate (and illicitly practise) abandoning clerical dress and from some directions an increasingly strident call comes for lay celebration of the eucharist. Such stance, together with the notion of 'enabling', became prominent. The consequent image was of a minister/leader sitting at home at the computer sending messages to his/her collaborators for implementation by ministry groups led by other ministers/leaders.[15]

Andrew Dawswell, in a survey of the implementation of Ministry Leadership Teams in an enthusiastic diocese, Lichfield, is also pessimistic about the practical working out of the CM paradigm:

> There are a number of teams which have been a significant source of conflict in their parishes. Many 'medium performing' teams do not yet seem to have repaid the time and energy invested in them. Far from providing a release from previous burdens on clergy, managing and leading the team in many instances seems simply to add to the long list of tasks to be done. Even in the more obviously 'successful' teams, significant tensions and differences of understanding can sometimes be observed.[16]

So what is the KGH priest to do? I think it is important to realize that a false dichotomy has been presented to us in the last 25 years. We have been told that the choice is between 'the Parson in God's stead' and all-member ministry, between 'the benign priesthood shepherding a passive flock'[17] and 'all Christians are called through baptism to share in the ministry and mission of the church'.[18] We have been told there are two broad areas of justification for this: insights from scripture and insights from modern business management. Neither area is as clear as the advocates of CM would like to think.

As Dawswell points out, Greenwood's insistence on the primacy of 'social trinitarianism' as the organizing principle of the Church's ministry requires certain scriptural witness to be set to one side: 'If a truly biblical trinitarianism were applied to the relationship between clergy and laity, then the willing obedience of the son displayed in the garden of Gethsemane narrative [for example] . . . could in fact offer considerable support to the "father knows best" style of ministry.'[19]

Similarly, the influence of a collaborative working model in secular business upon the Church actually ignores the breadth. As Watts, Nye and Savage point out,[20] much of the change in the Church's method in decision-making derives from the work in the early 1970s of two social psychologists, Victor Vroom and Philip Yetton. Vroom and Yetton in *Leadership and Decision-making* developed a 'normative theory' (that is, describing a preferred method of working, and not just neutrally describing what might be actually possible) of four different methods in making decisions. These methods they labelled A (for 'Autocratic'),

C ('Consultative'), G ('Group') and D ('Delegated'). Some of the methods had variants, depending on whether or not the problem being decided belongs to groups or individuals. So, for example, decision method AI functions this way: 'You solve the problem or make the decision yourself, using information available to you at the time.'[21]

I think that Vroom and Yetton's method can be both simplified and nuanced. The KGH priest should have six different methods for making a decision within parish ministry, and they can be represented in table form:

A1	Autocratic	The priest makes a decision entirely unilaterally, using available information, and their own judgement and discernment.
A2	Directive	The priest seeks information from others, but then makes a decision unilaterally, using their own judgement and discernment.
C1	Consultative *(Individual)*	The priest consults members of the congregation individually, asking for their judgement and discernment, but then makes a decision unilaterally.
C2	Consultative *(Group)*	The priest consults within a group, asking for the judgement and discernment of others, but then makes a decision unilaterally.
G1	Group *(Democratic)*	The priest consults within a group, asking for the judgement and discernment of others, and the decision is reached through discussion and a vote.
G2	Group *(Consensus)*	The priest consults within a group, asking for the judgement and discernment of others, and the decision is reached through discussion and consensus.

Surely, this is heresy? We all know people who have no sense of humour, but we know of no one who admits to it. Similarly, which priest today would, willingly, admit to being autocratic (without also being self-consciously and tediously 'old school')? But, think about it. CM surely does not mean that *every* decision in a parish should be made by the widest possible grouping. There are some decisions which are relatively trivial (Which notices need to be removed from the church hall notice board? Is it OK to leave some bags of compost behind the boiler room for the churchyard working party? Can the junior school visit the church on Wednesday week?). There are also decisions which are properly reserved for the parish priest (Can a Muslim be a godparent in a christening? Can a wedding service include Queen's 'Don't Stop Me Now'? May Uncle Bert's ashes be interred in the churchyard?). There are also some decisions which, neither trivial nor reserved for the parish priest, could be made by the priest for the sake of the parish's better functioning: a long argument in the PCC meeting over the system for booking the church hall peters out into deadlock. Everyone is tired and bored by the process. The priest, after a thoughtful pause, says 'I sense there is no clear feeling one way or another on this matter. Neither can I see any clear path from where we are at the moment towards being able to make a decision. I therefore think, for the sake of moving on, that we will (decide to do x/decide not to make a decision at this time and return to the matter in a year's time.)' Everyone breathes a deep sigh of relief, and the meeting, and the mission of the Church, turns to more fruitful matters.

Another reason to be suspicious of consensus as the panacea for all decision-making processes within the Church is the phenomenon known as 'groupthink'. The word was coined by William Whyte in an article for *Fortune* magazine in 1952:

> Groupthink being a coinage – and, admittedly, a loaded one – a working definition is in order. We are not talking about mere instinctive conformity – it is, after all, a perennial failing of mankind. What we are talking about is a rationalized conformity – an open, articulate philosophy which holds that group values are not only expedient but right and good as well.[22]

The idea was developed by Irving Janis in his analysis of the mistakes made by the American foreign policy in the post-war period, especially in what happened at the Bay of Pigs disaster. He defined 'groupthink' as 'a mode of thinking that people engage in when they are deeply involved in a cohesive in-group, when the members' strivings for unanimity override their motivation to realistically appraise alternative courses of action'.[23]

In other words, people really *want* to work towards consensus, and human psychology is such that people will tend towards consensus, even when it is a foolish and irrational consensus. A visitor to the rectory door once gave me, for reasons never adequately explained, a fridge magnet which said, 'Beware the power of stupid people in large groups' (illustrated with a fetching portrait of Ronald Reagan in his leading man days): this is true and wise. A more pertinent warning for church leaders would be 'Beware the stupidity of *wise and clever* people in large groups'.

The dangers of groupthink are another reason why the KGH priest should not strive officiously for consensus at all times and in all meetings. Sara Savage, following Janis, recommends seven strategies to prevent group decision-making succumbing to groupthink:

1 Groups should have a clearly defined process for making decisions which begins with identifying the outcome of any decision and the values the group holds which will be expressed by that outcome.
2 The group could set up several independent groups to work on the problem, and allow those groups to consult outsiders.
3 The consequences (intended and unintended) of alternative outcomes should be assessed.
4 The group leader (the KGH priest) should refrain from participating in the decision-making process, and should especially not prejudice the framing of the process at its beginning.
5 Members of the group should take turns in playing devil's advocate, expressing potential objections to any decision.
6 The group should use outside expertise. It needn't necessarily be from paid consultants, but might be from within the church community; just not someone who has emotionally invested in any possible decision.
7 The group's process should be integrated into the life of the parish: it shouldn't become isolated – 'smoke-filled rooms' lead to bad decisions.

If this seems too weighty a system for making important decisions (and why should it?) Savage alternatively suggests that Chairs of PCCs should mutter under their breath 'Remember the Bay of Pigs' whenever equanimity breaks out.[24]

These processes are far more complicated, subtle and effective than the simple choice between 'Father says' and 'Whatever you want'. It will be hard work to introduce, especially to a church community which says it wants the latter (What do we want? Lay autonomy! When do we want it? Now! etc.) but secretly longs for the security and co-dependency of clerical hegemony. It might also seem to be far from the simple bromide of CM, CM and nothing but CM. However, as Savage concludes:

> Most of us in leadership tend to develop a decision style we feel comfortable with and use this inflexibly. According to this research, however, good leaders take account of the situation, and select the best decision strategy that accords with it . . . Choosing decision strategies is a skill that develops with practice, evaluation of previous decisions, and feedback from others.[25]

The next question which might occur to the parish priest emerging from Herbertian captivity is, 'How do you find time to manage all these demands?'

The Herbertian model has truly died in this aspect. As Robin Greenwood says (and Michael Hocking recommends!) until the 1970s the daily pattern of the parish priest's life was: 'The morning was for the study (really studying, yes even the New Testament in Greek) and the afternoon for visiting women and the elderly.'[26] The administrative changes of the 1980s and 1990s mean that the parish priest now has to be something of an 'ecclesiastical manager'.* How to manage that (and not go crazy)? How to fulfil the obligations of transparent administration, with efficiency and probity, and keep some time to do the priestly stuff as well?[27]

Guy Wilkinson acknowledges the difficulty of achieving this in the reality of a parish priest's life:

> Too often [administration] can be much more a case of just accepting each need as it comes along, than as part of a more or less deliberate patterning of the day or the week . . . [our approach becomes] . . . essentially responsive, with the urgent driving out the important and

* In the memorable words of an advert for a House for Duty post in a diocese in the south east of England, as printed in the *Church Times* in 2005.

> the separation of different areas of ministry from one another becoming more difficult with all the consequences for effectiveness that follow.[28]

The solution is to adopt a 'deliberate patterning'. John Truscott calls this deliberate patterning 'administry', a lovely portmanteau word which honours the importance of what it is that administration sets out to serve: 'Administration is the organization and co-ordination of the earthly resources that are available in the service of Christ.' Like the servant leadership of Christ, administry serves every other ministry; that is, it is in a *subordinate* position (despite the best efforts of some diocesan secretariats, the primary purpose of the parish church is not to get the October Usual Sunday Attendance figures in!); but it also *enables* every other ministry. Because the church community is about community, because the KGH priest is a Weaver, the ministry which enables every other ministry should be 'a creative, people-centred ministry'.[29]

So how do we approach this ministry? At best, we write 'To do' lists! Guy Wilkinson says:

> There's no substitute for keeping a running list that has your main current activities as headings and a subsidiary list of things you have to do under each. How satisfying it is to be able physically to cross them off. I have even been known to add an item that I have just completed just to have the satisfaction of crossing it off.[30]

The only response of the KGH priest to such advice is '!' – which signifies open-mouthed horror. What use is a 'To do' list if a priest does things which aren't on it? Where were those tasks being 'carried' (that is, being kept in the priest's awareness), if they weren't written down on the list? The KGH priest realizes that such a form of administration is nothing more than Herbertian idolatry, the worshipping of the great god Overwork.

What is the KGH priest's approach, then? The first step in achieving administry Nirvana is to buy, read, mark, learn and inwardly digest this book: David Allen, *Getting Things Done: The Art of Stress-Free Productivity*. David Allen understands the besetting problem for people working in the complex world of ideas, relationships and knowledge that defines much of the business world today: that problem is, inelegantly, 'stuff'. 'Stuff' gets in the way of doing your work; there's too much 'stuff' to deal with, and, if you are not careful, you start responding to the stuff in an unstructured, even panicked way. The noisiest stuff gets your attention first – or, worse, the easiest. 'Stuff' makes discerning the relative importance you should assign to each piece difficult if not impossible. And what is this 'stuff'? 'Here's how I define "stuff": anything you have allowed into your psychological or physical world that doesn't belong where it is, but for which you haven't yet determined the desired outcome and the next action step.'[31] If you have 'things to do', things which are floating around in the back of your mind, or scribbled down on the back of a service sheet, or exist as a knot in your handkerchief, then you are expending psychological and emotional energy in keeping that 'stuff' in existence. There is a subconscious process in your brain which is dedicated solely to making sure you don't forget to attend to that 'stuff'. It doesn't always work. Sometimes there is so much 'stuff' that your subconscious mind just says 'Go hang', and the important wedding visit, the tax return form and the article for the diocesan newsletter just don't get done. Allen calls this form of 'stuff' an 'open loop'.[32] It requires energy, energy which is almost entirely unproductive. As Merlin Mann says:

> So you sprint from fire to fire, praying you haven't forgotten anything, sapped of anything like creativity or even the basic human flexibility to adapt your own schedule to the needs of your friends, your family or yourself. Your 'stuff' has taken over your brain like a virus now, dragging down every process it touches and rendering you spent and virtually useless.[33]

Sound familiar? Allen's solution, *Getting Things Done* (GTD), has three basic requirements to process 'stuff', to manage the energy-sapping open loops.

1 Any responsibility you have which isn't completed needs to be recorded somewhere outside your head in a 'trusted system' (more on what constitutes a 'trusted system' in a moment).
2 You need to clarify what is your commitment to this responsibility, and what you need to do to act upon this commitment.

3 You need to organize a clear system of reminders and reviews to ensure that the actions are actually happening.

At this point you might actually think that the traditional 'To do' list will do just fine. Mark Forster, another time management guru, points out the weakness of the traditional list: it makes no distinction between what needs to be done, and what might be done, what is easy to do and what is difficult to do. Forster says that the traditional 'To do' list is an 'open list':

> . . . anything can be added to it. There is no line drawn at the bottom. You might start off your day with a list of twenty items. As you go through the day you action some of the items, but at the same time you are adding new things on the end of the to-do list. . . . There is always a big chunk of items that gets transferred from day to day without ever getting done. Very often it is the more difficult and challenging items that get left. These are likely to be the very items that will take your business or work forward.[34]

Think of an example from your own ministry. Have you ever had a 'To do' list which included such classes of items as 'Change posters on church hall noticeboard' and 'New stewardship programme' and (simply and unhelpfully) 'Youth worker?'? Both Allen and Forster argue that the traditional 'To do' list is an unhelpful way of organizing this sort of work-flow.* Mixed up here are completely different classes of things: some are actions, some are projects and some are aspirations. Allen gives a simple example of how to distinguish between the three. Consider the situation or problem which is most on your mind right at this moment – it doesn't matter what it is. It could be 'I really need a holiday'; it might be 'Dad can't manage living on his own any more'; it might be 'The PCC is no longer working as a team'. This is the *project*. Now, write down what it would take for this situation or problem to be resolved, completed. So, using our previous examples, resolutions might be: 'Go to the Riviera for two weeks in October', 'Have Dad

* This is not to say that some fantastic things haven't been achieved using 'To do' lists, but rather to say it is amazing they have been achieved despite using such a system. See multi-tasking/switch-tasking on pages 169–70.

move in with us in a granny flat', 'Reconstitute the PCC'. This is the *resolution*. Then, finally *write down the very next physical action necessary to move from the former to the latter*. 'Physical' action is very important here. It is not enough to put 'Muse about destinations'; 'Think about nursing homes', or 'Wonder about team-building exercises'. A physical action would be 'Fetch brochures from travel agent'; 'Telephone Age Concern to research options'; 'Arrange appointment with Parish Development Officer'. This is the *action*. Projects are anything which requires more than one action to resolve. Actions are physical things done (the clue is in the name), not aspirations.

Your projects and aspirations are up to you. Allen gives you a method for achieving them. He provides a five-stage system to manage, not your time, nor your information nor your priorities, but *your actions*. The five stages for Allen are *Collect*, *Process*, *Organize*, *Review* and *Do* (which might be a little overwhelming on first glance). But if we rename one of the stages, we get *Collect*, *Handle*, *Organize*, *Review* and *Do*: *CHORD*. The key to GTD is *CHORD*(!).

1 *Collect*. Everything that is on your mind, everything which is nibbling away at your subconsciousness, everything which you feel in some way is your responsibility, needs to be collected: written down and placed in a single spot. Allen calls this the 'collection bucket'. It doesn't matter what you use: in-tray, notebook, PDA, smartphone, tape recorder, computer, whatever. The only requirement here is that collection is 100 per cent: nothing should be left in your head.

2 *Handle* (what Allen calls 'Process'). The collection bucket needs to be emptied. There is no point in collecting all your anxieties and projects in one place if nothing is ever done to them. Emptying is begun by 'handling': this means going through everything in the collection bucket (notebook, in-tray, electronic file), and deciding what they are, and what you need to do with them. You do this by asking a single question: 'Does this need action (now)?'

   If the answer is 'No', then choose one of these three actions: put it in a reference file (it might contain information useful for some time in the future, but be ruthless with this – you'll be surprised how many things you file away for 'future reference' and never need again); put it in a 'Someday/Maybe' file ('Someday I will want to think about doing a distance MPhil. in Liturgics, but not this year'); or, most satisfyingly, bin it.

If the answer is 'Yes', then decide: is it someone else's responsibility? If so, delegate it. Is it my responsibility and can it be done in less than two minutes? If so, do it. Is it my responsibility but it will take more than two minutes to achieve? Defer it.*

3 *Organize*. This is the heart of the GTD system. This is where everything that either can't be done in two minutes or isn't someone else's responsibility gets apportioned planned attention time. Yes, organizing according to GTD involves lists, but these are not the traditional, mixed, action/aspiration/project/daydreaming type of 'To do' list. These are sorted: 'power lists'! There are only two basic types:
   (a) *Next Action*: this is the answer to the 'next action' question we explored above. Although you might want to achieve something complicated and nebulous, there will always be a step which needs to be taken first. This is the 'next action': 'the next, physical, visible activity that needs to be engaged in, in order to move the current reality toward completion'.[35]
   (b) *Waiting For*: this is the list by which you keep track of all the actions you have delegated to other people: Waiting for a telephone call to be returned? Expecting a reply from the diocesan finance officer about parochial fees? Waiting for a wedding couple to make decisions about hymn choices? All these go on the 'Waiting For' list. You will have an opportunity to chase them up in the next step.

Along with the two basic lists, there are two other categories which need to be applied to each item: 'Project' and 'Context'. 'Project' means, as we have seen, 'any desired result that requires more than one action step'.[36] So, in our original example of a 'To do' list, 'Youth worker?' is a project, the project of identifying, resourcing and employing a youth worker for your parish. The next action might be 'Call diocesan youth officer to discuss potential job descriptions'. We assign multiple-step actions a project name so

* I know of a priest who has a three-category handling process: 'stuff' gets assigned to either FRO ('Go away'), NMFP ('Not my problem') or AIDI ('Alright, I'll do it'). Almost GTD in its simplicity!

that we can track how we are doing in working towards the completion of that project. Not every next action can happen in the same place. Some actions need to use a telephone, or a computer for email, or a library for reference. Some actions even happen away from the vicarage desk ('Visit Harry Stamp')! It helps greatly in the final stage if each action is assigned to a context, a place where the job can happen. In this way it is possible to review a number of different actions which can happen when you are in the right context. For example, you note two or three things which need to be bought next time you are in a shopping centre: a pen for the parish registers, an item of school uniform, a copy of the Archbishop of Canterbury's latest book – all for different projects, purposes and parts of your life. But, if each action is assigned to the 'Errands' context, then you will be easily able to lump all three together, saving time and energy. Allen makes a number of suggestions for different contexts (see pp. 192–3 in his book), and everyone who implements GTD will have to find ones most appropriate for their own situation: contextual contexts! I happen to find the following list works well for my parish ministry: @Office, @Computer, @Phone, @Visits, @Errands, @Home, @Alone (useful for assigning 'thinking/considering' time), and, of course, @Church. Allen recommends adding the '@' prefix to each context to distinguish contexts from other types of list, and, if you're using computer-based lists, the @ sign ensures that the contexts will be sorted to the top of all other lists.

4 *Review*. It doesn't matter how well you sort out your projects and actions if you don't keep track of them. Reviewing your lists helps you trust them, releasing that subconscious energy used up by not trusting them for more productive purposes. How often, and when, you review will depend on your own needs, and what sort of a worrier you are. Allen suggests a weekly maintenance review, but many people will find a smaller daily review (a quick glance over everything on the 'Action' and 'Waiting for' list) helpful too. The weekly review is where you reconnect projects to actions, look at items in the Someday/Maybe category (is it now time to begin that MBA?), are there any messages, bits of paper, emails, 'stuff' hanging around that haven't been tied into the system? 'Review' keeps the system working, helping you to integrate what you would like to be

doing (a vertical axis) with what you are being required to do by others (a horizontal axis). Like Guy Wilkinson's pleasure in crossing off items on a 'To do' list, it is emotionally satisfying; but, in this case, it actually moves you forward.

5 *Do*. The point of GTD is, not surprisingly, getting things done. The first four stages, CHOR, might seem like a bit of a chore, but they are designed to make the final stage as painless and productive as possible: CHOR becomes CHORD. GTD builds a very low threshold to applying yourself to your work: indecision caused by overwhelming responsibilities has been sorted; vague and imprecise tasks ('Bring the kingdom of God to St Paphnutius's') have been broken down into much simpler actions ('Fix date for course on the Gospel of Mark'). Almost everything that needs to be decided about how and what to do has been decided: things can be done. Look at your lists, and, according to the time you have available, the energy you have available and the priority of the task, just do the next thing.

There are real benefits to following this system, and for investing the (relatively small) time and energy in getting it off the ground. As Merlin Mann, one of the great evangelists for GTD says:

> So, basically, you make your stuff into real, actionable items or things you can just get rid of. Everything you keep has a clear reason for being in your life at any given moment – both now and well into the future. This gives you an amazing kind of confidence that a) nothing gets lost and b) you always understand what's on or off your plate.[37]

The genius of GTD for the life of the KGH priest is that the system makes no distinction between 'personal' and 'professional' lives. The same process that will keep track of business meetings, returning telephone calls and compiling tax returns is the same process that will keep track of sustaining friendships, getting to the children's parents' evening, making time to see your spouse. The permeable boundary between 'work' and 'home' in the parish priest's life is *not* something that has to be negotiated by two different ways of being.

The KGH priest will use these techniques to help put into practice all that he or she has learned to be important:

> . . . building the kingdom of God alongside the people of God, and promoting the encounter between the people of God and the reality of God. This is what is important. Not everything in parish or diocesan life acknowledges or allows that. But the priest will remember what Tim Ferriss has said:
>
> 1 Doing something unimportant well does not make it important.
> 2 Requiring a lot of time does not make a task important.[38]

What you do is infinitely more important than how you do it. Efficiency is still important, but it is useless unless applied to the right things.

14

Know how to manage conflict: Reconciling

> The art of leadership is saying no, not saying yes. It's very easy to say yes.
>
> (Tony Blair, 1994)

Early in our survey of the problems of Herbertism we looked at the stresses under which Church of England clergy operate. We saw in Yvonne Warren's study (p. 58ff.) how conflict was the major source of that stress, and a large part of the conflict came from internal pressures. Many of her respondents felt unable to accomplish anything; they were aware of the gap between the ideal Christian minister presented in, for instance, 1 Timothy 3.2 ('above reproach, married only once, temperate, sensible, respectable, hospitable, an apt teacher') and their own inner, publicly unadmittable frailties; they felt the pressure of dealing with the disbeliefs and doubts of others, which sometimes formed into conflicting belief systems within themselves; the difficulties in seeking affirmation from a hierarchy whose apparent agenda has moved on to management and discipline rather than pastoral care, and so on.[1] Some of this internal conflict arises in the discrepancies between the priest's rule and role; that is, the person he is and the function he is expected to fulfil, and some of the arising pressures can be relieved by putting into practice the earlier pillars of the KGH method. If your Rule of Life is clear, and humane, and workable and open, if your job description and role responsibilities within your parish or ministry are similarly known and owned by as wide a group as possible, then many of these internal conflicts fall away.

But internal conflicts were only part of Warren's equation; there remains *external* conflict, and all the way through this survey we have stressed how important the healthy and sustainable dealing with conflict will be for the post-Herbertian priest.

We recognize that conflict is inevitable in all human relationships. It is a sign (among other things) of personal investment: we conflict because we care. Dean Hoge and Jacqueline Wenger say:

> Church members and their pastors make a similar emotional commitment [as in marriage] to their church, bringing sometimes radically different, unacknowledged ideas of just how the church should function, and what its goals should be. In both cases, conflict is a strong indicator that people are invested – that they really care about their marriage or their church. Where conflict is present, apathy is not a problem.[2]

And yet conflict is very rarely celebrated as evidence of life, or as an antidote to apathy. Hoge and Wenger's book, a survey of why pastors leave local church ministry in the major Protestant denominations in the United States, finds that dealing with conflict within congregations was the second-largest reason for leaving parish ministry: 27 per cent of the sample, with a further 10 per cent who had left because of conflict with denominational leader. This latter group 'felt that their denominational officials were invested in the avoidance of conflict'.[3]

What structural reasons might there be for this experience of conflict? Sara Savage suggests three possible explanations.

First, most churches are voluntary organizations, and the responsibilities of church governance are held by volunteers. This is a fine and good thing, until a church wants to act in a co-ordinated and uniform way: at this point, volunteers 'are bound to discharge their responsibilities on their own terms'.[4] If they are 'encouraged' not to, to discharge their responsibilities on the terms of a wider group or even on the terms of the individual parish priest, it is very easy for people just to walk away from the responsibility: this leaves the parish priest with the difficulties, at best, of coping with *phulaxal* ministry (see p. 45), or, at worst, a rump of passive–aggressive resistance. Hoge and Wenger report the experiences of Frank, a pastor in the Assemblies of God: 'Sometimes, if anyone else tried to do anything, any ministry within the church, it was like they [the antagonists] would cause problems or complain or at times it even felt like they were trying to run some [other church members] off.'[5]

Second, developing from this, and as Hoge and Wenger also realized, most church communities come together because people care passionately about what it is the Church stands for and means. People therefore often 'have strong views about what ought to be done, and how things should be done. They derive emotional satisfaction from things being done in the way they prescribe.'[6] Layered upon this emotional satisfaction is theological principle; 'I am doing things this way, because this is the way God wants them done.' Once God is enlisted on one side or another of a conflict, no matter how trivial the presenting issue might be, it is very difficult for the conflict to be approached flexibly or pragmatically. To do so would be to deny the importance of the principle and the importance of God!

Third, and again developing from the first two points, it is very hard for a church to develop a coherent mission plan (or even any form of agreed strategic thinking). Different, deeply held personal visions, coupled with a lack of sanction against volunteers who don't sing from the same hymn sheet, mean that it is hard to both articulate and adhere to a specific strategic plan: 'Different people within a church often have different objectives, but these are rarely openly acknowledged.'[7] The most obvious difference is between those who are committed to maintenance and those who are committed to mission, with the added difficulty that it is a very rare church which admits that it cares not a jot for mission, and wants all its energies focused on its present membership: *every* church is mission-shaped, whether it is or not!

These three structural reasons combine into the interesting phenomenon that conflict in church life is considered taboo: it 'can provoke dread, fear or anger',[8] or worse. Sometimes the process is this: not agreeing* is understood as disagreement, which is understood as conflict, which is understood as failure. Frank, a former minister in the Evangelical Lutheran Church of the United States, experienced this 'conveyor-belt' interpretation: 'There is a sense I had, and I think it's common to pastors, that if there is a conflict, then you [the pastor] did something wrong. It's very subtle. It's like, "If you were really good at this, this wouldn't happen".'[9]

A priest was sent into a multi-parish benefice unbriefed that one of his churches had been treated for many years as if it were a private chapel by a small group of people, dominated by one particular woman. When he finally realized this, and saw the damage their domineering

---

* Meaning both 'dissenting from another's opinion' *and* 'not affirming another's opinion'.

did to the reputation of the church in the wider community, he attempted (very gently) to rein in her control. The immediate response was a letter of complaint to the bishop. The priest quickly received a telephone call from the bishop's chaplain asking him to go easy on the complainant, because 'we wouldn't want her to go to the newspapers'. At his next ministerial review, he was encouraged to find a more conciliatory way of working with the impossible people in this particular parish. In the meantime, church life has all but died.

So, in short: conflict is inevitable in all human relationships. Conflict in church is also inevitable, and perhaps more so, because church life deals with important matters of principle upon which people are prepared to make a stand, no matter how melodramatically or disproportionately. Unhappily, at the same time there is a lower tolerance for conflict within church circles and a higher expectation of perfection in the relationships between professing Christians and their ministers. As Sara Savage says: '. . . it is no wonder church life can act as a poultice, drawing out problems that need transformation'.[10] Or, more picturesquely:

> The group spirit, or 'ego' of a church, conspires to make conflict a gruelling experience. One contributing factor is a prevailing norm of niceness. People are supposed to be 'nice' in church. Translation: no anger, no disagreement, no problems, *no* conflict.[11]

Along with these structural causes of persistent conflict in parish life, the personal contribution of clergy themselves must be admitted. Colin Patterson expresses the bewilderment of many clergy when he says: 'I was trained to handle conflicting *ideas*, but not how to handle conflicting *people*.'[12] Patterson sets out six different ways in which the clergy themselves can exacerbate the conflict inherent within parishes, by behaviour and fundamental personality traits.

Clergy, subconsciously believing that disagreement equals conflict equals failure, can attempt to suppress any expression of any disagreement that might possibly lead to conflict. They act as the Red Adair of the relationship world, flying around the parish fire-fighting and extinguishing flames before they become blazes. Distressingly, this is also a fine way of stoking up resentment in people not allowed to express what they think or feel about any important matters. Here we see the 'power of the clergy' (the power which remains) used coercively.

Alternatively, some clergy allow the dominant people of the congregation to set the agenda and frame the terms of the debate. They act like Ledru-Rollin, running to stay two steps behind the movers and the shakers of a church community. Unhappily, if clergy allow the domineering to dominate, they will find that others become resentful at the lack of a forum in which the 'underbearing' can be heard. This is the 'power of the clergy' again used not at all.

Sometimes clergy will attempt to follow St Paul and become all things to all people (1 Corinthians 9.22). By such means they may be won for the kingdom. Sadly, although clergy might be comfortable in holding contradictory roles in creative tension, usually this will be seen as duplicity by parishioners, especially if the multiple roles assigned to the individual clergyperson haven't been negotiated openly as part of a job description. This is the 'power of the clergy' hidden under camouflage.

Related to this, some clergy attempt to 'softly, softly, catchee monkey', hiding their real motives or agenda. They act like Moses: content to tell the people of Israel neither where they are going nor that there will be a short detour on the way. Woefully, this will lead directly to mistrust and opposition: people don't like to be treated as mushrooms. This is the 'power of the clergy' used by stealth.

In some parishes, of a particular churchmanship I suspect, clergy may be tempted to use the pulpit for personal rebukes, addressing those people who are being difficult or destructive. Clergy act like Samuel Parris,* convincing themselves that they are acting on behalf of God or their good offices, when actually it is an expression of hurt or mistreated ego. This is the 'power of the clergy' used unequally.

The final contribution noted by Patterson is when clergy attempt to deny their own anger involved in the conflict. This is the clergy acting as Ned Flanders, so terrified by the expression of negative emotions that they suppress them and remain in denial.[13] To believe that a priest must not get angry is what Patterson calls 'another role-based problem'.[14] This is the 'power of the clergy' turned against its holder.

Sara Savage suggests[15] there are five separate modes commonly used in dealing with conflict. The KGH priest is aware of these five modes, and aware of which one he tends to favour in a given situation.[16]

* The anti-hero of the Salem witch trials and Arthur Miller's play *The Crucible*.

The first mode regards conflict as a zero-sum game in which there are either winners or losers, and nothing else: conflict as *Competition*. Here the goal is control; of the terms of the conflict and the outcome. Disagreement is discouraged and the primacy of the priest's own point of view is paramount. Conflict, in this mode, is about right and wrong, and a low value is ascribed to relationships *per se*. In a church context, this is the mode most susceptible to being theologized: 'Your way or God's way'.

The second mode judges the issue in dispute not to be worth the battle: conflict as *Accommodation*. Here the prime directive is to sacrifice personal interests, to assume that conflict will always lead to disaster and that relationships must have priority. The antagonist's point of view is accepted, and peace is kept at any price. In a church context, this can slide dangerously into self-sacrifice on the altar of 'Nice', and then result in co-dependency ('a tendency to attribute all goodness to others, and all badness to oneself, so one must please others in order to be accepted').[17]

The third mode is a variation of the second. Conflict is hopeless and will result in disaster, therefore it is best averted: conflict as *Avoidance*. This mode will require the priest to withdraw and become remote or divert attention from the issue at hand. Paradoxically, this mode has a low value for both relationships and issues. It says, in effect, the issue is not worth the fight and the relationship causes too much pain, therefore I will avoid both. In the church context, like accommodation, avoidance might be mistaken for peaceable virtue ('He's a very *holy* man'), even though its roots could lie in cowardice.

The fourth mode regards conflict as an opportunity to bargain, and counsels those involved that the best solution will lie somewhere between the two positions: conflict as *Compromise*. Is it possible to look for win/win, even if what is won is only part of what was originally sought? Moderation is the virtue here, and although issues are important, they are not so important that relationships can be routinely sacrificed for them. In a church context such a mode would work well within the democratic and pseudo-democratic structures (such as committees and other aspects of church governance). But Savage warns about the possibility of *moral* compromise in other situations ('Perhaps we could let the pagans use the church on the *third* Sunday of the month?').

The fifth mode is what Savage calls truly win/win, in which one's own views are asserted in the expectation that others will be able to express theirs as well: conflict as *Collaboration*. Differences are celebrated, and the main concern is to identify the (real) issues at stake and to invite as diverse a range of opinions as possible. Collaboration therefore functions as an *inquisitorial* mode rather than the *adversarial* nature of previous modes. The assumption here is that there surely exists a solution which meets as many different points of view as possible.* It places a high emphasis on the possible goals to be achieved and the relationships of those involved in the conflict. Unhappily, in a church context it depends on the view that conflict is natural, neutral, normal, and must be experienced before a resolution can be found.

There is a slight problem, I feel, with this fivefold differentiation in approaching conflict. It uses normative theory in setting out the alternatives, and so, rather like Niebuhr's descriptions of the relationship between Christ and Culture, there is a distinct preference expressed in the criteria and descriptions used. Collaboration is to be prized above all other models.

We saw the same assumptions made when considering the different methods to make decisions within church: collaboration has become the *ne plus ultra* of decision-making and leadership, and yet we saw how the pursuit of collaboration to the exclusion of any other method can lead to unnecessary friction and the expenditure of energy more usefully applied elsewhere. Just as different styles of decision-making can be applied in different contexts, perhaps there may also be occasions in which collaboration isn't the only appropriate method of dealing with conflict? Perhaps one of the other four modes outlined by Killman, Thomas and Savage would be a better tool? We can find encouragement in the *appropriate* application of the other modes in the Kraybill Conflict Style Inventory (KCSI), developed by Ronald S. Kraybill, and reproduced in an appendix to their book by Sara Savage and Eolene Boyd-MacMillan.[18] Here the five modes are named *Competing/Directing*; *Accommodating/Harmonizing*; *Avoiding*; *Compromising*; and *Collaborating/*

* An example of this assumption at work was in the article by Madeleine Bunting in the *Guardian* just before the Lambeth Conference of 2008: 'If Anglicanism achieved an extraordinary "middle road" of both unity and diversity in the 16th century, when Europe was tearing itself apart over religious doctrine, then why can't it take up again that remarkable vocation in however small a measure, this time globally? In short, if Anglicans could do it over transubstantiation 400 years ago, why can't they eventually find a way to do it about gay priests today?' (Bunting, 'If They Did It Over Transubstantiation', 2008.)

Co-operating. They are represented, endearingly, by five animals: respectively a lion, a panda, a tortoise, a fox and an owl. The KCSI asks two basic questions: 'How committed are we to our *own agenda*? How committed are we to the *relationship*?'[19] Depending on the way we answer those questions, we have the beginnings of a means of understanding how we should use the five different modes of conflict resolution. So, for example, it would be appropriate to use a *Competing/Directing* mode when the issue is raised in an emergency: as Kraybill says, you don't seek consensus and collaboration when the ship is sinking. It would be appropriate to use *Accommodating* if you ever find yourself in the unpleasant situation of being powerless and liable to retaliation, or, alternatively the issue is trivial. You might use an *Avoiding* mode when the relationship is not a significant one, or if the time needed for a conversation and consensus is not available.* *Compromising* is most appropriately used in situations when the relationship is important; but, again, time is limited, or 'efforts to co-operate will be misunderstood'.[20] *Collaborating/Co-operating*, rather than being the default or only mode of operation, would be most properly used when both issue and relationship are equally important, a creative solution is needed, and it is reasonably possible to expect such a solution.

The power of the KCSI is found in the way it describes the 'shadow' side to these modes as well. For every situation in which it is appropriate to use one of these modes, there is another in which it will be inappropriate or harmful. For example, co-operating will sometimes be wrong to use if you are 'overloaded with "processing"' or 'the goals of the other person are wrong beyond doubt'.[21] To discern positive side and shadow sides of these five modes is the mark of wisdom and self-understanding, and a critical appreciation of the intensity of the conflict that is being experienced.

To develop this discernment, to learn how to use the modes as consciously chosen tools, and *not* instinctively lapsing into psychologically comfortable patterns, KGH priests need to know something about their own psychology and something about the psychology of those who are opposing them. There are many different ways to find help in this. One

* This is the only technique employed by Reverend Walter Goodfellow, the vicar played by Rowan Atkinson, in *Keeping Mum* (written by Richard Russo and Niall Johnson, directed by Niall Johnson, Summit Entertainment, 2005). Of course, he turns out to be employing a homicidal housekeeper.

method would be to study the TKI, mentioned in note 16, or the KCSI, which has the great virtues of being both cheaper and has its origins in church-based conflict resolution. Another way would be to seek the support of the Mennonites within the UK and the USA: as Savage encouragingly says: 'The London Mennonite Centre has made conflict resolution in churches a cornerstone of its ministry of peacemaking.'[22] Colin Patterson, an assistant director of the Bridge Builders programme, and whose Grove Booklet we have already cited, sets out in that booklet a programme of exercises and education for church communities.

In the meantime, and aware of the complexity of all these issues, how does the KGH priest manage conflict? A flip answer, but a true one, is: 'Very carefully'. There is no such thing as a simple, 'one size fits all', method for managing, minimizing, eliminating conflict from your church. As Patterson says: 'If you see a book with a title like *Seven Simple Steps to Resolve your Church's Conflict*, do not buy it.'[23] Conflict is a difficult, tenacious and multifaceted aspect of being human, and therefore requires a series of complex, tenacious and multifaceted approaches.

There are, however, three attitudes or mindsets which, if made your own, can help the KGH priest in assembling a multifaceted approach to conflict.

First, *admit it*. Allow yourself to accept the fact that conflict will exist within your church, and when it does emerge, that is a good thing. It shows that your congregation is human (not always immediately apparent) and that things are changing, in some way, within the structure and relationships of the congregation. Change means life (or the potential for life). The only part of your church community in which there is no conflict is the graveyard, and even then, the descendants of the dead can more than make up for it. Give thanks to God for disagreements: these are opportunities to clarify what it is you believe and why, and opportunities to explain your (singular and plural) beliefs to those who may not have had the chance to understand them before. Realize that conflict is much more often about the situation or the subtext than it is about the presenting issue, especially if the presenting issue is you. People are much more often dealing with projection than reality, particularly if they fall within the range of 'inflexible, maladaptive personalities' identified by Sara Savage.[24]

Second, once you have accepted the inevitability and the possibilities of conflict within your own congregation, then *educate others*. As

Savage, again, says, there is a belief that 'church should be a conflict-free zone of heavenly peace. [But] far from being a sign of failure, conflict is a growth point; it is a rare arena in which religious people are forced to relate honestly with one another.'[25] If this is so (and it is so!), then educate the lay leadership of the parish about it. Work with the churchwardens, the ministry leadership team (if you have one or its equivalent), the PCC. Eventually, offer a study day/prayer morning/evening discussion group (whichever is more applicable to your context) for the wider congregation. As Kenneth Haugk argues, antagonists in church operate in the space allowed them by the passivity of everyone else.[26] Education both removes that passivity and narrows the space.

Third, remember that it is not just DVD players and iPods which are equipped with *pause buttons*. Very often, when faced with conflict, the KGH priest's first reaction is the wrong one, in common with the first reaction of every human being. Conflict requires action, our primitive evolution-inflected minds tell us. Now! Really! I mean it! Now! Act! And so we act quickly, instinctively and thoughtlessly. Who can then be surprised if we choose to act in instinctive and unmediated patterns? This is where the pause button comes in. When faced with conflict, when an antagonist says something unexpected, hurtful or unfair, stop. Pause. Don't say anything; or, if you must say something, then say something like, 'This requires some thought and prayer. I realize that what you have said is very important to you, and to respect that I will need to think about it. I will get back to you.' In doing so you will have given yourself a chance to reflect on both what has been said and what may be the most appropriate way of responding to it. You will also have given your interlocutor an unexpected opportunity to reflect: perhaps, just perhaps, the contention won't be quite so contentious when you both next meet. It is exaggeration to say there is nothing that cannot be solved by the judicious use of the pause button – the opposite is certainly true, though: there is no situation which cannot be made worse by flying off the handle.

Jeremy Taylor, the Bishop of Down and Connor who lived through the political and religious turmoil of the Civil Wars and Revolution of the mid-seventeenth century (and so knew something about conflict), said this: 'Whether is the wiser man of the two, he who thinks and deliberates what to say, or he that utters his mind as fast as it comes?'[27] Let this stand as the motto for the KGH priest when faced with the challenges of conflict and reconciliation.

15

Afterword: Standing by Herbert's grave

> The Anglican Church can lead the way in tackling the problems that confront it only if it digs down to its own foundations, which are the gospel of God, the sacramental life, and the soundest learning that its clergy and laity can possess.
>
> (Michael Ramsey, *The Gospel and the Catholic Church*, 1936)[1]

If you were to measure the public image of the Church of England, as presented in diocesan newspapers and synodical addresses (deanery, diocesan, national,) month by month, it would be most encouraging. More news of fresh triumphs! Innovative projects, fresh expressions, increased take-up of lay ministry training courses, record numbers baptized/confirmed/ordained/attending the cathedral for Christmas worship! Perhaps you would be content with this. Here we are, living in the best of all possible worlds, and the Church has never been in such good shape.

But then you might be tempted to look for an alternative depiction. Don't read the religious correspondence of the mainstream media; don't look at the commentariat of the cyber-church (that way madness and blindness lie). Look at the job adverts in the back of *Church Times.* You'll see adverts for posts involving four, five, six parishes in a single benefice, with the opportunity for further, 'creative' sector ministry tacked on. Look in *Crockford* and see the history of the amalgamation of these benefices. Look at the number of benefices now being served by half-time, house-for-duty priests, simultaneously fulfilling other, deanery or diocesan, responsibilities. The disconnect between what clergy are expected to do, to achieve ('Be a fresh expression! Keep paying the quota! Both! And!'), and the means by which clergy are expected to achieve all this (sustaining the pattern of Herbertism), is getting bigger and bigger. It is impossible. So they leave.

In the 1970s Towler and Coxon estimated that the percentage number of clergy leaving parochial ministry every year was about 6 per cent of the total.[2] One improvement in the way the Church is managed since those days is the collection of statistics. The Church Commissioners compile lists of clergy numbers and publish them for our enlightenment. The latest figures available are for 2006.[3] Therein we learn that on 31 December 1990 the Church of England had 11,076 full-time stipendiary clergy. By 2006 that had fallen to 8,496 (of whom 7,001 were men – that's me on the end!). Each year between the two dates includes numbers of those who leave through 'Deaths in service', 'Retirements', or, euphemistically, 'Other losses'.* Each category averages 24, 344 and 258 respectively over the seventeen years recorded: 625 clergy lost every year to full-time stipendiary ministry through death, retirement and 'other' reasons. The 'other' reasons aren't broken down. The exit route for the twenty-first-century parson isn't clear cut. Today a clergyperson can leave full-time paid ministry through doors marked sector ministry, specialized ministry, freelance work, NSM, house for duty or permission to officiate (PTO). The figures as published don't give us the reasons for leaving. One man might move to PTO because he wants to paint the pictures he has always wanted to paint: another woman might move to PTO because she can't stand the bullying and the conflict dumped upon her. One woman might retire because she has reached 65; another man retires because his physical and mental health have been broken. Of course, the Church of England will lose a number of clergy every year to *Anno Domini*: how many is she losing to other, preventable reasons? 50? 100? 200? To lose any more than one clergyperson for such reasons is more than unfortunate. It seems like . . . what? Surely something more than just carelessness?

When I began writing this book I made the mistake of telling a number of people the title and the thesis. Clergy in diocesan ministry (the so-called senior staff) looked bemused and changed the subject quickly. Laity were either puzzled ('Who's George Herbert?', 'What have you got against a hymn writer?'), or angry ('How can you say that about him? I love his poems!'). I then had to launch into an explanation

* As the preamble explains: 'The losses and gains recorded under headings include people who have moved to and from posts which are funded by external agencies such as National Health Service Trusts, the Prison Service, mission agencies or schools.' There is no breakdown of the different categories of retirement (age or medical related).

of how I loved his poems too, and I was even quite fond of his memory, but I felt increasingly alienated by the way a *false* memory of Herbert was being used to keep the clergy of the Church of England today, now in the twenty-first century, in a Babylonian captivity, a fantasy of what we were, what we are and who we ought to be. This land is our land, this Church is our Church, this parish is our parish, this ministry is our ministry, because 'George Herbert', the icon, has granted it to us. Uniformly, clergy in parochial ministry responded enthusiastically: 'Yes! That's exactly it. Tell me what conclusions you come up with.'

My intention, in the first part of this book, was to show that the Herbertian fantasy has become a captivity, one that is no longer possible to endure in today's Church and society. There are connections, ecclesiastical and social sinews, between George Herbert's ministry and context (or, rather, what we fondly *imagine* Herbert to be) and where we actually are. But those connections have become so thinned and attenuated that, insisting on them, we will, at best, expect our clergy to fulfil a role which distracts from the real pastoral and parochial ministry required of us – or at worst, live a lie. We should read *The Country Parson*, just as we should read the spate of how-to books from the 1960s and 1970s, for historical interest, to examine the challenges our predecessors faced, and to see what they decided was important in their ministry. But we shouldn't think that the ministry of a council estate in 1950s Bristol, or the suburbs of south London in the 1970s, can be mapped onto our own circumstances, any more than we should expect the pattern of rural life in seventeenth-century Wiltshire to work for us today.

And yet, as I have shown in the second part of the book, there is a better theoretical underpinning for parochial ministry available, one based on the teaching and writing of people like Rowan Williams, Stanley Hauerwas, Dietrich Bonhoeffer, and (even) Benedict XVI, in which the 'right, good, old way' of Nicholas Ferrar[4] might be followed. Actually how old, how perennial, this right, good way is can be seen by the quotation from Michael Ramsey at the head of this chapter. Who could deny that the Church of England faces problems? Who can deny that foundations of gospel, life lived sacramentally, and sound learning, might just be the place from which to rebuild? And Ramsey suggested that 70 years ago!

In the final section I have proposed five different pillars upon which the KGH priest might build his or her own ministry, appropriate to their community and for their context: a ministry prepared for the reality of twenty-first-century life, and less concerned with replicating old, falsely learned patterns. This does not involve the overthrow of the parish system. I don't advocate, as some clergy have done in recent years, handing the keys to our parish churches back to some suitable authority (who? English Heritage? the local council?), and wandering off to rediscover house churches. (I feel a little like Mohandas Karamchand Gandhi, who, when asked by a patronizing English journalist, 'Mr Gandhi! What do you think of Western civilization?' replied, 'I think it would be a good idea!'. 'KGH priest! What do you think of the parish ministry?' 'I think it would be a good idea!'). The parish system, despite the advocacy of those inside and outside the church hierarchy, is not broken: it just needs setting free, and a step to setting it free would be setting its clergy free from the burden of Herbertism.

We stand at the grave of George Herbert, the unmarked grave somewhere in the chancel of St Andrew, Bemerton, and we join with the tens of thousands of our clergy predecessors in throwing the good earth of England upon his grave: 'earth to earth, ashes to ashes, dust to dust'. This is the reason we bury the dead, so we don't have to carry them around with us. Instead, we celebrate his ministry (of its time and place), and we celebrate his poetry (for all times and in all places), and we look to be priests of the Church in our own right (as much as we can be) and not in the shade of George Herbert.

My book began with an Anglican adaptation of a Zen story: if you meet the icon of your faith in your journey, be very suspicious, as it is more likely to be a projection of your fantasies than the real Buddha, the real George Herbert. Perhaps, then, it would be appropriate to finish with another Zen story, one which exemplifies the clear-sighted, confident and fearless attitude needed by the descendants of the parson of Bemerton today.

When a rebel army swept into town in Korea, all the monks of the Zen temple fled except for the Abbot. The general came into the temple and was annoyed that the Abbot did not receive him with respect. 'Don't you know', he shouted, 'that you are looking at a man who can run you through without blinking?'

'And you', replied the Abbot strongly, 'are looking at a man who can be run through without blinking!' The general stared at him, made a bow and retired.[5]

Appendix: A Rule of Life, based upon the Four Pillars of the Dominican Constitution

1 Prayer

Devote yourselves to prayer, keeping alert in it with thanksgiving. (Colossians 4.2)

Private prayer: I will begin each day in mindful meditation, aware of the presence of God in all my words, actions and thoughts throughout each day.

Common prayer: I will be diligent in sharing in the Common Prayer of the whole Church, by observing the canonical offices, and encouraging those in my spiritual charge to observe them with me.

Eucharist: I will celebrate the indiscriminate generosity of Christ by daily participation in the Eucharist, and so attempt to live eucharistically, in constant surrender and thanksgiving.

Confession: Recognizing that the call to live in truth and freedom requires me to surrender my illusions and self-camouflage, I will be regular in observing sacramental confession.

Retreat: With the example of Jesus's withdrawal from his public ministry before me, I will be conscientious in setting aside time for retreats, both directed and eremitical. I will undertake an annual week-long retreat and two night-away retreats before Advent and Lent.

2 Study

One does not live by bread alone, but by every word that comes from the mouth of God. (Matthew 4.4)

Daily: In reading the scriptures of the daily offices I will read them prayerfully, expecting God to speak to me through my reading of them. In doing so, I will 'waste time with God'.

Weekly: I will spend one working day a week in study, away, if necessary, from the rectory. This period of study will not be directed solely to preparation for preaching on the coming Sunday or Feast day; that is an additional task.

Annually: I will allot ten days a year for continuing ministerial education, possibly including a weekend. A budget for this will be agreed with the parish, supplementing, if necessary, the CME allocation from the diocese.

3 Community

Day by day, as they spent much time together in the temple, they broke bread at home and ate their food with glad and generous hearts, praising God and having the goodwill of all the people. And day by day the Lord added to their number those who were being saved. (Acts 2.46–47)

Family: God gave me my vocation to my family before he called me into ordained ministry. My family are the people and the place in which God has given me my wholeness, so I will honour this gift by paying them the appropriate time and attention. I will remember, and I will teach others in the community of believers, that my vocation to the priesthood and pastorate is mine alone, and is not shared by my family. They should not be treated as if they did.

Friendships: I will cultivate friendships inside and outside the parish, and allow myself the time to do so.

Parish: I will participate in all those activities of the church community which build up and foster loving regard for one another. I will cultivate a discernment of the needs of the parish, and seek to lead the parish in ways of love and reconciliation. I will watch especially for those who, through handicaps of body, mind, or manner, are unable to participate fully or easily in the life of the community, and will work towards ways of integrating them more fully into the life of the community, so that the wholeness for which Christ prays may be more perfectly seen. I will strive for unanimity, even if I do not always succeed in achieving it, for the striving is a sure guarantee of the working of the Holy Spirit.

Diocese: I will participate fully in the life of the wider Church, at deanery, diocesan and national levels, offering my skills and time and prayers to the service of the Church.

Society: I will spend one-twentieth of my time in non-church voluntary work.

Balance: I will seek to model a life lived in balance between work and leisure, commitments for which I am obliged and commitments for which I choose to respect. I will divide each week into 21 sessions (morning, afternoon, evening), and will plan to work no more than fourteen sessions, or 50 hours in a week. If exceptional circumstances require me to work more than this, then I will TOIL.* I will take one full day and two full evenings for personal refreshment (not 'off') every week, and as much of Saturday as circumstances allow me.

Accountability: I recognize that I am a priest under discipline, with legal and moral obligations. I will make use of the Diocesan Ministerial Review programme. I will agree four annual goals for my parochial ministry with the PCC, and those goals will be specific, concrete, measurable and obtainable. I will agree an annual goal for my wider ministry with the counsel and direction of my confessor, to whom, *in loco dei*, I will be accountable.

4 Ministry

With great power the apostles gave their testimony to the resurrection of the Lord Jesus, and great grace was upon them all. (Acts 4.33)

Preaching: 100 people might be in church on a given Sunday morning. Their presence gives a ten-minute sermon 1,000 minutes of attention. There may be 4,500 years of lived experience represented by the congregation. Can that attention and that lived experience be adequately and respectfully addressed by something prepared in no more time than it takes to preach? My sermons, therefore, will take a week to prepare, a session to write and a lifetime to follow.

Teaching: I will remember that my teaching ministry is not limited to those who choose to come to church on Sundays, and who are willing to listen to sermons. I will provide different forums in which people may learn: talks, films, house groups, exercises and activities. I will discover what needs to be taught in collaboration with the *laos*, and I will seek to improve my teaching with feedback, exploration and being taught myself. I will endeavour to find new ways to allow those *outside* the ecclesial community to hear the challenge and promise of Christ. I will be prepared to teach in places and forms that might be unrecognizable to earlier generations of worshippers. Preaching to those outside the Church has as much right to demand my time as preaching to those who choose to follow Christ within this community.

* Time Off In Lieu.

Notes

Part 1: Death to Herbertism

1. Sam Norton, 'Workload, Priorities, Vocation', *Elizaphanian*, 29 January 2007, <http://elizaphanian.blogspot.com/2007/01/workload-priorities-vocation.html>.

Chapter 1: Lin-Chi, the curate and the Anglican divine

1. Burton Watson, *The Zen Teachings of Master Lin-Chi: A Translation of the Lin-chi lu*, p. 52.
2. Isaak Walton, 'The Life of Mr George Herbert', p. 101–2.
3. Diarmaid MacCulloch, 'The Myth of the English Reformation', p. 10.
4. MacCulloch, 'Myth', p. 14.

Chapter 2: '. . . how many live so unlike him now . . .'

1. Arthur Waugh, introduction to *George Herbert: Poems*. Quoted in T. S. Eliot, *George Herbert*, p. 20.
2. Edward Herbert, *The Life of Edward, First Lord Herbert of Cherbury Written by Himself*, p. 36.
3. In George Herbert, *The Complete Works in Verse and Prose of George Herbert*, p. 449. Seemingly this is the only translation of Herbert's orations into English.
4. Barnabas Oley, 'A Prefatory View of the Life of Mr Geo. Herbert', p. 79 (spelling and punctuation modernized).
5. John Donne, 'A Sermon of Commemoration of the Lady Danvers', from *The Sermons of John Donne*, Vol. 8, pp. 90–1 (spelling and punctuation modernized).
6. Kenneth Mason, *George Herbert Priest and Poet*, p. 1.
7. T. S. Eliot, 'George Herbert', in *The Spectator*, 12 March 1932. Reprinted in Patrides, *George Herbert*, pp. 333, 334.
8. Patrides, *George Herbert*, p. 335.
9. T. S. Eliot, *George Herbert*, p. 25.
10. Peter Porter, 'Introduction', in T. S. Eliot, *George Herbert*, p. 9.
11. Mario A. Di Cesare and Rigo Mignani, *A Concordance to the Complete Writings of George Herbert*.
12. Quotations from *The Country Parson* are taken from John N. Wall Jr (ed.), *The Country Parson, The Temple*.
13. Elizabeth Clarke, 'The Character of a Non-Laudian Country Parson', p. 480.
14. See the fascinating description of the publication history of *The Country Parson* in Clarke, 'Character'.

Chapter 3: The only thing I don't run

1. Thomas Hinde, *A Field Guide to the English Country Parson*, p. 4.
2. Sandy Mitchell, 'Britain's Best-loved Parson', pp. 85–6.
3. Figures up to 1976 taken from Anthony Russell, *The Clerical Profession*, pp. 262–3. Figures for 2004/2005 taken from the Church of England's Statistics website: <www.cofe.anglican.org/info/statistics/churchstats2004/statisticspg26.htm> (accessed 14 June 2007).
4. J. J. Blunt, *The Parish Priest: His Acquirements, Principal Obligations, and Duties* (1856), quoted in Anthony Russell, *The Clerical Profession*, pp. 53–4.
5. John Clubbe, *A Letter to Free Advice to a Young Clergyman* (1770), in Russell, *Profession*, p. 80.
6. Russell, *Profession*, p. 85.
7. Russell, *Profession*, p. 88.

8. Russell, *Profession*, p. 101.
9. William Jesse, *Parochialia, or Observations of the Discharge of Parochial Duties* (1785), in Russell, *Profession*, pp. 114–15.
10. Russell, *Profession*, p. 187.
11. Russell, *Profession*, p. 143.
12. Diana McClatchey, *Oxfordshire Clergy, 1777–1869* (1960), quoted in Russell, *Profession*, p. 152.
13. Charles Kingsley, *Politics for the People* (1848), quoted in Russell, *Profession*, p. 168.
14. Alexander Gerard, *The Pastoral Care*, (1799), quoted in Russell, *Profession*, p. 170.
15. Herbert, ch. 23, 'The Parson's Completeness', in Wall (ed.), *Parson, Temple*, p. 88.
16. Russell, *Profession*, p. 219.
17. Richard H. Hall, 'Professionalization and Bureaucratization', pp. 92–104.
18. Hall, 'Professionalization', p. 93.
19. Hall, 'Professionalization', p. 93.
20. Russell, *Profession*, p. 233.
21. Martyn Percy, *Clergy: The Origin of the Species*, p. 26.
22. *The Times*, 5 November 1900, quoted in Callum G. Brown, *Religion and Society in Twentieth-century Britain*, p. 44.
23. Quoted in Adrian Hastings, *A History of English Christianity 1920–1990*, p. 71.
24. Hastings, *History*, p. 71.
25. Charles Forder, *The Parish Priest at Work*, p. 127. Emphasis added. I am grateful to the Very Revd R. M. C. Jeffery for directing me to Forder's book.
26. Forder, *The Parish Priest*, p. 76.
27. Percy Dearmer, *The Parson's Handbook*, Michael Hocking, *The Parish Seeks the Way*, Trevor Beeson, *New Area Mission*, Ernest Southcott, *The Parish Comes Alive*, Robert Martineau, *The Office and Work of a Priest*.
28. Paul Ferris, *The Church of England*, p. 95f.
29. Rowan Williams, *Anglican Identities*, p. 110.
30. Mark Chapman, 'Theology in the Public Arena: The case of South Bank Religion', p. 97.
31. Nicolas Stacey, *Who Cares*, p. 97.
32. Stacey, *Who Cares*, p. 197.
33. Stacey, *Who Cares*, p. 158.
34. Nick Stacey, 'How the Church Could Survive'.
35. Eric Mascall and Bryan Wilson, responses to 'How the Church Could Survive', in *The Observer Weekend Review*, 30 May 1965.
36. Quoted in James Bogle, *South Bank Religion*, p. 26. Emphasis added.
37. Bogle, *South Bank Religion*, p. 26.
38. Stacey, *Who Cares*, p. 77.
39. Chapman, 'Public Arena', p. 93.
40. Donald Hughes, 'Neo-Matins', p. 68.
41. Stuart Jeffries, 'Fay Weldon: Lie back and think of Jesus', p. 10.
42. I don't give a reference for this article, as I don't want to identify, even by the name of the newspaper, the clergyman and his wife.
43. Yvonne Warren, *The Cracked Pot*, p. 13.
44. Skye Jethani, 'iChurch'.
45. Hastings, *History*, pp. 614–15.
46. Bryan Wilson, quoted in Paul Ferris, *The Church of England*, p. 12.
47. Bryan Wilson, *Religion in Secular Society*, pp. 81–4.
48. R. Towler and A. Coxon, *The Fate of the Anglican Clergy*, p. 54–5.
49. Rowan Williams, 'The Christian Priest Today'.
50. Humphrey Mynors, 'What I Look for in My Parish Priest', p. 64. Emphasis added (although you could fairly italicize the whole passage). This is taken from an address to the Guildford Diocesan Clergy Conference, and Sir Humphrey (yes, really!) was deputy governor of the Bank of England, and the son, nephew and grandson of six priests.

Chapter 4: The Cult of Nice

1. Leslie Paul, *The Deployment and Payment of the Clergy*, pp. 228–30.
2. Paul, *Deployment*, p. 72.
3. Paul, *Deployment*, pp. 72–3.
4. Paul, *Deployment*, pp. 86, 87.
5. Michael Hare Duke, 'Psychological Implications of the Paul Report', *Prism*, No. 91, November 1964, pp. 28-9.
6. Warren, *The Cracked Pot*.
7. Sara Savage, 'On the Analyst's Couch'.
8. Savage, 'Analyst's Couch', p. 17.
9. Savage, 'Analyst's Couch', p. 18.

10. Savage, 'Analyst's Couch', p. 19.
11. Savage, 'Analyst's Couch', p. 22.
12. Paul, *Deployment*, p. 86f.
13. Warren, *Cracked Pot*, p. 54
14. Warren, *Cracked Pot*, p. 57.
15. Martyn Percy, *Clergy: The Origin of the Species*, p. 166
16. Percy, *Origin of the Species*, pp. 114ff.
17. Robert Jeffery, 'Self Understandings of the Church Today', unpublished lecture delivered at St Stephen's House, Oxford, 8 March 2007.
18. Percy, *Origin of the Species*, p. 115.
19. Giles Fraser, 'Resurgent Religion has Done Away with the Country Vicar', the *Guardian*, 13 April 2006, p. 33.
20. Savage, 'Analyst's Couch', p. 22.
21. *Church Times*, 6 January 2006
22. Warren, *Cracked Pot*, pp. 205ff.
23. Warren, *Cracked Pot*, p. 206.
24. Savage, 'Analyst's Couch', p. 24.
25. Savage, 'Analyst's Couch', p. 25.
26. Savage, 'Analyst's Couch', p. 25.
27. Savage, 'Analyst's Couch', pp. 25f.
28. Lydia Polgreen and Laurie Goodstein, 'At Axis of Episcopal Split, an Anti-Gay Nigerian', *The New York Times*, 25 December 2006, Section A, p. 1.
29. Savage, 'Analyst's Couch', p. 26.
30. Archbishops' Council, 'The Ordination of Priests, also called Presbyters', *Common Worship: Ordination Services (Study Edition)*, p. 32.
31. Warren, *Cracked Pot*, p. 44
32. Paul, *Deployment*, p. 86.
33. Savage, 'Analyst's Couch', p. 27.
34. Savage, 'Analyst's Couch', p. 27.
35. Warren, *Cracked Pot*, pp. 154f.
36. Church House Publishing, *A Time to Heal: A Report for the House of Bishops on the Healing Ministry*, p. 148.
37. Savage, 'Analyst's Couch', p. 28.
38. Dean R. Hoge & Jacqueline E. Wenger, *Pastors in Transition*, p. 130.

Chapter 5: A little soft round the edges

1. 'Bishop Regrets Attack on Softies', *Church Times* (No. 7254), 8 March 2002.
2. William Shakespeare (?), poems from *The Passionate Pilgrim*, in Stanley Wells and Gary Taylor (eds), *The Oxford Shakespeare: The Complete Works*, p. 780.
3. Eric Partridge, *A Dictionary of Slang and Unconventional English*, Vol. 1, p. 111. Partridge records this meaning as having become standard English by 1900.
4. Graham Greene, *A Burnt-Out Case*, p. 110.
5. *Psychotherapy*, Vol XII/1 (1973).
6. Herbert Freudenberger, 'Staff Burnout', *Journal of Social Issues*, Vol. 30/1 (1974), pp. 159–65.
7. William N. Grosch and David C. Olsen, 'Clergy Burnout', p. 620.
8. Herbert J. Freudenberger and Geraldine Richelson, *Burn-out: The High Cost of High Achievement*, p. 22.
9. Wilmar Schaufeli and Dirk Enzmann, *The Burnout Companion to Study and Practice: A Critical Analysis*, p. 102.
10. Schaufeli and Enzmann, *Burnout Companion*, p. 6.
11. Christina Maslach, *Burnout: The Cost of Caring*, p. 2.
12. Schaufeli and Enzmann, *Burnout Companion*, pp. 12–17.
13. Schaufeli and Enzmann, *Burnout Companion*, p. 13.
14. Schaufeli and Enzmann, *Burnout Companion*, p. 15.
15. Schaufeli and Enzmann, *Burnout Companion*, p. 14.
16. *Draft Ecclesiastical Offices (Terms of Service) Legislation* (GS1637-9X), a report presented to General Synod in February 2007.
17. Maslach, *Burnout*, p. 18.
18. Maslach, *Burnout*, p. 20.
19. Church House Publishing, *A Time to Heal*, p. 147.
20. Church House Publishing, *A Time to Heal*, p. 147.
21. Maslach, *Burnout*, p. 14.
22. BALM: 'Bullying and Spirituality', Available online from: <www.balmnet.co.uk/spirituality.htm.>. Accessed 20 August 2007. Emphasis in the original.
23. Douglas W. Turton and Leslie J. Francis, 'The Relationship Between Attitude Toward Prayer and Professional Burnout Among Anglican Parochial Clergy in England', p. 70.
24. Christopher Lewis et al., 'Clergy Work-

related Psychological Health, Stress, and Burnout', p. 2.

Chapter 6: +ABC and the three Ws

1. Michael Ramsey, *The Christian Priest Today*.
2. P. T. Forsyth, *The Church and the Ministry* (1917), quoted in Ramsey, *Christian Priest*, p. 4.
3. A. A. K. Graham, 'Should the Ordained Ministry Now Disappear?', pp. 242–50.
4. Ramsey, *Christian Priest*, p. 7.
5. Ramsey, *Christian Priest*, p. 8.
6. Ramsey, *Christian Priest*, p. 8.
7. Ramsey, *Christian Priest*, p. 9.
8. Ramsey, *Christian Priest*, p. 10.
9. Ramsey, *Christian Priest*, p. 10.
10. Ramsey, *Christian Priest*, p. 111.
11. Rowan Williams, 'The Christian Priest Today'. The talk is available from the Archbishop's website: at <http://www.archbishopofcanterbury.org/1185>. All otherwise unattributed references in this chapter are to the text published on that website.
12. In Douglas Dales, *Glory Descending*, pp. 163–75.
13. And also so very popular: 3.76 million visits and counting! <www.brank.org/gibbon>.
14. Bernard Cornwell, *The Winter King* (1995), *Enemy of God* (1996), *Excalibur: A Novel of Arthur* (1997), (The Warlord Chronicles; London: Penguin Books).
15. Compare this with Pritchard's images (John Pritchard, *The Life and Work of a Priest*: sixteen different roles for the priest to fulfil, from 'Presiding genius?' to 'Artful story-teller' to 'Weather-beaten witness' and, best of all, 'Flower arranger'.
16. Rowan Williams, 'Community Well-Being'.

Chapter 7: Witness

1. Edward Schillebeeckx, *Ministry: A Case for Change*, p. 34.
2. Hans Küng, *The Church*, p. 355.
3. Küng, *Church*, pp. 355–6. Emphasis in the original.
4. Hans Küng, *Structures of the Church*, p. 161
5. Küng, *Structures*, pp. 165–6.
6. Küng, *Church*, p. 366.
7. Küng, *Church*, p. 367.
8. Schillebeeckx, *Ministry*, p. 34.
9. Schillebeeckx, *Ministry*, p. 33.
10. Schillebeeckx, *Ministry*, pp. 36–7.
11. The will of Adam, Lord Gifford, 21 August 1885, available online from: <www.giffordlectures.org/will.asp>. Accessed 10 November 2007.
12. 'Natural theology', in *The Concise Oxford Dictionary of World Religions*.
13. 'History of the Gifford Lectures', available online from: <www.giffordlectures.org/online.asp>. Accessed 11 November 2007.
14. Stanley Hauerwas, *With the Grain of the Universe*, p. 142.
15. Hauerwas, *Grain of the Universe*, p. 207.
16. Hauerwas, *Grain of the Universe*, p. 207.
17. John Howard Yoder, *The Priestly Kingdom*, p. 56. Quoted in Hauerwas, *Grain of the Universe*, p. 223.
18. Irenaeus, in *Adversus haereses (Against Heresies)*, (c. AD 175–85); 4.20.7.
19. Yoder, *Priestly Kingdom*, pp. 50–4. The New Testament examples that Yoder gives are John 1.1–14; Hebrews 2.8–9; Colossians; Philippians 2 and Revelation 4.1–5.4.
20. Yoder, *Priestly Kingdom*, p. 53.
21. Michael Ramsey, *The Glory of God and the Transfiguration of Christ* (1949/1967), pp. 89–90. Reprinted in Douglas Dales (ed.), *Glory Descending*, p. 84.
22. Michael G. Cartwright, 'Being Sent', p. 483.
23. Yoder, *Priestly Kingdom*, p. 54.
24. John Howard Yoder, *The Royal Priesthood: Essays Ecumenical and Ecclesiological*, ed. Michael G. Cartwright, p. 74. Quoted in Cartwright, 'Being Sent', p. 484.
25. Elias Chacour, *We Belong to the Land*, pp. 30–1. Also quoted in Cartwright, 'Being Sent', p. 482.
26. Chacour, *We Belong*, p. 32.
27. Cartwright, 'Being Sent', p. 486.
28. Cartwright, 'Being Sent', p. 486.
29. Cartwright, 'Being Sent', p. 486.
30. Cartwright, 'Being Sent', p. 492.
31. Christine D. Pohl, *Making Room*, p. 42. Michael Cartwright has also explored the

centrality of hospitality to Christian witness in his own context of university ministry: see Michael G. Cartwright, *Giving and Receiving Hospitality: Ecumenical and Interfaith Programs at the University of Indianapolis*. See also Michael G. Cartwright, *Offering Hospitality under the Cross and Flame: United Methodists and Higher Education in Indiana*.

32. Pohl, *Making Room*, p. 31.
33. Pohl, *Making Room*, p. 33. The quotation is from Gregory Nazianzen, Oration 40 §31 AD 381, 'On Holy Baptism', Nicene and Post-Nicene Fathers, Series II, Vol. 7. The whole of Pohl's book is a masterful restatement of the importance of hospitality in the Christian tradition.
34. Yoder, *Priestly Kingdom*, p. 61.

Chapter 8: Watchman

1. J. R. R. Tolkien, 'The Grey Havens', *The Lord of the Rings: The Return of the King*, pp. 1068–9.
2. Rowan Williams, 'The Christian Priest Today'. All otherwise unattributed references in this chapter are to the text published on that website. The Archbishop's comment reminds me of the acerbic quip attributed variously to Robert Runcie or Bill Vanstone that 'Church of England is a swimming pool in which all the noise comes from the shallow end'. The source of the Runcie attribution seems to be an address given to the AGM of the Romney Marsh Historic Churches Trust, 5 June 1999. Available online from: <http://members.aol.com/huddnp/runcie.htm>, accessed 1 March 2008. The alternative, Vanstone, origin seems to have its roots in his obituary published in *The Daily Telegraph*, 15 March 1999, republished in Trevor Beeson (ed.), *Priests and Prelates: the Daily Telegraph Clerical Obituaries*, pp. 214–16.
3. Judith Maltby, 'Face to Faith', p. 35.
4. Samuel Butler, *Erewhon*, pp. 137–8.
5. Benedict XVI in an address to the clergy of Warsaw, 25 May 2006, reported via Zenit.org. Available online from: <www.zenit.org/article-16119?l=english>. Accessed 14 August 2007.
6. Benedict XVI, Address to the clergy of Warsaw.
7. Benedict XVI, in the record of 'The Meeting of the Holy Father Benedict XVI with the Clergy of the Dioceses of Belluno-feltre and Treviso', Church of St Justin Martyr, Auronzo di Cadore, 24 July 2007. Available online from: <www.vatican.va/holy_father/benedict_xvi/speeches/2007/july/documents/hf_ben-xvi_spe_20070724_clero-cadore_en.html>. Accessed 14 August 2007.
8. H. Richard Niebuhr, *Christ and Culture*.
9. Martin E. Marty, 'Foreword', p. xiii.
10. Glen H. Stassen (probably), 'Preface' to Glen H. Stassen et al., *Authentic Transformation*, p. 9.
11. Niebuhr, *Christ and Culture*, pp. 1, 2.
12. Niebuhr, *Christ and Culture*, p. 11.
13. Niebuhr, *Christ and Culture*, p. 13.
14. Niebuhr, *Christ and Culture*, pp. 18, 19.
15. Niebuhr, *Christ and Culture*, p. 19.
16. Niebuhr, *Christ and Culture*, p. 27.
17. Niebuhr, *Christ and Culture*, p. 28.
18. Niebuhr, *Christ and Culture*, pp. 28–9.
19. Niebuhr, *Christ and Culture*, p. 30.
20. Niebuhr, *Christ and Culture*, p. 32. Niebuhr acknowledges his debt to Bronislaw Malinowski's article on 'culture' in *The Encyclopedia of Social Sciences*, published by Macmillan in New York in the 1931. ('Culture', *Encyclopedia of the Social Sciences*, Vol. 4, pp. 621–46).
21. Niebuhr, *Christ and Culture*, p. 33.
22. Timothy J. Gorringe, *Furthering Humanity*, p. 14.
23. Niebuhr, *Christ and Culture*, p. 83.
24. Niebuhr, *Christ and Culture*, pp. 41, 116.
25. Niebuhr, *Christ and Culture*, p. 121.
26. Niebuhr, *Christ and Culture*, p. 157.
27. Niebuhr, *Christ and Culture*, p. 156.
28. Gorringe, *Furthering Humanity*, p. 15.
29. Gorringe, *Furthering Humanity*, p. 15.
30. Niebuhr, *Christ and Culture*, p. 1. Emphasis added.
31. George Marsden, 'Christianity and Cultures'.
32. Gibbon, *The Decline and Fall of the Roman Empire*, Vol. 1. Ch. XV §2. Misquoted in Niebuhr, *Christ and Culture*, p. 5.
33. John Howard Yoder, 'How H. Richard

Niebuhr Reasoned', p. 41.
34. James M. Gustafson, Preface, p. xxiii. What an amazing admission, not to have read Yoder's essay, which was published three years before Gustafson wrote his preface!
35. Yoder, 'How Niebuhr Reasoned', p. 55.
36. Yoder, 'How Niebuhr Reasoned', p. 47.
37. Yoder, 'How Niebuhr Reasoned', p. 59.
38. Craig A. Carter, 'The Legacy of an Inadequate Christology: Yoder's Critique of Niebuhr's *Christ and Culture*'.
39. Karl Barth, 'Church and Culture', pp. 334–54. Originally published in German in 1928.
40. Barth, 'Church and Culture', p. 337.
41. S. Eck, in *Religion in Geschichte und Gegenwart*, quoted by Barth, 'Church and Culture', p. 337. The similarity of Eck's definition and Neibuhr's can't be coincidental. It seems unbelievable that there could be no relationship of dependence between them.
42. Barth, 'Church and Culture', p. 337.
43. Barth, 'Church and Culture', p. 338.
44. Barth, 'Church and Culture', p. 339.
45. Barth, 'Church and Culture', pp. 338, 341.
46. Gorringe, *Furthering Humanity*, p. 18.
47. Gorringe, *Furthering Humanity*, p. 18.
48. Francis Bacon, 'The Advancement of Learning', p. 132.
49. Gorringe, *Furthering Humanity*, p. 20.
50. Barth, 'Church and Culture', p. 344.
51. Barth, 'Church and Culture', p. 349.

Chapter 9: Weaver

1. Sarah Murray, 'Responsible Neighbours Invest in Local Causes', *Financial Times*, 3 July 2007, p. 10; William Keegan, 'Gordon has Fought for Sterling – But Can he Now Defend the Realm?', *The Observer*, 17 June 2007, p. 8; Siân Griffiths, 'Don't Blame Us', *The Sunday Times*, 22 July 2007, p. 12; Michael Evans, 'Blogs and Chat Rooms Out of Bounds in MoD Gag Order on Troops', *The Times*, 10 August 2007, p. 2.
2. Rowan Williams, 'The Christian Priest Today'.
3. This is actually Clifford Green's gloss on Barth. Less succinctly but in reality, Barth regarded *Sanctorum Communio* with 'the deepest respect', because its conclusions were so unusual in Berlin at the time (the late 1920s): Karl Barth, *Church Dogmatics*, p. 641. For the punchier judgement see Clifford Green, 'Human Sociality and Christian Community', p. 122.
4. Geffrey B. Kelly and F. Burton Nelson, *The Cost of Moral Leadership*, p. 8.
5. Dietrich Bonhoeffer, *Sanctorum Communio*, p. 34. Emphasis in the original. Most quotations from Bonhoeffer's works will be taken from the definitive series being produced by Fortress Press, translations of the German critical edition *Dietrich Bonhoeffer Werke* (DBW), 17 vols. Edited by Eberhard Bethge et al. (Munich and Gütersloh: Chr. Kaiser-Gütersloher Verlagshaus, 1986–1999).
6. Bonhoeffer, *Sanctorum Communio*, p. 33.
7. 'Sociality, a.1.a, 2' *The Oxford English Dictionary*, <http://dictionary.oed.com/cgi/entry/50229738>
8. Green, 'Human Sociality', p. 114.
9. Nicholas Lash, 'Conversation in Context', in *Theology for Pilgrims*, pp. 157–8. Lash glosses his explanation further: 'For those readers who prefer to have these things clothed in academic dignity, I am suggesting that our ecclesiology is shaped by whatever anthropology we simply take for granted, and that our anthropology, in turn, is shaped by whatever ontology we simply take for granted' (note 12 on p. 158).
10. Green, 'Human Sociality', p. 115.
11. Bonhoeffer, *Sanctorum Communio*, note 1 on p. 60.
12. Bonhoeffer, *Sanctorum Communio*, pp. 80–1. The translation is taken from p. 53 of an earlier English edition (Collins, 1963).
13. Bonhoeffer, *Sanctorum Communio*, note 1 on p. 60.
14. Bonhoeffer, *Sanctorum Communio*, note 1 on pp. 60–1.
15. Williams, 'Christian Priest Today'.
16. Bonhoeffer, *Sanctorum Communio*, pp. 156–7.
17. Martin Luther, 'Fourteen Consolations

for those who Labour and are Heavy-Laden' (1520), in Martin O. Dietrich (ed.), *Luther's Works*, Vol. 42, pp. 121–66. Quoted in Bonhoeffer, *Sanctorum Communio*, note 47, p. 180.
18. Bonhoeffer, *Sanctorum Communio*, p. 183.
19. Williams, 'Christian Priest Today'.
20. Green, 'Human Sociality', p. 120.
21. See, for example, Bonhoeffer, *Sanctorum Communio*, p. 121.
22. Stephen Plant, 'The Sacrament of Ethical Reality: Dietrich Bonhoeffer on Ethics for Christian Citizens', p. 78.
23. Quite! Eberhard Bethge, *Dietrich Bonhoeffer*, p. 349.
24. Bethge, *Dietrich Bonhoeffer*, p. 348.
25. Kelly and Nelson, *Cost of Moral Leadership*, p. 25.
26. Geffrey B. Kelly and John D. Godsey (eds), *Discipleship* (DBWE Vol. 4.).
27. Dietrich Bonhoeffer, *Life Together*. Another very common edition of *Life Together* is that translated by J. W. Doberstein and published by SCM. It is superseded in every way by the DBWE edition.
28. Kelly and Nelson, *Cost of Moral Leadership*, p. 145.
29. Bonhoeffer, *Life Together*, p. 31.
30. Bonhoeffer, *Life Together*, p. 33.
31. Bonhoeffer, *Life Together*, pp. 34, 43.
32. Bonhoeffer, *Life Together*, n. 2, p. 27, or p. 47.
33. Bonhoeffer, *Life Together*, pp. 51, 78
34. Bonhoeffer, *Life Together*, p. 62.
35. Bonhoeffer, *Life Together*, p. 73.
36. Bonhoeffer, *Life Together*, p. 83.
37. Green, 'Human sociality' p, 125.
38. Kelly and Nelson, *Cost of Moral Leadership*, p. 165
39. Bonhoeffer, *Life Together*, p. 36.
40. Bonhoeffer, *Life Together*, p. 36.
41. Bonhoeffer, *Life Together*, p. 90.
42. Bonhoeffer, *Life Together*, p. 93.
43. Bonhoeffer instructed the seminarians of Finkenwalde never to speak of a brother in his absence, or, if they did so, to explain it to him afterwards: 'almost as much was learned from the failure to observe this simple rule and from the renewed resolution to keep it as from sermons and exegeses', Eberhard Bethge, *Dietrich Bonhoeffer*, p. 349.
44. Bonhoeffer, *Life Together*, p. 98.
45. Bonhoeffer, *Life Together*, p. 99.
46. Bonhoeffer, *Life Together*, p. 95, 100–2.
47. Bonhoeffer, *Life Together*, p. 108.
48. Bonhoeffer, *Life Together*, p. 111.
49. Bonhoeffer, *Life Together*, pp. 113–14.
50. Kelly and Nelson, *Cost of Moral Leadership*, p. 171.
51. Bonhoeffer, *Life Together*, p. 118.
52. Gerhard Ludwig Müller and Albrecht Schönherr, 'Editors', p. 128.
53. Bonhoeffer, *Life Together*, p. 116.
54. 'The extemporaneous prayer at the close of daily worship normally will be said by the head of the house. But in any case it is best that it is always said by the same person. That places an unexpected responsibility on this person'. Bonhoeffer, *Life Together*, p. 69.
55. Bethge, *Dietrich Bonhoeffer*, pp. 349, 351, 363.
56. Bethge, *Dietrich Bonhoeffer*, p. 350.
57. Vincent J. Donovan, *Christianity Rediscovered: An Epistle from the Masai*, p. 15.
58. Donovan, *Christianity Rediscovered*, p. 86.
59. Donovan, *Christianity Rediscovered*, p. 146.
60. Donovan, *Christianity Rediscovered*, p. 143.
61. Donovan, *Christianity Rediscovered*, p. 145, 146.
62. Williams, 'Christian Priest Today'.
63. For another description of this community differentiation, see Tom Wright, *Simply Christian*, pp. 180–1.
64. Canterbury Cathedral Mission Statement, based on John 12.20: <www.canterbury-cathedral.org/community/index.aspx#mission>. Accessed 30 July 2008.

Chapter 10: Know who you are: Rule

1. Robert C. Fuller, *Spiritual, but not Religious: Understanding Unchurched America*, p. 5.
2. Fuller, *Spiritual*, p. 156.
3. Abraham H. Maslow, *Religions, Values and Peak-experiences*, p. viii.
4. Gore Vidal, 'America First? America Last? America at Last?', Lowell Lecture,

Harvard University, 20 April 1992. Available online from: <www.dce.harvard.edu/pubs/lowell/gvidal.html>. Accessed 29 August 2008.

5. 'The Deer's Cry' in Alister E. McGrath, *Christian Literature*, p. 134.
6. 'St Patrick's Breastplate', attributed to St Patrick (372–466); tr. Cecil Frances Alexander (1818–95), for a St Patrick's Day service in 1889, and printed in *The English Hymnal*, 1906.
7. See 'Religion', in *The Oxford English Dictionary*, <http://dictionary.oed.com/cgi/entry/50202047>, and particularly definition 5.a.
8. Stephen Conway, 'Public Ministry, in David Ison et al., *The Vicar's Guide: Life and Ministry in the Parish*, ed. David Ison, p. 166.
9. Malcolm Grundy, *What They Don't Teach You at Theological College: A Practical Guide to Life in the Ministry*, p. 163.
10. C. Edmondson, *Fit to Lead: Sustaining Effective Ministry in a Changing World*, pp. 46–7.
11. Harold Miller, *Finding a Personal Rule of Life*.
12. Miller, *Personal Rule*, p. 4.
13. See for example, Paul Ballard, 'The Emergence of Practical and Pastoral Theology in Britain', in James Woodward et al., *The Blackwell Reader*, p. 64. For Thornton's original work see Martin Thornton, *Pastoral Theology*.
14. Martin Thornton, *Christian Proficiency*.
15. Thornton, *Christian Proficiency*, p. xi.
16. Richard Templar, *The Rules of Work: A Definitive Code for Personal Success; The Rules of Management: A Definitive Code for Managerial Success; The Rules of Life: A Personal Code for Living a Better, Happier, More Successful Kind of Life; The Rules of Wealth: A Personal Code for Prosperity; The Rules of Parenting: A Personal Code for Bringing up Happy, Confident Children.*
17. Thornton, *Christian Proficiency*, p. 46. Emphasis in the original.
18. Grundy, *What They Don't Teach You*, p. 163.
19. Felicity Lawson, 'Spiritual Life', in *Vicar's Guide*, p. 43.
20. Thornton, *Christian Proficiency*, p. 52.
21. Grundy, *What They Don't Teach You*, p. 172.
22. Thornton, *Christian Proficiency*, p. 49.
23. Miller, *Personal Rule*, p. 24.
24. See, for example, 'I really believe that any spirituality worth its salt will have a strong emphasis on the individual's personal relationship with his or her Lord' (p. 16); or 'the rest of the booklet is geared towards finding a "personal" pattern' (p. 13).
25. *The Rule of St Benedict*, 'Chapter 1: The Kinds of Monk'.
26. Thornton, *Christian Proficiency*, pp. 51–2.
27. Mark Mills-Powell, *St Benedict for Today*, pp. 6–7.
28. Theodore Austin-Sparks (an independent Baptist Minster, d. 1971) in the journal *A Witness and A Testimony*, May–June 1963, Vol. 41/3, published by Honor Oak Christian Fellowship of London, quoted by Frank Viola, *Reimagining Church*, p. 31. With the greatest respect to Mr Austin-Sparks and Mr Viola, we're not talking mainstream Christian scholarship here!
29. Douglas W. Turton and Leslie J. Francis, 'The Relationship Between Attitude Toward Prayer', p. 66.
30. From Benedict XVI's address to the clergy of Warsaw, 25 May 2006, quoted more fully on page 110 above.
31. '*Contemplari et contemplata aliis tradere*', often said to derive from *Summa Theologica* II.II q.188 a.6.
32. Donald Goergen OP, 'The Pillars Revisited', pp. 192.
33. T. S. Eliot, *The Four Quartets: Little Gidding* (1942).
34. Eugene H. Peterson, *The Contemplative Pastor*, p. 43.
35. From the Prologue to the *Primitive Constitutions* (1228) of the Order of Preachers, quoted in Simon Tugwell OP, *Early Dominicans*, p. 457.
36. Rowan Williams, 'The Christian Priest Today'.
37. Williams, 'The Christian Priest Today'.
38. Williams, 'The Christian Priest Today'.
39. This quotation, regularly and confidently ascribed to Antoine de Saint-Exupéry in his book *The Wisdom of the Sands*, trans.

Stuart Gilbert from *Citadelle* (Gallimard, 1948), (London: Hollis & Carter, 1952), isn't actually found in that volume. Another one of those quotations which *ought* to have been said.

Chapter 11: Know what you are for: Role

1. Benjamin R. Doolittle, 'Burnout and Coping Among Parish-based Clergy', p. 37.
2. William N. Grosch and David C. Olsen, 'Clergy Burnout', p. 623.
3. Guy Wilkinson, 'The Changing Role of the Vicar', in *The Vicar's Guide*, p. 5.
4. Fr George Morelli, 'Understanding Clergy Stress: A Psychospiritual Response', published on the website of the Antiochian Orthodox Church, available online from: <www.antiochian.org/morelli/understanding-clergy-stress>. Accessed 6 September 2008.
5. John Davey, *Burnout*, p. 31.
6. John Truscott, 'Job Descriptions'.
7. See *Ecclesiastical Offices (Terms of Service) Legislation Summary* (July 2008), available online from: <www.cofe.anglican.org/lifeevents/ministry/workofmindiv/dracsc/rctshomepage/summary.doc>. Accessed 5 September 2008.
8. Truscott, 'Job Descriptions', p. 2.
9. Truscott, 'Job Descriptions', p. 3.
10. John Vernon Taylor (1914–2001), Bishop of Winchester, from the Diocesan Service of Institution, quoted in Rowell et al., *Love's Redeeming Work*, p. 716.
11. John Truscott, 'The Minister's Role in Larger Churches', p. 2.
12. Merlin Mann, 'Time & Attention Presentation: "Who Moved My Brain?"', 14 August 2008, on www.43folders.com. Available online from: <www.43folders.com/2008/08/14/who-moved-my-brain>. Accessed 8 September 2008.
13. David Allen, *Getting Things Done: The Art of Stress-Free Productivity*; Merlin Mann, 43Folders.com, 2004B, www.43folders.com; Dave Crenshaw, *The Myth of Multitasking: How 'Doing It All' Gets Nothing Done.*
14. Crenshaw, *Myth of Multitasking*, p. 48.
15. Truscott, 'The Minister's Role', p. 3.
16. Truscott, 'The Minister's Role', p. 3.

Chapter 12: Know who you are set over: Responsibility

1. Ludwig von Bertalanffy, *General System Theory; Foundations, Development, Applications.*
2. Michael G. Roskin, 'Political Science', in *Encyclopædia Britannica*. Available online from: <www.britannica.com/EBchecked/topic/467721/political-science>. Accessed 10 September 2008. See also the explanation in William N. Grosch and David C. Olsen, 'Clergy Burnout', p. 623.
3. Walter Wink, *Unmasking the Powers*, p. 4. For the initial delineation of the powers, see Walter Wink, *Naming the Powers.*
4. Jim Herrington, Robert Creech and Trisha L. Taylor, *The Leader's Journey*, p. 33.
5. Wink, *Unmasking the Powers*, p. 70.
6. Wink, *Unmasking the Powers*, p. 80. If you want to follow an excellent programmatic version of Wink's book, then look at Robert Warren's *The Healthy Churches' Handbook*, which sets out a series of exercises to identify the angel of a particular church community. Remember, the identification must happen in the context of the community as well!
7. Wink, *Unmasking the Powers*, p. 80.
8. Wink, *Unmasking the Powers*, p. 81.
9. John Adair, *Effective Leadership*, p. 201.
10. Rowan Williams, 'The Stable Door is Open. Anyone Can Come In', *The Times*, 24 December 2007, p. 17.
11. Like most political comments, it is unlikely that Ledru-Rollin said anything like this. Alvin R. Calman, the historian of the Second Republic, says Ledru-Rollin's use of 'I am their chief; I must follow them' is probably apocryphal: Alvin Rosenblatt Calman, *Ledru-Rollin and the Second French Republic*, p. 374.
12. Wesley Carr, 'Leading Without Leadership, p. 76.
13. See Charles Handy, 'One Question and Ten Answers', pp. 24–31, especially the

pitiful anecdote on pp. 27–8 involving a motivated but misguided churchwarden.
14. Elizabeth Welch, 'Leadership with Vision', p. 135.
15. David Brown, *Making Room for Church Leadership*, p. 7.
16. Brown, *Making Room*, p. 5.
17. Brown, *Making Room*, p. 3.
18. Brown, *Making Room*, p. 5.
19. Michael Spencer, 'Church Quitting in Evangelicalism'.
20. See 'The Declaration', in *The Ordination of Priests* from *Ordination Services: Study Guide, Common Worship: Services and Prayers for the Church of England* (Church House Publishing, 2007), pp. 37–9.
21. John Adair, *The Leadership of Jesus*. Peter Shaw's Grove booklet, *Mirroring Jesus as Leader*, also has some interesting conceptualizations for Jesus's leadership: Jesus as a visionary, servant leader, teacher, coach, radical and healer.
22. Adair, *Leadership of Jesus*, p. 91.
23. Heifetz and Linsky, *Leadership on the Line*, p. 142.
24. Adair, *Leadership of Jesus*, p. 117.
25. Lehr, *Clergy Burnout*, p. 11.
26. Lehr, *Clergy Burnout*, p. 11. Gerald May's book is *Addiction and Grace*.
27. Fraser Watts, 'Clergy' in Watts, Nye, and Savage, *Psychology for Christian Ministry*, p. 263.
28. Lehr, *Clergy Burnout*, pp. 15–16.
29. Shaw, *Mirroring Jesus*, p. 6.
30. Lehr, *Clergy Burnout*, p. 55.
31. Nigel Melville, 'Rugby Union', p. 9. Johnson is Australian, which might explain the forcefulness of his expression!
32. See 'Presidential Medal of Freedom Nominee Chaplain Rev. Mychal Judge O.F.M.', *Presidential Medal of Freedom (Official Site)*, n.d. Available online from: <www.medaloffreedom.com/MychalJudge.htm>. Accessed 19 September, 2008.
33. Adair, *Leadership of Jesus*, p. 139.
34. Herrington, Creech and Taylor, *Leader's Journey*, p. 164.
35. Sara Savage and Eolene Boyd-MacMillan, *The Human Face of Church*, p. 149.
36. Savage and Boyd-MacMillan, *Human Face*, p. 150.
37. Murray Bowen, *Family Therapy in Clinical Practice*.
38. Savage and Boyd-MacMillan, *Human Face*, p. 169.
39. Herrington, Creech and Taylor, *Leader's Journey*, p. 18.
40. William N. Grosch and David C. Olsen, 'Clergy Burnout', p. 621. This article has an especially valuable exploration of 'overfunctioning', in which clergy work excessively hard in order to achieve the praise which was missing in their upbringing.
41. Savage and Boyd-MacMillan, *Human Face*, p. 170.
42. For example, look at the chapters on co-dependency in Lehr, *Clergy Burnout*; Savage and Boyd-MacMillan, *Human Face*, has a series of exercises to follow on developing self-awareness and healthy church relationships; The Beta Course ('Being Christian. Becoming whole. Building community' allows church groups to encounter these ideas: <www.beta-course.org>.

Chapter 13: Know how to make decisions: Reckoning

1. George Herbert, *The Country Parson, The Temple*, p. 82.
2. Robin Greenwood, 'Understanding New Patterns of Management in Ministry', pp. 100–1.
3. Greenwood, 'Understanding New Patterns', p. 100.
4. This is Greenwood's list in 'Understanding New Patterns', p. 101. He means Michael Ramsey, Roland Allen, Frank Russell Barry, John Robinson, Hans Küng, Edward Schillebeeckx, Leonardo Boff, Léon-Joseph Suenens, Jurgen Möltmann, and John Zizioulas
5. Anglican–Roman Catholic International Commission (ARCIC I), *Authority in the Church*, § 5 & 6.
6. Advisory Council for the Church's Ministry, *Education for the Church's Ministry*. For the Archbishop of Canterbury's reservations about this

approach, see the opening of his lecture 'The Christian Priest Today' (2004)

7. Robin Greenwood's summary in *Transforming Priesthood*, p. 183. See also the handy paragraph by paragraph summary on pp. 56–9. Greenwood's approval for ACCM 22 can be seen in the title he gives to the chapter examining it: 'The Dawning of a New Era'. Bliss was it in that dawn to be alive, but to be ACCM was very heaven!
8. Andrew Bowden and Michael West, *Dynamic Local Ministry*, p. 19.
9. Brighton and Hove Deaneries Pastoral Strategy Review Group, *Strengthening the Church*. I don't mean to disparage the work of Brighton and Hove Deaneries: this report is a fine piece of work, once you accept the initial premise of §1.2.
10. The 'Hind Report'. Ministry Division, Archbishops' Council, *Formation for Ministry Within a Learning Church*, §1.3.
11. Convocations of Canterbury and York, *Guidelines for the Professional Conduct of the Clergy*, esp. §6.3.
12. The Archbishop's Council, *Draft Ecclesiastical Offices*, §31.1.
13. Ministry Division of the Archbishops' Council, *Review of Clergy Terms of Service*, Annex 6: Revised Capability Procedure, §2.
14. Hilary Ineson and Bernard Kilroy, 'Appropriate Professional Support and Development', p. 161; and John Walker, 'Quality Ministry,' p. 145, both in Nelson, *Management and Ministry*.
15. Wesley Carr, 'Leading Without Leadership, p. 77.
16. Andrew Dawswell, *Ministry Leadership Teams*, p. 5.
17. Greenwood, *Transforming Priesthood*, p. 51.
18. Advisory Board of Ministry of the Church of England, *Stranger in the Wings*, §3.1.
19. Dawswell, *Ministry Leadership Teams*, p. 12. Dawswell cites Luke 22.42: 'Father, if you are willing, remove this cup from me; yet, not my will but yours be done' and John 6.38: '. . . for I have come down from heaven, not to do my own will, but the will of him who sent me.'
20. Watts et al, *Psychology for Christian Ministry*, chapter 12, 'The Church as an Organization'.
21. Victor Vroom and Philip Yetton, *Leadership and Decision-making*, Table 2.1, p. 13.
22. William H. Whyte Jr, 'Groupthink', in *Fortune* (March 1952). Quoted by Safire in 'On Language'.
23. Irving Janis, *Victims of Groupthink*, p. 9.
24. Sara Savage, 'The Church as an Organisation', box 12.4 on p. 245, and the section on Groupthink on pp. 245–7.
25. Sara Savage, 'The Church as an Organization', p. 230.
26. Greenwood, 'Understanding New Patterns', p. 100.
27. In December 2007, the Revd David Faulks, rector of four rural parishes in Peterborough Diocese, was found 'culpably inefficient' in his administration of parochial fees and the management of the parish magazine's finances. His inability to 'keep full and accurate financial records for the parish magazine' and other charges amounted to 'neglect and inefficiency in the performance of his duties of office and financial conduct unbecoming or inappropriate to his office and work'. See Rachel Harden, 'Verdict on Sick Rector', in *Church Times*, 1 February 2008, p. 8. The Clergy Discipline Measure has made administration a serious priority for the KGH priest.
28. Guy Wilkinson, 'Parish Systems', p. 99.
29. See John Truscott, 'Christian Administration?'.
30. Wilkinson, 'Parish Systems', p. 100.
31. David Allen, *Getting Things Done: The Art of Stress-Free Productivity*, p. 17.
32. Allen, *Getting Things Done*, p. 12.
33. Merlin Mann, 'Getting Started with "Getting Things Done"', blog post on 43Folders.com, 8 September 2004. Available online from: <www.43folders.com/2004/09/08/getting-started-with-getting-things-done>. Accessed 13 September 2008.

34. Mark Forster, *Do It Tomorrow*, pp. 99–100, 145.
35. Allen, *Getting Things Done*, p. 34.
36. Allen, *Getting Things Done*, p. 37.
37. Mann, 'Getting Started'.
38. Timothy Ferriss, *The 4–Hour Workweek*, p. 68.

Chapter 14: Know how to manage conflict: Reconciling

1. See Yvonne Warren, *The Cracked Pot*, pp. 205 ff, and the discussion on p. 54 above.
2. Dean R. Hoge and Jacqueline E. Wenger, *Pastors in Transition*, pp. 76–7.
3. Hoge and Wenger, *Pastors in Transition*, p. 114.
4. Sara Savage, 'The Church as an Organisation', p. 225.
5. Quoted by Hoge and Wenger, *Pastors in Transition*, p. 89.
6. Savage, 'The Church as an Organisation', p. 225.
7. Savage, 'The Church as an Organisation', p. 225.
8. Savage, 'The Church as an Organisation', p. 233.
9. Quoted by Hoge and Wenger, *Pastors in Transition*, pp. 95–6
10. Savage, 'The Church as an Organisation', p. 233.
11. Sara Savage and Eolene Boyd-MacMillan, *The Human Face of Church*, p. 57.
12. Colin Patterson, *How to Learn Through Conflict*, p. 3.
13. See especially Steve Young (writer) and Bob Anderson (director), 'Hurricane Neddy'.
14. Patterson, *Learn Through Conflict*, p. 13.
15. In both Sara Savage, 'On the Analyst's Couch', p. 24, and, in much more detail, 'The Church as an Organisation', pp. 234–6.
16. The five modes are adapted from Ralph H. Kilmann and Kenneth W. Thomas, 'Developing a Forced-Choice Measure of Conflict-Handling Behavior, pp. 309–25, which has now turned into the 'Thomas-Kilmann Conflict Mode Instrument (TKI)', 'the world's best-selling instrument for understanding how different conflict-handling modes, or styles, affect interpersonal and group dynamics and for learning how to select the most appropriate style for a given situation' (according to CPP, which sells TKI: <www.cpp.com/products/tki/index.asp>). 'Mode' stands for 'Management-of-Differences Exercise', another acronym in search of a convincing origin!
17. Savage, 'The Church as an Organisation', p. 235. See also pp. 181–2 above.
18. Savage and Boyd-MacMillan, *Human Face*, Appendix 2: Questionnaires, pp. 266–79.
19. Ron Kraybill, *Style Matters*, p. 9. Available from Riverhouse Press: <www.riverhouseepress.com/Conflict_Style_Inventory.htm>.
20. Kraybill, *Style Matters*, p. 15.
21. Kraybill, *Style Matters*, p. 15.
22. Savage, 'Analysts' Couch', p. 24. The London Mennonite Centre can be contacted via <www.menno.org.uk>: their programme is called Bridge Builders. In the USA, the Mennonite Office on Justice and Peacebuilding can be contacted through <http://mcc.org/us/peacebuilding>. Ronald Kraybill was the founding director of the Mennonite Conciliation Service, the Office on Justice and Peacebuilding's predecessor.
23. Patterson, *Learn Through Conflict*, p. 17.
24. Savage, 'Analysts' Couch', p. 25. See the discussion on p. 60 above.
25. Savage, 'Analysts' Couch', p. 24.
26. Kenneth C. Haugk, *Antagonists in the Church*, esp. ch. 4, 'Why Antagonism Happens in Congregations'.
27. Jeremy Taylor, *The Whole Works of Jeremy Taylor*, Vol. 5, p. 261.

Chapter 15: Afterword: Standing by Herbert's grave

1. Michael Ramsey, *The Gospel and the Catholic Church* (1936/1956 repr. 1990), quoted in Douglas Dales (ed.), *Glory Descending*, p. 113.
2. R. Towler and A. Coxon, *The Fate of the Anglican Clergy*, p. 180.

3. 'Full-time stipendiary clergy losses and gains 1990B2006', as part of *Church Statistics 2005/6*, <www.cofe.anglican.org/info/statistics/churchstats2005/statisticscontent.html>. Accessed 19 September, 2008. Curiously the statistics are presented in two separate tables for men and women clergy. The figures I quote are the combined figures.
4. A. L. Maycock, *Nicholas Ferrar of Little Gidding*, p. 294.
5. Trevor Leggett, ed., *A Second Zen Reader*, p. 160.

Bibliography

John Adair, *Effective Leadership: A Modern Guide to Developing Leadership Skills* (London: Pan, 1988).

——, *The Leadership of Jesus and Its Legacy Today* (Norwich: Canterbury Press, 2001).

Advisory Board of Ministry of the Church of England, *Stranger in the Wings: A Report on Local Non-Stipendiary Ministry*, GS Misc 532 (London: Church House, 1998).

Advisory Council for the Church's Ministry, *Education for the Church's Ministry: The Report of the Working Party on Assessment of the Committee for Theological Education*, ACCM Occasional Papers 22 ([London]: ACCM, 1987).

David Allen, *Getting Things Done: The Art of Stress-Free Productivity* (New York: Viking, 2001).

Anglican–Roman Catholic International Commission (ARCIC I), *Authority in the Church: A Statement on the Question of Authority, Its Nature, Exercise, and Implications* (London: SPCK: Catholic Truth Society, 1976).

Archbishop's Council, *Draft Ecclesiastical Offices (Terms of Service) Regulations*, General Synod GS 1638 (2007)

——, *Ordination Services: Study Guide*, Common Worship: Services and Prayers for the Church of England (London: Church House Publishing, 2007).

Francis Bacon, 'The Advancement of Learning (1605)', in *The Oxford Francis Bacon*, ed. Michael Kiernan (Oxford: Clarendon Press, 2000)

Karl Barth, *Church Dogmatics: The Doctrine of Reconciliation*, Vol. IV, Part 2 (Edinburgh: T&T Clark, 1958).

——, 'Church and Culture (1926)', in *Theology and Church: Shorter Writings 1920–1928* (London: SCM, 1962), pp. 334–54.

Trevor Beeson, *New Area Mission: The Parish in the New Housing Estates* (London: A. R. Mowbray, 1963).

—— (ed.), *Priests and Prelates: the Daily Telegraph Clerical Obituaries* (London: Continuum, 2002).

St Benedict, *The Rule of Saint Benedict*, tr. and ed. by Abbot Parry OSB, with an introduction by Esther de Waal (Leominster: Gracewing, 1990).

Ludwig von Bertalanffy, *General System Theory; Foundations, Development, Applications* (New York: G. Braziller, 1969).

Eberhard Bethge, *Dietrich Bonhoeffer: Theologian, Christian, Contemporary*, ed. Edwin Robertson, tr. Eric Mosbacher (London: Collins, 1970).

Tony Blair in Terry Coleman, 'The New Churchill . . . or the New Bambi?', *The Mail on Sunday*, 2 October 1994, pp. 8, 10, 13.

James Bogle, *South Bank Religion: The Diocese of Southwark 1959–1969* (London: Hatcham, c. 2002).

Dietrich Bonhoeffer, *Life Together and Prayerbook of the Bible*, eds Gerhard Ludwig Müller, Albrecht Schönherr and Geffrey B. Kelly, *Dietrich Bonhoeffer Works English Edition, Volume 5* (Minneapolis: Fortress Press, 1996).

——, *Sanctorum Communio: A Theological Study of the Sociology of the Church*, eds Clifford J.

Green and Joachim von Soosten, tr. Reinhard Krauss and Nancy Lukens, *Dietrich Bonhoeffer Works English Edition, Volume 1* (Minneapolis: Fortress Press, 1998)

Andrew Bowden and Michael West, *Dynamic Local Ministry* (London: Continuum, 2000).

Murray Bowen, *Family Therapy in Clinical Practice* (New York: Aronson, 1978).

John Bowker (ed.), *The Concise Oxford Dictionary of World Religions* (Oxford: Oxford University Press, 2000).

Brighton and Hove Deaneries Pastoral Strategy Review Group, *Strengthening the Church for God's Mission* (Chichester: Diocese of Chichester, 21 June 2003). Available online from:<www.diochi.org.uk/content/review/brighton-hove/Final-Consult.pdf>. Accessed 12 September 2008.

Callum G. Brown, *Religion and Society in Twentieth-century Britain* (Harlow: Longman, 2006).

David Brown, *Making Room for Church Leadership* (Foundation for Church Leadership, 2008), Available online from: <www.churchleadershipfoundation.org/website_documents/david_brown_making_room.pdf>. Accessed 10 September 2008.

Madeleine Bunting, 'If They Did It Over Transubstantiation, They Can Find a Way Over Gay Priests', the *Guardian*, 14 July 2008, p. 25. Available online from: <www.guardian.co.uk/commentisfree/2008/jul/14/anglicanism.religion>. Accessed 17 September 2008.

Samuel Butler, *Erewhon* (English Library Series; London: Penguin Classics, [1872/1901] 1970).

Alvin Rosenblatt Calman, *Ledru-Rollin and the Second French Republic*, Columbia Studies in the Social Sciences, No. 234 (New York: Octagon Books, 1980 [1922]).

Wesley Carr, 'Leading Without Leadership: Managing Without Management', in *Creative Church Leadership*, ed. John Adair and John Nelson (Norwich: Canterbury Press, 2004), pp. 75–87.

——, *The Priestlike Task: A Model for Developing and Training the Church's Ministry* (London: SPCK, 1985).

Craig A. Carter, 'The Legacy of an Inadequate Christology: Yoder's Critique of Niebuhr's *Christ and Culture*', *Mennonite Quarterly Review*, Vol. LXXVI/3 (July 2003). Available online from: <www.goshen.edu/mqr/pastissues/july03carter.html>. Accessed 7 March 2008.

Michael G. Cartwright, 'Being Sent: Witnesses', in *The Blackwell Companion to Christian Ethics*, ed. Stanley Hauerwas and Samuel Wells (Oxford; Malden, MA: Blackwell, 2004).

——, *Giving and Receiving Hospitality: Ecumenical and Interfaith Programs at the University of Indianapolis* (Indianapolis, IN: University of Indianapolis Office of Ecumenical and Interfaith Programs, ND [2003?]). Available online from: <http://eip.uindy.edu/publications/givingreceiving.pdf>. Accessed 7 February 2008.

——, *Offering Hospitality under the Cross and Flame: United Methodists and Higher Education in Indiana*, available online from: <www.inareaumc.org/together/offering_hospitality.htm>. Accessed 7 February 2008.

Mario A. Di Cesare and Rigo Mignani, *A Concordance to the Complete Writings of George Herbert* (Cornell Concordances), (Ithaca: Cornell University Press, 1977).

Elias Chacour, *We Belong to the Land: The Story of a Palestinian Israeli Who Lives for Peace and Reconciliation*, with Mary E. Jensen, 2nd rev. edn (Notre Dame, IN: University of Notre Dame Press, 2001 [1990]).

John Chandler, 'The Country Parson's Flock: Bemerton in 1632', a paper presented at the conference 'George Herbert's Living Legacies: George Herbert's Pastoral: Poetry and Priesthood, Past and Future', Sarum College, Salisbury, October 2007. Available online from <www.georgeherbert.org.uk/Docs/Chandler%20Lecture.pdf>. Accessed 23 February 2009.

Mark Chapman, 'Theology in the Public Arena: The Case of South Bank Religion', in Jane

Garnett et al., *Redefining Christian Britain.*
Church House Publishing, *A Time to Heal: A Report for the House of Bishops on the Healing Ministry* (London: Church House Publishing, 2000).
Elizabeth Clarke, 'The Character of a Non-Laudian Country Parson', in *Review of English Studies*, Vol. 54 No. 216 (September 2003), pp. 479–96.
The Convocations of Canterbury and York, *Guidelines for the Professional Conduct of the Clergy* (London: Church House Publishing, 2003).
Stephen Conway, 'Public Ministry', in David Ison et al., *The Vicar's Guide: Life and Ministry in the Parish*, ed. David Ison (London: Church House Publishing, 2005).
Dave Crenshaw, *The Myth of Multitasking: How 'Doing It All' Gets Nothing Done* (San Francisco: Jossey-Bass, 2008).
Stephen Croft (ed.), *The Future of the Parish System: Shaping the Church of England for the Twenty-First Century* (London: Church House Publishing, 2006).
Douglas Dales, *Glory Descending: Michael Ramsey and his Writings* (Norwich: Canterbury Press, 2005).
John Davey, *Burnout: Stress in the Ministry* (Leominster: Gracewing, 1995).
Andrew Dawswell, *Ministry Leadership Teams: Theory and Practice in Effective Collaborative Ministry*, Grove Pastoral Series P93 (Cambridge: Grove Books, 2003).
Percy Dearmer, *The Parson's Handbook* (multiple editions from 1899 to 1965).
Martin O. Dietrich (ed.), *Luther's Works*, Vol. 42 (Devotional Works 1), (Philadelphia: Fortress Press, 1969), pp. 121–66.
John Donne, *The Sermons of John Donne*, ed. Evelyn M. Simpson and George R. Potter (Berkeley: University of California Press, 1953–62)
Vincent J. Donovan, *Christianity Rediscovered: An Epistle from the Masai*, 2nd edn (London: SCM, 1982).
Benjamin R. Doolittle, 'Burnout and Coping Among Parish-based Clergy', in *Mental Health, Religion & Culture* (10/1), January 2007, pp. 31–8.
C. Edmondson, *Fit to Lead: Sustaining Effective Ministry in a Changing World* (London: Darton, Longman & Todd, 2002).
T. S. Eliot, *George Herbert* (Writers' and Their Work Series; Plymouth: Northcote House, 1994 [1962]).
Paul Ferris, *The Church of England* (London: Gollancz, 1962).
Timothy Ferriss, *The 4-Hour Workweek: Escape 9–5, Live Anywhere, and Join the New Rich* (New York: Crown Publishers, 2007).
Charles Forder, *The Parish Priest at Work* (2nd rev. edn) (London: SPCK, 1959).
Mark Forster, *Do It Tomorrow: And Other Secrets of Time Management* (London: Hodder & Stoughton, 2006).
Herbert J. Freudenberger and Geraldine Richelson, *Burn-out: The High Cost of High Achievement* (Garden City, NY: Anchor Press, 1980).
Robert C. Fuller, *Spiritual, but not Religious: Understanding Unchurched America* (New York: Oxford University Press, 2001).
Jane Garnett, et al. (eds), *Redefining Christian Britain: Post-1945 Perspectives* (London: SCM Press, 2007).
Donald Goergen OP, 'The Pillars Revisited: A Fresh Look at Dominican Spirituality', *Spirituality* 13/73 (July/ August 2007).
Timothy J. Gorringe, *Furthering Humanity: A Theology of Culture* (Aldershot: Ashgate, 2004)
A. A. K. Graham, 'Should the Ordained Ministry Now Disappear?', *Theology* (LXXI/576), June 1968, pp. 242–50.
Clifford Green, 'Human Sociality and Christian Community', in *The Cambridge Companion to Dietrich Bonhoeffer*, ed. John W. de Gruchy (Cambridge: Cambridge University Press, 1999), pp. 113–33.

Graham Greene, *A Burnt-Out Case* (London: Penguin Classics, 1992 [1960]).

Robin Greenwood, 'Understanding New Patterns of Management in Ministry', in *Management and Ministry: Appreciating Contemporary Issues*, ed. John Nelson, MODEM (Norwich: Canterbury Press, 1996), pp. 99–108.

——, *Transforming Priesthood: A New Theology of Mission and Ministry* (London: SPCK, 1994).

Paul J. Griffiths, 'Witness and Conviction in *With the Grain of the Universe*', *Modern Theology* 19/1 (January 2003), pp. 67–75.

William N. Grosch and David C. Olsen, 'Clergy Burnout: An Integrative Approach', in *Journal of Clinical Psychology* (56/5), May 2000, pp. 619–32.

John W. de Gruchy (ed.), *The Cambridge Companion to Dietrich Bonhoeffer* (Cambridge: Cambridge University Press, 1999).

Malcolm Grundy, *What They Don't Teach You at Theological College: A Practical Guide to Life in the Ministry* (Norwich: Canterbury Press, 2003).

James M. Gustafson, Preface to the fiftieth anniversary expanded edition of H. Richard Niebuhr, *Christ and Culture* (New York, HarperSanFrancisco, [1951] 2001).

Richard H. Hall, 'Professionalization and Bureaucratization', in *American Sociological Review*, Vol. 33 No. 1. (February 1968).

Charles Handy, 'One Question and Ten Answers', in *Creative Church Leadership*, ed. John Adair and John Nelson (Norwich: Canterbury Press, 2004), pp. 24–31.

Adrian Hastings, *A History of English Christianity 1920–1990* (3rd edn), (London: SCM, 1991).

Stanley Hauerwas, 'Why Did Jesus Have to Die?: An Attempt to Cross the Barrier of Age', in *The Princeton Seminary Bulletin* 28/2 (2007), pp. 181–90.

——, *With the Grain of the Universe: The Church's Witness and Natural Theology: Being the Gifford Lectures Delivered at the University of St Andrews in 2001* (London: SCM Press, 2002).

——, 'Hooks: Random Thoughts by Way of a Response to Griffiths and Ochs', *Modern Theology* 19/1 (January 2003), pp. 89–101.

Kenneth C. Haugk, *Antagonists in the Church: How to Identify and Deal with Destructive Conflict* (Minneapolis: Augsburg Publishing House, 1988).

Ronald A. Heifetz, *Leadership Without Easy Answers* (Cambridge, MA: Belknap Press of Harvard University Press, 1994).

Ronald A. Heifetz and Martin Linsky, *Leadership on the Line: Staying Alive Through the Dangers of Leading* (Boston, MA: Harvard Business School Press, 2002).

Edward Herbert, *The Life of Edward, First Lord Herbert of Cherbury Written by Himself*, ed. J. M. Shuttleworth (Oxford: Oxford University Press, 1976).

George Herbert, *The Complete Works in Verse and Prose of George Herbert; For the First Time Fully Collected and Much Enlarged*, ed. Alexander B. Grosart (London: printed for private circulation, Robson and Sons, printers, 1874).

Jim Herrington, Robert Creech and Trisha L. Taylor, *The Leader's Journey: Accepting the Call to Personal and Congregational Transformation* (San Francisco: Jossey-Bass, 2003).

Thomas Hinde, *A Field Guide to the English Country Parson* (London: Phoebe Phillips/ Heinneman, 1984).

Michael Hocking, *The Parish Seeks the Way: A Strategy for a Working Class Parish* (London: A. R. Mowbray, 1960).

——, *A Handbook of Pastoral Work* (London: Mowbrays, 1977).

——, *A Handbook of Parish Work*, rev. edn (London: Mowbrays, 1984).

Dean R. Hoge and Jacqueline E. Wenger, *Pastors in Transition: Why Clergy Leave Local Church Ministry* (Grand Rapids, MI: William B. Eerdmans, 2005).

Donald Hughes, 'Neo-Matins', in *Prism*, No. 85, May 1964.

Hilary Ineson and Bernard Kilroy, 'Appropriate Professional Support and Development', in

Management and Ministry: Appreciating Contemporary Issues, ed. John Nelson, MODEM (Norwich: Canterbury Press, 1996), pp. 155–69.

Irving Janis, *Victims of Groupthink: A Psychological Study of Foreign-Policy Decisions and Fiascoes* (Boston, MA: Houghton, Mifflin, 1972).

Stuart Jeffries, 'Fay Weldon: Lie Back and Think of Jesus', the *Guardian G2*, 5 September 2006, p. 10.

Skye Jethani, 'iChurch: All We Like Sheep: Is Our insistence on Choices Leading Us Astray?', in *Leadership Journal*, Summer 2006, Available online from: <www.christianitytoday.com/le/2006/003/3.28.html>. Accessed 20 August 2007.

Geffrey B. Kelly and John D. Godsey (eds), *Discipleship* (DBWE Vol. 4.), translated by Barbara Green and Reinhard Krauss (Minneapolis: Fortress Press, 2000), originally published in English as *The Cost of Discipleship*, tr. R. H. Fuller (London: SCM, 1948).

Geffrey B. Kelly and F. Burton Nelson, *The Cost of Moral Leadership: The Spirituality of Dietrich Bonhoeffer* (Grand Rapids, MI: William B. Eerdmans, 2003).

Ralph H. Kilmann and Kenneth W. Thomas, 'Developing a Forced-Choice Measure of Conflict-Handling Behavior: The "Mode" Instrument', in *Educational and Psychological Measurement* (37/2), July 1977, pp. 309–25.

Ron Kraybill, *Style Matters: The Kraybill Conflict Response Inventory* (Harrisonburg, VA: Riverhouse ePress, 2005).

Hans Küng, *Structures of the Church* (London: Burns & Oates, 1965).

——, *The Church* (London: Burns & Oates, 1967).

Nicholas Lash, 'Conversation in Context', in *Theology for Pilgrims* (London: Darton, Longman & Todd, 2008).

Trevor Leggett (ed.), *A Second Zen Reader: The Tiger's Cave and Translations of Other Zen Writings* (Rutland: Charles E. Tuttle, 1988).

John Frederick Lehr, *Clergy Burnout: Recovering from the 70 Hour Week and Other Self Defeating Practices* (Minneapolis: Fortress Press, 2006)

Christopher Lewis et al., 'Clergy Work-related Psychological Health, Stress and Burnout: An Introduction', in *Mental Health, Religion & Culture* (10/1), January 2007, pp. 1–8.

Diarmaid MacCulloch, 'The Myth of the English Reformation', in *The Journal of British Studies* (30/1), January 1991.

Judith Maltby, 'Face to Faith: Epiphany Shows How Both the Life of the Mind and that of the Heart Can Be Good', the *Guardian*, 6 January 2007, p. 35.

George Marsden, 'Christianity and Cultures: Transforming Niebuhr's Categories', *Insights: The Faculty Journal of Austin Seminary* 115, No. 1 (Fall 1999). Available online from: <www.religion-online.org/showarticle.asp?title'517>. Accessed 29 February 2008.

Robert Martineau, *The Office and Work of a Priest* (Oxford: A. R. Mowbray and Co. Ltd, 1972).

Martin E. Marty, 'Foreword' to the fiftieth anniversary expanded edition of H. Richard Niebuhr, *Christ and Culture* (New York, HarperSanFrancisco, [1951] 2001).

Christina Maslach, *Burnout: The Cost of Caring* (Cambridge, MA: Malor Books, 2003).

Abraham H. Maslow, *Religions, Values and Peak-experiences* (Harmondsworth: Penguin, 1976 [1964]).

Kenneth Mason, *George Herbert, Priest and Poet* (Oxford: SLG Press, 1980).

A. L. Maycock, *Nicholas Ferrar of Little Gidding* (London: SPCK, 1938).

Gerald May, *Addiction and Grace* (San Francisco: Harper & Row, 1988).

Alister E. McGrath, *Christian Literature: An Anthology* (Oxford: Blackwell, 2001).

Nigel Melville, 'Rugby Union: Six Nations: Gloom in the Valleys but Johnson's Red Army are Confident', the *Guardian Sports*, 24 February 2006, p. 9.

Harold Miller, *Finding a Personal Rule of Life*, Grove Spirituality series No. 8, 3rd edn (Cambridge: Grove Books, 2003 [1984]).

Mark Mills-Powell, *St Benedict for Today*, Grove Spirituality series S103 (Cambridge: Grove Books, 2007).

Ministry Division of the Archbishops' Council, *Formation for Ministry Within a Learning Church: The Structure and Funding of Ordination Training*, General Synod GS 1496 (London: Church House, 2003), otherwise known as the 'Hind Report'.

——, *Review of Clergy Terms of Service: Part 2*, General Synod GS 1564 (London: Church House Publishing, 2005).

Sandy Mitchell, 'Britain's Best-Loved Parson', *Country Life*, 22 September 2005.

Gerhard Ludwig Müller and Albrecht Schönherr, 'Editors' Afterword to the German Edition', in Bonhoeffer, *Life Together*.

Humphrey Mynors, 'What I Look for in My Parish Priest', *Theology* (LXXI/572), February 1968.

John Nelson (ed.), *Management and Ministry: Appreciating Contemporary Issues*, MODEM (Norwich: Canterbury Press, 1996).

H. Richard Niebuhr, *Christ and Culture* (New York, HarperSanFrancisco, [1951] 2001).

Peter Ochs, 'On Hauerwas' *With the Grain of the Universe*', *Modern Theology* 19/1 (January 2003), pp. 77–88.

Barnabas Oley, 'A Prefatory View of the Life of Mr Geo. Herbert' (1652) in Patrides, *Herbert*.

The Oxford English Dictionary, 2nd edn, 1989, *OED* Online. Oxford University Press.

Eric Partridge, *A Dictionary of Slang and Unconventional English* [5th edn] (London: Routledge & Kegan Paul, 1961), Vol. 1.

C. A. Patrides (ed.), *George Herbert: The Critical Heritage* (London: Routledge & Kegan Paul, 1983).

Colin Patterson, *How to Learn Through Conflict: A Handbook for Leaders in Local Churches*, Grove Pastoral Series P96 (Cambridge: Grove Books, 2003).

Leslie Paul, *The Deployment and Payment of the Clergy: A Report* (Westminster: Church Information Office for the Central Advisory Council for the Ministry, 1964).

Martyn Percy, *Clergy: The Origin of the Species* (London: Continuum, 2006).

Eugene H. Peterson, *The Contemplative Pastor: Returning to the Art of Spiritual Direction* (Grand Rapids, MI: William B. Eerdmans, 1993).

Stephen Plant, 'The Sacrament of Ethical Reality: Dietrich Bonhoeffer on Ethics for Christian Citizens', *Studies in Christian Ethics*, 18 (2005).

Christine D. Pohl, *Making Room: Recovering Hospitality as a Christian Tradition* (Grand Rapids, MI: William B. Eerdmans, 1999).

John Pritchard, *The Life and Work of a Priest* (London: SPCK, 2007).

Michael Ramsey, *The Christian Priest Today* (London: SPCK, 1972, 1985).

Bruce D. Reed, *The Dynamics of Religion: Process and Movement in Christian Churches* (London: Darton, Longman & Todd, 1978)

Geoffrey Rowell, Kenneth Stevenson and Rowan Williams (eds), *Love's Redeeming Work: The Anglican Quest for Holiness* (Oxford: Oxford University Press, 2001).

The Rule of St Benedict, 'Chapter 1: The Kinds of Monk', in a translation by Abbot Parry, OSB, (Leominster: Gracewing, 1990).

Anthony Russell, *The Clerical Profession* (London: SPCK, 1980).

William Safire, 'On Language: Groupthink', *The New York Times*, Section 6, 8 August 2004, p. 16.

Sara Savage, 'The Church as an Organisation', in *Psychology for Christian Ministry*, eds Fraser Watts, Rebecca Nye, and Sara Savage, (London: Routledge, 2002), p. 224–49.

——, 'On the Analyst's Couch: Psychological Perspectives on Congregations and Clergy', in *The Future of the Parish System: Shaping the Church of England for the Twenty-First Century*, ed. Stephen Croft (London: Church House Publishing, 2006).

Sara Savage and Eolene Boyd-MacMillan, *The Human Face of Church: A Social Psychology and*

Pastoral Theology Resource for Pioneer and Traditional Ministry (Norwich: Canterbury Press, 2007).

Wilmar Schaufeli and Dirk Enzmann, *The Burnout Companion to Study and Practice: A Critical Analysis* (Issues in Occupational Health Series), (London: Taylor & Francis, 1998).

Edward Schillebeeckx, *Ministry: A Case for Change* (London: SCM, 1981).

William Shakespeare, poems from *The Passionate Pilgrim*, in Stanley Wells and Gary Taylor (eds), *The Oxford Shakespeare: The Complete Works* (Oxford: Clarendon Press, 1999).

Peter Shaw, *Mirroring Jesus as Leader*, Grove Ethics series E135 (Cambridge: Grove Books, 2004).

Ernest Southcott, *The Parish Comes Alive* (London: A. R. Mowbray, 1956).

Michael Spencer, 'Church Quitting in Evangelicalism', podcast, 10 September 2008, *Internet Monk Radio Podcast*, Episode 110: www.internetmonk.com/archive/internet-monk-radio-podcast-110.

Nick Stacey [Nicolas Stacey], 'How the Church Could Survive', in *The Observer Weekend Review*, 23 May 1965.

Nicolas Stacey, *Who Cares* (London: Anthony Blond, 1971)

Glen H. Stassen, D. M. Yeager and John Howard Yoder (eds), *Authentic Transformation: A New Vision of Christ and Culture* (Nashville: Abingdon Press, 1996).

Jeremy Taylor, *The Whole Works of Jeremy Taylor*, ed. Reginald Heber, ed. and revised by Charles P. Eden, Vol 5 (London: Longman, Brown, Green, 1859).

Richard Templar, *The Rules of Life: A Personal Code for Living a Better, Happier, More Successful Kind of Life* (Harlow: Pearson Prentice Hall, 2006).

——, *The Rules of Management: A Definitive Code for Managerial Success* (Harlow: Prentice Hall Business, 2005).

——, *The Rules of Parenting: A Personal Code for Bringing up Happy, Confident Children* (Harlow: Prentice Hall, 2008).

——, *The Rules of Wealth: A Personal Code for Prosperity* (Harlow: Prentice Hall Business, 2007).

——, *The Rules of Work: A Definitive Code for Personal Success* (London: Prentice Hall Business, 2003).

William Temple, 'Christian Unity and Church Reunion: Speech to the Canterbury Convocation, 25 May 1943', published in *The Church Looks Forward* (London: Macmillan, 1944).

Martin Thornton, *Pastoral Theology: A Reorientation* (London: SPCK, 1956).

——, *Christian Proficiency* (London: SPCK, 1959).

J. R. R. Tolkien, 'The Grey Havens', *The Lord of the Rings: The Return of the King* (London: HarperCollins, 1991 [1955]).

R. Towler and A. Coxon, *The Fate of the Anglican Clergy: A Sociological Study* (London: Macmillan, 1979).

John Truscott, 'Christian Administration? A Theological Introduction', Leaflet A15 in his series on Administration (2006). Available online from: <www.john-truscott.co.uk/resources/articles/a15.pdf>. Accessed 13 September 2008.

——, 'Job Descriptions: Advice and Examples for Staff and Volunteers', Leaflet A6 in his series on Management (2008 [2003]), Available online from: <www.john-truscott.co.uk/resources/articles/a6.pdf>. Accessed 5 September 2008.

——, 'The Minister's Role in Larger Churches', Leaflet TN6 in his series on Leadership (2007 [2001]). Available online from: <www.john-truscott.co.uk/resources/training/tn6.pdf>. Accessed 6 September 2008.

Simon Tugwell OP, *Early Dominicans: Selected Writings*, The Classics of Western Spirituality (New York: Paulist Press, 1982).

Douglas W. Turton and Leslie J. Francis, 'The Relationship Between Attitude Toward Prayer and Professional Burnout Among Anglican Parochial Clergy in England: Are Praying Clergy Healthier Clergy?', in *Mental Health, Religion & Culture* (10/1), January 2007, pp. 61–74.

Frank Viola, *Reimagining Church: Pursuing the Dream of Organic Christianity* (Colorado Springs, CO: David C. Cook, 2008).

Victor Vroom and Philip Yetton, *Leadership and Decision-making* (Pittsburgh: University of Pittsburgh Press, 1973).

John Walker, 'Quality Ministry', in *Management and Ministry: Appreciating Contemporary Issues*, ed. John Nelson, MODEM (Norwich: Canterbury Press, 1996), pp. 141–6.

John N. Wall (ed.), *George Herbert: The Country Parson, The Temple*, (Classics of Western Spirituality; New York: Paulist Press, 1981).

Isaak Walton, 'The Life of Mr George Herbert', in *Lives of Done and Herbert*, ed. S. C. Roberts (Cambridge: Cambridge University Press, 1928 [1670]).

Robert Warren, *The Healthy Churches' Handbook: A Process for Revitalizing Your Church* (London: Church House Publishing, 2004).

Yvonne Warren, *The Cracked Pot: The State of Today's Anglican Parish Clergy* (Stowmarket: Kevin Mayhew, 2002).

Burton Watson, *The Zen Teachings of Master Lin-Chi: A Translation of the Lin-chi Lu* (New York: Columbia University Press, 1999).

Fraser Watts, Rebecca Nye and Sara Savage, *Psychology for Christian Ministry* (London: Routledge, 2002).

Arthur Waugh, *George Herbert: Poems* (The World's Classics; Oxford: Oxford University Press, 1907).

Elizabeth Welch, 'Leadership with Vision: A Challenge for the Churches?', in *Creative Church Leadership*, ed. John Adair and John Nelson (Norwich: Canterbury Press, 2004), pp. 134–45.

Guy Wilkinson, 'Parish Systems', in *The Vicar's Guide: Life and Ministry in the Parish*, ed. David Ison (London: Church House Publishing, 2005), pp. 93–109.

Rowan Williams, *Anglican Identities* (London: Darton, Longman & Todd, 2004).

——, 'The Christian Priest Today', lecture given at Ripon College, Cuddesdon, 28 May 2004. Available online from: <www.archbishopofcanterbury.org/1185>. Accessed 25 January 2008.

——, 'Community Well-Being', a speech given at Rose Street Methodist Centre, Wokingham, 30 July 2004. Available online from: <www.archbishopofcanterbury.org/1058>. Accessed 25 January 2008.

Bryan Wilson, *Religion in Secular Society: A Sociological Comment* (London: C. A. Watts, 1966).

Walter Wink, *Naming the Powers: The Language of Power in the New Testament*, The PowersVol. 1 (Philadelphia: Fortress Press, 1984).

——, *Unmasking the Powers: The Invisible Forces that Determine Human Existence*, The Powers Vol. 2 (Philadelphia: Fortress Press, 1986).

James Woodward, Stephen Pattison and John Patton (eds), *The Blackwell Reader in Pastoral and Practical Theology* (Oxford: Blackwell Publishing, 2000).

Tom Wright, *Simply Christian* (London: SPCK, 2006).

John Howard Yoder, *The Priestly Kingdom: Social Ethics as Gospel* (Notre Dame: University of Notre Dame Press, 1984).

——, *The Royal Priesthood: Essays Ecumenical and Ecclesiological*, ed. Michael G. Cartwright (Grand Rapids, MI: Eerdmans, 1994).

——, 'How H. Richard Niebuhr Reasoned: A Critique of Christ and Culture', in *Authentic Transformation: A New Vision of Christ and Culture*, eds Glen H. Stassen, D. M. Yeager and John Howard Yoder, (Nashville: Abingdon Press, 1996).

Steve Young (writer) and Bob Anderson (director), 'Hurricane Neddy', *The Simpsons*, Ep. 161/808, first broadcast 29 December 1996.

Index